Riot City: Prot... and Re...

Riot City is a fluent, well-researched and compe...
he student demonstrations the year before. Sharp, articulate analysis and a thoughtful account
f the national mood and social conditions in the capital put the story into context. Bloom has
lone an excellent job in giving us a lively, blow-by-blow account of those tumultuous days while
eeping a balanced and factual tone throughout. A book that shows authority and clear historical
nderstanding, this must surely be the definitive account from an author who is already an expert in
he field.' – Michael Binyon, Leader Writer for The Times

There is another London, hiding behind the Olympics, the Jubilee, the palaces and stadiums – the
ondon of riot and rebellion. Clive Bloom takes us on a breathtaking tour of the politics of disorder,
iowing what happens, and why, when the battle for progress turns violent.' – Danny Kruger,
rmer speechwriter to David Cameron

' brilliant documentation, analysis and commentary on the recent wave of popular protests – their
ms, methods and effects – and how the state has responded to these challenges to its power and
ithority.' – Peter Tatchell, Human Rights Campaigner

ı Riot City, Clive Bloom offers the first indepth study of the student protests of 2010 and the
mmer riots of 2011, revealing how these different forms of unrest emerged from very different
ıses of entitlement. His insightful, thoughtful and balanced reading of these disturbances
ould be required reading for activists, policymakers and academics alike.' – Dr Ted Vallance,
ehampton University

iolent London: 2000 Years of Riots, Rebels and Revolts

ı exhilarating rush through countless riots, insurrections and full-blown street wars...written in a
y and accessible style ... As I read this superb history, I looked out at my quiet suburban garden,
appointed not to hear the sound of trumpets.' – J.G. Ballard, Daily Telegraph

ı ambitious and erudite chronicle ... Bloom is a polymath.' – The Times

ıis isn't just a history of riots and revolts ... this is a political history which is made all the more
eresting because it concentrates on the flashpoints, and the events which caused them.' – The
ardian

oom is a card-carrying public intellectual, a regular media commentator and ... prolific author ...
short, he has street cred.' – Times Higher Education Magazine

Also by Clive Bloom

Violent London: 2000 Years of Riots, Rebels and Revolts (Palgrave Macmillan, 2010)

Bestsellers: Popular Fiction Since 1900 (Palgrave Macmillan, 2008)

Gothic Horror: A Guide for Students and Readers (Palgrave Macmillan, 2007)

Cult Fiction: Popular Reading and Pulp Theory (Palgrave Macmillan, 1996)

Clive Bloom is Emeritus Professor of English and American Studies at Middlesex University, UK. A respected broadcaster, he is also the author of *Violent London: 2000 Years of Riots, Rebels and Revolts* (Palgrave Macmillan, 2003; 2010), *Literature, Politics and Intellectual Crisis in Britain Today* (Palgrave Macmillan, 2000), *Cult Fiction: Popular Reading and Pulp Theory* (Palgrave Macmillan 1996) and many other titles.

RIOT CITY

PROTEST AND REBELLION IN THE CAPITAL

Clive Bloom

palgrave
macmillan

First published 2012 by
PALGRAVE MACMILLAN

Palgrave Macmillan in the UK is an imprint of Macmillan Publishers Limited, registered in England, company number 785998, of Houndmills, Basingstoke, Hampshire RG21 6XS.

Palgrave Macmillan in the US is a division of St Martin's Press LLC, 175 Fifth Avenue, New York, NY 10010.

Palgrave Macmillan is the global academic imprint of the above companies and has companies and representatives throughout the world.

Palgrave® and Macmillan® are registered trademarks in the United States, the United Kingdom, Europe and other countries.

ISBN 978–1–137–02935–5

This book is printed on paper suitable for recycling and made from fully managed and sustained forest sources. Logging, pulping and manufacturing processes are expected to conform to the environmental regulations of the country of origin.

A catalogue record for this book is available from the British Library.

A catalog record for this book is available from the Library of Congress.

10 9 8 7 6 5 4 3 2 1
21 20 19 18 17 16 15 14 13 12

Printed and bound in Great Britain by
CPI Antony Rowe, Chippenham and Eastbourne

This one for my mum who'd hang 'em all

The future isn't written yet.

Tony Blair, *New Labour/New Britain* Centenary Membership leaflet (1997)

And we're going to start by taking power away from central government and giving it to people.

David Cameron, Conservative Party Conference (Birmingham, 6 October 2010)

We're all in this together.

George Osborne, Chancellor of the Exchequer (6 October 2009)

The capital is a ticking bomb.

David Cesarini, letter to the *Evening Standard,* 20 April 2012

This is the merit of entire, or collected, narrative. Isolated facts, doubts, suspicions, conjectures, give way to … homogeneity.

Bram Stoker, *The Jewel of Seven Stars* (Chapter 9)

CONTENTS

LIST OF FIGURES

LIST OF PLATES

ACKNOWLEDGEMENTS

Thanks are due to the following: Nancy Langfeldt and the librarians at the Bishopsgate Institute; Catherine Coulthard at the City of London Police; the press office at the Metropolitan Police; Karyn McCluskey of the Violence Reduction Unit, Strathclyde Police; the press office at Her Majesty's Inspectorate of Constabulary; Sue Toper and Lynne McKay of the Essex Probation Service; Sabarah Rob of the Central Criminal Court; the press office at the Ministry of Justice; the press office at 10 Downing Street; the press office at Conservative Party Head Office; the press offices at both the House of Lords and the House of Commons; Professor Jenny Shaw and her colleagues in the Forensic Psychiatry Association who allowed me to try ideas in front of a professional audience; Dr Susan Harvey; the press office of the National Union of Students; Nick Hamilton of Resonance FM; again Malcolm Hopkins of Housmans Bookshop; Newham Bookshop for its unstinting support; David B. Lawrence, whose correspondence on revolutionary flags was most enlightening; 'Heathcote' and his radical companions, whose knowledge of current alternative politics is second to none and whose sincerity cannot be questioned; Amber and Matthew Hall for their help with sourcing illustrations; the Eastside Young Leader's Academy Newham; Dr Richard Heffernan of the Open University; Danny Kruger of Only Connect; the various editors of *The Independent*, the *Financial Times*, *The Times*, *The Guardian*, *Der Spiegel*, *The Times Higher Education* magazine, *Nuts* magazine, *Time Out*, *BBC History magazine* and the *Irish Times* who have invited me to air my opinions at various times of disturbance in London; the BBC, especially Robert Elms; everyone at the Whitechapel Society and the Sohemian Society; Lesley, Esther, Jonathan and James Bloom for all their help as always and Jonathan especially for his photography; Barry Forshaw for his kind words; and, finally, Michael Strang, Ruth Ireland, Abby Coften and Maddie Voke at Palgrave Macmillian who put up with my nagging, Clare Mence for helping with pictures and Jenny McCall who encouraged more than merely the last push. Lastly, a thank you to Jonathan Fryer (who I have never met) for his careful reading of the second edition of *Violent London* and his subsequent comments.

PERMISSIONS

Information on Alfie Meadows in Chapter 4 was first published in the *Times Higher Education* magazine (20 January 2011).

Appendix 1 was first published in a slightly different version as Chapter 6 in Clive Bloom, *Literature, Politics and Intellectual Crisis in Britain Today* (Basingstoke: Palgrave, 2001).

1

2000: PREFACE TO DISORDER IN THE TWENTY-FIRST CENTURY

Since 2000 we have seen unprecedented levels of unrest in London. The capital has become the battleground for a host of new demands and new ideological standpoints, so much so that protesters and authority alike have had to invent new tactics to cope with the pressure of new demands. Once extra-parliamentary protest was relatively rare. There were exceptions, of course, in the Suffragette movement before the First World War, the rallies of fascists and their opponents during the 1930s, the Aldermaston Marches of the 1950s and 1960s, and the CND and anti-Vietnam protests. Each was a response to a specific crisis and each (excluding the Vietnam protests) ultimately recognised parliamentary action as the supreme goal. Nowadays, there is no confidence in Parliament or the perceived chiselling of its members, and the House of Lords seems merely to be a chamber packed with political appointees and technocrats; the police are still seen as the active agents of state repression.

Since the millennium there have been growing political movements whose focus is no longer on parliamentary decisions, but instead is based upon direst action – the action of committed people disillusioned with the apparent collusion of politicians and financiers. These new political activists have named themselves the spokespeople for the '99 per cent' of the population that they perceive have no power and they have vowed to bring to account the one per cent who have it all. This movement, more anarchist-communal than Marxist-communist, has grown as perceived inequality has grown in the first ten years of the new century; the banking crisis of 2008 crystallised its demands for a fairer system. It is natural justice that needs re-affirming, say protesters, and not laws that need changing. The old cry that the whole system is corrupt and needs demolishing rises once again; students in 2010 and the poor in 2011 knew why they were there. London is still Babylon, the 'Great Wen' of the radical William Cobbett, but in the belly of the beast something rises: a new politics.

What is this that is coming? The ghosts of old promises whisper in the atmosphere of new dreams. Lenin, in the midst of Bolshevik triumph, could confidently feel that the fact 'that the socialist revolution in Europe must come, and will come, is beyond doubt. All our hopes for the *final* victory of socialism are founded on this certainty'.[1] He was incorrect; there are no mathematical certainties in politics, but he was not wholly wrong. International political resistance is stronger than it has been for many years and there are new challenges and new demands, but always the same corrupt system, ever the same authorities barring the way, but ever the same goal, ever the same promise of equality, liberty and justice; always on a distant horizon and always illusory, but always to be striven towards.

Protest constantly changes in London, and in recent years much has changed. Not perhaps in quantity or in levels of violence, although violence has increased as much from the authorities as from protesters. What has come to prominence since the May Day and Guerrilla Gardening exploits at the turn of the millennium is a moral agenda defining but outside of the political sphere proper. When voters feel impotent or when protestors are ignored by Parliament, anger and frustration replace political debate with calls for natural justice and rightness – a moral agenda replaces political talk as people spill onto the street. The Iraq War, climate change, fox hunting legislation, the greed of world bankers and their bonuses, and politicians who are seen to be working the system whilst others are laid off infuriate and frustrate the public, who feel ignored by their representatives and who believe that they are treated with contempt by those who seem to be above the law and beyond legal redress.

More importantly, the servants of the general public, the police, have increasingly been perceived as the instruments of the rulers, so much so that they themselves were forced to address the issue of public confidence in a report produced by Her Majesty's Inspectorate of Constabulary in July 2009 called *Adapting to Protest*, which followed the G20 and other difficult protests that year.[2] The essential message of the report was that the policing of public order events must be lawful, consensual and legal, not provocative and aggressive.

The right way to live for protesters has become the right lifestyle to have: not a single-issue argument as in the old days, but a whole package of values, some anarchist, some libertarian, but just as often a rather old-fashioned Trotskyist socialism (usually unarticulated) in which anti-Americanism, anti-capitalism, anti-airport expansionism and anti-fat-cat-ism mix: a higgledy-piggledy composition of the positive virtues of environmental concern, support for Palestine and a new world based on citizenship of 'Planet Earth'. There is no one cause anymore, there are only a plurality of causes. It is this pluralism that will unite groups as disparate as Class War, Anonymous, Greenpeace, UK Uncut and the International Union of Sex Workers. To some extent, it is the old revolt of youth against age, of the powerless against those in power, of radicalism and alternative lifestyle against the innate conservatism of those who rule.

For the most part, all the usual suspects will turn up, the same folks who turn up for any anti-authority gig, whatever the actual cause. They number from a few hundred to a mere few thousand hardcore young people and students or those who were young in the days of the squatting movement of the 1970s and 1980s. The new counter culture is small and self-defining, keeping in contact through current media – the Internet, blogs, websites, streaming, texting, Twitter, MSN, BlackBerry – in many respects using communication systems only known to a relative few with media savvy and ironically thereby restricting the number of activists to a small group and effectively creating a virtual ghetto for their ideas, which do not then reach a wider public and are therefore subsequently frequently misunderstood.

Even the language of protest often sounds like it was borrowed from the enemy's latest corporate buzzwords. Thus, there is talk of 'open sourcing' and 'working groups', 'break out' sessions and other phrases glibly borrowed from an alien rhetoric to describe a situation of 'open' alliances and friendships. Nevertheless, through personal involvement and actual activity in real space and time, revolutionaries may rally many thousands and this may be helped

Figure 1.1 Coalition of Resistance flyer (courtesy of Coalition of Resistance)

by the simple reporting of newspapers and television as much as by personal electronic equipment.

For the most part, the new urban warriors of the twenty-first century began secretively and defensively, breaking the windows of banks or trouncing McDonald's as acts of petty defiance in the cause of the revolution. In 2010, this timidity changed as Conservative Campaign Headquarters was attacked and children defied police. In 2011, these new militants (mostly students and schoolchildren) were joined by another class, ill educated, hedonistic, raucous and ill prepared to do what they traditionally had been instructed to do by their so-called betters. Another class entirely, one left out of the political debate because its members were inarticulate and badly educated, joined the street party: the urban poor were willing to loot shops, burn buildings and fire guns at the police to get their point across.

The silent majority may not remain silent for long either. The suburban and rural middle classes are also willing to protest if the issue is one that affects their lifestyle or moral perspective. The combination of conservatism, traditionalism, middle-England values and single-issue 'moral' politics is often likely to end up succeeding where other causes fail. The middle classes already have knowledge and power on their side and know how to articulate grievances (remember the 'Poll Tax' protests of 1990), especially when such grievances contain values which are ignored or ridiculed by the intellectual elite, Parliament and 'hippy do gooders'.

Yet, since 2000, they too have been defeated time and again by those in power. Real political power now seems beyond not only the impoverished underclasses but also the middle classes, whose votes seem to evaporate as government is formed. In 1832, the middle classes won the franchise which promised political power and a say in the running of the nation. Changes to the franchise promised real democracy. The Labour Party arose to defend worker's rights. New Labour, with its 'authoritarian' political viewpoint, seemed to reverse a process which had lasted over 160 years. The banking crisis put a complete stop to 'democratic' opportunities. The people no longer had to be consulted; technocratic government would see to that. Between 2001 (the start of New Labour's second term) and 2012, the middle classes, who make up the backbone of the politically engaged, seemed further from power than ever. Nowhere was this more evident than in the history of their recent protests.

The emergence of the Countryside Alliance in the opening years of the new century, which came together around a combination of issues that were understood by supporters to have been ignored by the metropolitan elite, was cause for thought. The rally on 22 September 2002 was a force with the potential to change laws by the very presence of the numbers of protesters who were law-abiding citizens and conscientious voters. The importance of this rally compared to the later and much bigger 'Not in My Name' rally of 2003, which mobilised similar people against Tony Blair's policy in Iraq, was simply that the Countryside Alliance was fighting against legislation and attitudes that directly affected its members' incomes and way of life, something far more potent and practical than a march, however large, based upon moral values and legalistic principles alone and one unwilling to apply the violence that erupted at the fox hunting protest in Parliament Square. Nevertheless, the outcome was the same for both protests – abject failure. Thus, the middle classes learned the lesson that the state no longer served their needs.

There is, however, still a place for the dedicated individual. Brian Haw's longstanding encampment and vigil against a war and a war culture he considered immoral could claim a precedent in the one-man campaign for liberty waged by John Lilburne in the seventeenth century. Such protest was later renewed in the campaign of the Barking activist Billy Bragg, who refused to his pay taxes while big bonuses were handed to the bosses of the Royal Bank of Scotland (his particular precedent being, perhaps, Henry David Thoreau in mid-nineteenth-century America). Such individual protests were focused reminders of the difference between what is perceived to be natural justice and what is seen to be parliamentary law, which are too often nowadays seen to be in opposition to one another.

It would be naïve simply to take the claims of opposition movements as valid merely on their say so. After all, the state and governmental authority are pillars of social cohesion and stability and may not be rocked with impunity. There are always dangers to be avoided. The emergence of the English Defence League (EDL) has been one symptom of a growing number of new threats posed by right-wing groups, Islamic terrorists and environmental protesters – organisations which pose new problems for internal security.[3] The various services dedicated to fighting these threats have had to adjust to areas of significance that are no longer focused on the Soviet

Union or Irish nationalism, which is not to say that the threat from both is not real, but simply that it is diminishing. After the murder in London of Alexander Litvinenko in November 2006, the deterioration of the relationship between Russia and the UK was so 'serious' that a large part of the budget of the secret services had to be redirected to Cold-War-style counter intelligence, there being 'no decrease in the numbers of undeclared Russian intelligence officers in the UK ... conducting covert activity', and there still remained lingering concerns regarding the potential activities of the Real IRA, the Continuity IRA and Northern Irish loyalists.[4]

As well as the immediate threat to the country of terrorism, there remains the perceived threat to the planet. The environmental agenda may not be as strongly represented as it once was, given the sharp diminishment of general public interest in global issues during 2010, but environmentalism will certainly not have vanished. To reinforce the idea that human-induced climate change is a reality and not more government propaganda to increase taxation, climate change protest may become more vociferous and extreme as the 'message' ceases to get through. This means that smaller, more targeted and possibly more 'violent' protests will occur at organisations that are perceived to be the worst polluters. Where climate change protest may succeed is in the area of restricting air traffic and saving local villages and green belt land. Such protests have a large public base of support and seem to follow the logic of various governments that have preached about the carbon footprint of excessive air travel. Here the wishes of the voting public and government policy often do coincide.

There are other subtle ways in which the demands of voters and the needs of the state have diverged. Since 2007, there has been a growing criminalisation of space and movement, and authority has tightened its grip through sophisticated surveillance against physical protest. Such authority nevertheless remains porous, subject as it is to intense pressure from the media, from watchdogs and from activists using cyberspace. Whilst it appears that current protests pit a multiplicity of interests against a stubborn singularity of authority (visible in the ranks of helmeted police officers), this is not the case, and the forces of security are themselves divided in terms of their aims and actions; the watchers are now watched by their own surveillance methods (especially CCTV and mobile phones). Will the nature of protest change to meet the new demands of forbidden geography and the importance of mass media?

This time the revolution will be televised. Protestors have for a decade embraced modern methods of communication and organisation, but they have also realised the importance of the world's cameras and the possibilities of 'virtual' protest and of 'staging' an event, whether the smashing of a bank's windows by a single person or creating carnivalesque situations that disarm authority and provide the media with the best photo opportunity. All active dissent is marked by an adversarial position and a sequential course of events. Television and newspapers only operate in terms of the latter and as such protest may have to become more photo-friendly and less ideological if it wishes to be noticed. Such post-modern protests, in which the action stops in order for an 'event' to be properly filmed, suggest that simulation rather than participation will create pastiche protest or simulations organised precisely to be 'looked at' later in photographs, on mobile phone videos and on the Internet.

Yet the camera distorts; the multiplicity of images bewilders. The image exists not in neutral space but within the media context of business, and its proliferation is only partially a matter of personal choice. The continuous television broadcast distorts by extension and manipulation of time sequences (what 'has been' is endlessly repeated in a loop of violence contained within a soundbite – it is always the present moment, frozen in time). Images are juxtaposed to create metaphors and similes, televised interviews with participants make 'characters' out of protestors and produce narratives of action. Moreover, 'celebrity activists' make protest into a 'market of struggle', reducing actions to personalities and campaigns into advertising.[5]

Every image comes with its corporate compensation; every Facebook entry or BlackBerry image (and every 'tweet') is subject to public and private surveillance. The photo is never neutral but is fixed in a politics of visual imagery that is itself toxic, because it seems so safe, so 'non-hierarchical, so 'leaderless'. Nevertheless, its very horizontality may mask vertical forms of control:[6]

> When the Forward Intelligence Teams (FIT) aggressively film us, when we are only let out of kettles on condition we have our faces filmed, when we are arrested *en masse* in Trafalgar Square for breach of the peace just so our personal details can be taken, when police cameramen turn up to community meetings of environmentalists or to student occupations – when any of these occur, the message is clear: we control data, and we control you. By protecting what is ours, we deny the state control.[7]

Real lives, virtual architecture: the protest group 'Anonymous', a decentralised collective of cyber-culture enthusiasts, started in 2003. The 'organisation', which began as entertainment on the Internet, is a loosely organised and open network of 'hactivists' who use humour and cyber-attacks to further protest on behalf of absolute freedom of information and speech. The movement exists as an anarchic, free-flowing intelligence or 'hive' brain that organises and reorganises itself spontaneously and simultaneously through virtual contact. Its most successful campaigns have been to shut down government and financial websites in distributed denial of service (DDoS) attacks. The most publicised of these was in 2010 after the arrest of WikiLeaks founder Julian Assange, when PayPal, MasterCard and Visa were attacked after WikiLeaks' assets were frozen, whilst on 3 February 2012, Anonymous successfully hacked into communications between the FBI and London Metropolitan Police.

These varied potent forms of new media activism became visible to the general public around the time of the attack on Conservative Campaign Headquarters at 30 Millbank in late 2010. Then the papers reported that police had tried to coax protesters from the roof using Twitter, a situation that allowed Richard Littlejohn in the *Daily Mail* to speculate on the imbecility of the authorities trying to use the communications networks of their opponents, a method doomed to failure, not least because it was so ludicrously patronising and transparent.[8] Where force may once have been used to restore order, there was merely the police tweeting; the signs of disorder had been misread.

The *Evening Standard* ran an article on the use of social media in January 2011, highlighting the use of social networks to organise demonstrations like 'Dance Against the Deficit', a lunchtime groove held in front of the Bank of England. Focusing on the new 'clicktivism' of those who use blogs, Twitter, online petitions and Facebook, the paper concentrated on the demands of UK Uncut who were then targeting high-street store owners and bank CEOs who avoided paying their taxes. With 13,000 online supporters in early 2011, the organisation seemed one to watch, as was '38 Degrees', whose petition for dismissal of MPs by grassroots voters before an election received government support; or 'False Economy', set up partly with the Trades Union Congress and union donations, an information platform or hub, to show what was happening locally; or the 'National Campaign Against the Cuts', a network of students unaffiliated to the National Union of Students and set up after a conference, which campaigns for free education and became one of the major bodies behind the student strikes in 2010.[9]

The authorities in the UK and elsewhere have become very aware of cyber-attack and have acted swiftly to shut down hactivists, making numerous arrests around the world, including a number in the UK. These protest groups do not just act in cyberspace, they also still act in the real environment of the streets, but when they demonstrate, they do so anonymously and wearing masks (the *V-mask* from the film *V for Vendetta* was first worn by 'Anonymous' in 2006).

Such masks are a provocation, and although there are police powers to remove facial coverings, the government and the opposition have united in calling for more enforcement. In the spring of 2011,

Figure 1.2 'Anonymous' (author's collection)

both the Home Secretary, Theresa May, and her opposite number on Labour's front benches, Yvette Cooper, agreed that the police should be asked if they needed greater powers to enforce the law. Cooper went further, asking if May would 'consider co-ordinated action against so-called anarchist groups' as well.[10] Thus, the protest movement as a whole has managed to unite both main parliamentary parties as never before and in doing so has effectively abolished the official differences between the left and the right that previous politics had taken as a given.

'Anonymous' is protean and leaderless. This new form of leaderless protest has replaced the old leader-led protest of the past. The revolt of the faceless masses produces not only anonymity but also 'agility', as 'generalising [the] struggle depends on generalising representation' and 'democratising [the] voice'. No longer will the ego be allowed to speak for the people; instead, protesters exclaim 'look into the crowds hurling paint and bricks at cops; put on a mask and say it: "We're not going to be famous."'[11]

Nevertheless, the physical political manifestation of leaderless protest began to emerge in the early years of the twenty-first century. The Piratpartiet or Pirate Party was founded in 2006 by the Swedish activist Rick Falkvinge with a manifesto that argued for the reform of laws that restricted freedom of information, that reinforced rights to privacy and that argued for the transparency of government. It is the first political party that comes from, and speaks to, the Internet generation. It is also a party of the disenchanted but technically savvy young, who now seem to have made a link between green politics and the information-led post-modernism their lifestyles are meant to exemplify. Indeed, in Sweden the Pirate Party actually surpassed the green vote in 2008, making it the third largest party in the country and gaining it two members in the European Parliament in 2009. There are Pirate Parties in Austria, Denmark, Finland, Germany, Morocco, Poland and Spain, as well as Tunisia (where the recent revolution has seen members of the party persecuted) and even the UK.

The Pirate Party UK boasts a membership of 3,000 – not many perhaps, but made up of motivated and active young people, especially students involved with the recent demonstrations and interested in libertarian, social justice or information politics. There is talk amongst students of this being something new and refreshing in politics, and something for their generation.

'In recent years', the Pirates argue, 'we have seen an unprecedented onslaught on the rights of the individual. We are treated like criminals when we share entertainment digitally, even though this is just the modern equivalent of lending a book or a DVD to a friend. We look on helpless as our culture and heritage, so important for binding our society together, is eroded and privatised. Now there is a democratic alternative ... we, the people, can overturn the fat cats and the corrupt MPs who hold our nation's cultural treasures to ransom, ignore our democratic wishes and undermine our civil liberties.'[12]

However, the movement is based on a certain naïve idealism: a party that 'admits it doesn't always have all the answers, is willing to listen and that wants to give voters more rights, not burden them with any more taxes' suggests the moral high ground but little else besides. It is thin gruel, but who would be so mealy-mouthed as to argue with such fine sentiments, especially now that no one trusts mainstream politicians?

Succinctness is a virtue in politics and a necessity for the Twitter generation, and the Pirates are nothing if not succinct. Even the description of the Party is short and sweet. Its main plank is that the 'world is changing' and that the Internet has turned everything into a 'global village', an expression borrowed and revived from the sayings of Marshall McLuhan, the 1960s media guru who predicted that the 'medium is the massage' long ago, now not only reborn as a reality but also as an ideological sensibility, something he could not have predicted.

This is a new politics of tweeting, texts and blogs, of P2P streaming and 'Pirate Bay', of communities that simply exist in virtual space or that come together in temporary communities at festivals, demos or flash mobs. It is no less serious for all that. This is also, at least in part, a lifestyle movement aligned to neither the old right nor the left of the political spectrum, a party of moral outrage for the emotionally important sensibilities of a generation in waiting, advocates of Black Bloc and UK Uncut.

There are currently 50 Pirate Parties in existence across the world. There is no funding, just good wishes and occasional donations. The PPI (the international congress of the movement) allegedly has all of 600 euros in its accounts at one time, but much of its effort has gone towards supporting WikiLeaks. This is its most timely coup, with the older political hegemony discredited by its constant threat to gag alternative political beliefs. The USA is again cast as the bad guy, its borders guarded by satellites and lawyers attempting to patrol the briny ocean of cyber information against piratical libertarians.

Indeed, the moral support the PPI lends to Julian Assange is probably the greatest recruiter to individual Pirate Parties. Make no mistake, WikiLeaks is a new form of intelligence warfare conducted on the Internet. The wars of the twenty-first century, which have become so worrying to British generals, will not be fought, we are told, only with tanks or aircraft carriers, but increasingly with intelligence, passwords and encryption. The new enemy may not be al-Qaeda at all, but the pirates of the communications highways. So it seems we must all go and buy a hoodie, wrap our faces in a scarf or wear a 'V-mask' in order not to reveal our identities or show authority the anger on our faces. Beware the image and read the literature of protest: 'cover your face: today we can do nothing as somebody or something as nobody'.[13]

Just what is it that makes today's riots so different, so appealing? The revolution reappears strangely different, strangely the same, a litany of frustration when 'trapped people get angry'; history repeats itself, but appears as if it is happening for the first time. 'Manifestations of acts of resistance' lead to resistance and revolution: bubbles rising to the surface of long-extinct volcanoes, from the 'long-term alienation' of those for whom the 'future is slain'. The collective is still alive and well with its denial of egotism and its concern for anonymity – as old as the international and as young as yesterday. Squatting too has returned from the abyss of the 1970s, reclaiming those ever-empty derelict spaces for 'free schools' and living space. For contemporary protesters, the 'Big Society' means nothing more than weak citizens, lack of community through economic degradation, the production of subservient functionaries through an education system that is geared towards money and power and management (just as, they note, the Situationists warned in 1967); the reproduction of capital disguised in the corporate language of 'sustainability'.

Some commentators have even suggested that the autonomous, participating and interventionist citizen is now defunct, but there is no need to accept a model predicated upon an essentialist and absolute version of a totally 'free' citizen versus a totally trapped consumer. The concept of 'active citizenship' propagated by the right and the left (both Conservative and Labour) denies the very nature of citizenship, it is now suggested, by leaving no role for common effort and democratic process (both once expressed through the support of elected governments and the rule of law). Individualism, it is argued, essentially turns everyone into an entrepreneurial vigilante and is no better than an appeal to authoritarian, anti-liberal populism.

Authority still wears blue. The police still attract the old hostility of the politically dispossessed. 'In as far as we express ourselves politically', they cry, 'the police are our enemy.'[14] Because the police are the 'armed wing of the state', they are in direct conflict with whoever protests against the state. Indeed, students suggest that being a copper is in direct conflict with radical political activism per se because the police 'defend the very same state which criminalises those who challenge the very structures that produce crime in the first place: state regulation on behalf of neo-liberalism!'.[15] The 'dominated', whether students, unemployed teenagers, ethnic minorities or poor families, are still the victims of the violence of authority. Even as they struggle for self-expression, the baton and riot shield give warning of their subservience:

> Violence is of course [the] most visible weapon [of the police] ... More subtly, however, the police attempt to suppress us through simple data collection of our faces, our names, our location and our political acts. When, via the police, the state collects the politically active citizens, treating them in the process as criminals-in-waiting, it expresses its preference for weak citizenship. The range of discretionary powers possessed by our state bureaucracies mean that the collection and use of this data is completely sovereign: we have no say or influence over what our data is used for, nor where it is stored. In this respect we are dominated.[16]

Nevertheless, protesters today are not quite the demonstrators of the past. For one thing, there are the multiplicity of causes and the multiverse of expression. The nature of binary oppositions and of left and right have been ditched in favour of the idea of temporary communities of political interest in the widest sense, whose enemy, however, remains class in the narrowest political sense. Without clear leaders, whom the protest movement disparages, it embraces utopian horizontality and non-hierarchical decision making, reminiscent of anarchism rather than Marxist-Leninism, where boundaries may 'remain permeable' in an architecture where protest itself is in 'opposition to boundaries' altogether and in which the architecture (the space of occupied buildings) remains only a temporary resource; here there is no inside or outside, nor any sense of them and us. The occupation has become the anti-occupation.[17]

There is still a touch of 1990s terminology, perhaps: fluffy or spiky, not left or right but pacifist protest or violent action. On the one hand, there is 'Occupy the City', a worldwide protest organisation who camp and party; on the other hand, there are the more violent waves of student protest and inner-city rioting of 2010 and 2011. The aim is to make the future and make it now, maybe out of 'fluffy' peace-loving politics (with its oppositionary boundary with 'spiky' violence and disorder), but always out of necessary political conflict driven by economic inequality and social dominance, in the full maturity of ideological and practical civil disobedience.

This book is the companion book to *Violent London: 2000 Years of Riots, Rebels and Revolts*. This book gives the first full and consecutive historical account of the student riots of 2010 and the inner-city riots of 2011, and offers the first account and explanation of how the two sets of riots are related. It also gives a clear historical analysis of the main British protest groups and their aims and tactics in the twenty-first century, and demonstrates that security forces and others in authority predicted the riots of August 2011 as long ago as 2010, but failed to act on the information. Consequently, the book also investigates police responses and strategy in a rapidly changing environment and explores police failings of advance intelligence and tactics. Finally, it offers an historically-based context for the recent London riots from the race riots of 1981 and the protest movements of the 1960s and 1970s, back to the Gordon Riots of 1780, the Bawdy House Riots of the seventeenth century and the anti-banking movement of the twelfth century. My approach is, perhaps, holistic, an attempt to combine the latest official documentation, police reports, security briefings, reportage and parliamentary reports with information from the rioters, revolutionary groups and historical evidence. This work, like its predecessor, is about the heartbeat of contemporary London.

The political action on the streets in the last few years has suggested that London is again in a period of fluidity. Eruptions of street violence have always followed periods when London's population has felt frustrated through disengagement with the political process, disinherited of its perceived rights, disenchanted with its rulers or dispossessed of its economic security. All of these factors have come together in recent years and are likely to continue. Grassroots protest stems from frustration and moral indignation, whether it be students attacking Conservative Campaign Headquarters or looters attacking Foot Locker. These factors, alongside perceived economic hardship and the indifference of those in Parliament or those with money, are powerful stimuli for disturbance. This book is a story of refusal and protest, of a renewal of political consciousness and the new ways in which it is displayed by those who feel left out by the system, whether students, anti-capitalists or the unemployed youthful poor; an analysis of the emergence of new protest in the twenty-first century but concentrating on two riotous and momentous periods separated by a mere ten months.

Commonalities stretch over a long history of rioting and disturbance in London and cover many centuries. All riots are different, but similarities may also be drawn across time and synchronically. Of course, London is no stranger to civil unrest. From Wat Tyler to the G20 and from the Gordon Riots of the eighteenth century to the 'summer riots' of 2011, London has an alternative history, one outside the framework of parliamentary procedures and endless committees, where there is direct political confrontation by the people with the state to bring about fundamental social change. It is a story of street fighting and slum warfare, assassination and bombing, whether the fight is against monarchy or draconian laws, and it is filled with demagogues and democrats, bigots and revolutionaries from the extremes of the left and the right of politics: anarchists, libertarians, Trotskyists and communists, environmentalists and anti-capitalists. The nature of those involved has changed over the years, as have their demands, and even the landscape of protest has altered, morphed into cyberspace, as well as the dirty politics of the pavement, but live protest remains at the heart of our democracy and at the heart of what it means to live in a free society. It is the raw and vital edge of being a Londoner.

2

2010: OCCUPY EVERYTHING

A fire extinguisher falls in slow motion; a student revved on adrenalin holds a red flag and kicks the Cenotaph; protesters barricade a derelict pub called the Hand and Racquet near Leicester Square, raid restaurant dustbins and play with the plumbing; a bottle of bubbly is opened at a top London store, but no one pays; groceries and televisions, bottled water and wine taken at the plaza and in the high street; a girl in a mask holds two fingers up to the CCTV whilst her mum does more than window shop; a young boy helps dad with a stolen fruit machine; 'BlackBerry' phones and text messages; 24-hour news images; glass shattering everywhere, burning trash, burning buildings; a woman jumps as her flat crashes to the ground; fire licks around a furniture store; a hoodie on a chopper bike, a cop on a radio; a robbed man and a dead man; the imprint of sudden dread; a carnival for the disinherited. Such are the fragments of the images of the riots of November and December 2010, and March and August 2011; images of social breakdown and of political and urban decay; of the impotence of authority and the insouciance of youth.

Images silhouetted against an unprecedented economic depression; no Plan B; a faltering Plan A; tales of the euro spinning out of control, television footage of Greeks and Italians, the Portuguese and Spaniards throwing petrol bombs and fighting riot police; the Arab Spring; the fall of dictators in distant lands; the death toll in Afghanistan; anti-capitalism in Wall Street, anti-democracy in Syria and Russia; universal repression; the highest unemployment for a decade; the lowest number of jobs; the shadow of tuition fees; severe government cutbacks, including those on jobs and pensions in the public sector; the restructuring and further privatisation of the National Health Service; unprecedented banker's bonuses and unprecedented tax savings for the rich; hacking scandals at the *News of the World*; the endless snow of the riots of 2010 and the endless warm nights of the riots of 2011. Images of despair against a backcloth of emergent joy: the London Olympics 2012.

In 2011 there was also the end of a long series of legal tangles left unresolved from previous demonstrations and incidents: £117,000 was paid in compensation to 30 protestors at the G20 protests by the Metropolitan Police and a final inquest was held to review evidence regarding the death of Ian Tomlinson. An officer, Simon Harwood, was eventually charged in May 2011 with 'unlawful killing' by the office of the Director of Public Prosecutions after a new inquest jury found that he used 'excessive and unreasonable force': he pleaded 'not guilty' in October 2011 and stood trial at the Old Bailey in June 2012. Tomlinson's last words were apparently 'they got me, the fuckers got me'; the 7/7 inquest brought to its legal finality, the endless suffering of the victims and relatives of those killed; in November and December, the Metropolitan Police produced two reports on the summer riots, one of which followed the report of the Riots, Communities and Victims Panel, and these were themselves followed by the reports of *The Guardian*/London School of Economics studies and that of Her Majesty's Chief Inspectorate of Constabulary. The Stephen Lawrence murder trial also finally ground to its end with the conviction of Gary Dobson and David Norris, but left other potential prosecutions still hanging in the air.[1] It was a year of attempts at closure and new beginnings.

Do the years 2010 to 2011 represent an awakening or mere frustration, a new beginning or mere repetition? Whilst so many have sought to separate the politics of the student movement from those looting Nando's, they have failed to see that the breaking of glass at 30 Millbank and the stealing of mobile phones from the local electrical store do have things in common.

The destruction at Millbank on 10 November 2010 changed the shape of extra-parliamentary politics. Here were young people who had taken their fight to the centre of power, who had shown no fear of authority and who had wrong-footed the police and, for a short moment, who had rekindled the energy of political struggle. It was in that respect defining. The fight was ostensibly about students refusing to become consuming cogs in the corporate machine, their professors turned into vocational managers, students now merely 'calculating investors' in their own overpriced future.[2]

Indeed, it took them little time to understand that their struggle was not just against rising tuition fees, but was also about class struggle where those that have and those that have not were locked in combat once again. And the question was a simple one: who owns the future? 'Where's my future' proclaimed a banner on 10 November 2010; in other words, where is hope in the bleak landscape of austerity, a landscape precisely the opposite of that which greeted the protesters of the 1960s? What was wanted was a new kind of hope, one devoid of personal gain and existential longing, but one produced in social space in 'an age of scarcity'. 'We are entering', students argued, 'an age of scarcity of the future' where neo-liberal policies preached only the salvation of the few and the aspirational politics of acquisition. As the student agitators presciently observed:

> Hope is not evenly distributed – what hopes there are and who has access to them depend on where you are located (be you poor or black, disabled, a woman, young, living in the regions, etc). Neoliberal hope – aspiration – is increasingly restricted to an ever-smaller circle of people: those people doing well through the current crisis; those people above the buffer of the 'squeezed middle'. For the rest, there's the lottery. (To be clear, there have been 'no hopers' for quite some time – an underclass living a kind of social death of meaningless, pointless lives, hidden away behind ASBOs on estates. But this is to become the norm for many, many more people.)[3]

No wonder proponents of 'DIY protest' advocate stealing; 'shoplifting is an art' they said to beat capitalist domination:

> Within capitalism, most of us are either (1) alienated from our labour and hence dependent on the ruling classes for commodities as basic as food and clothing, (2) excluded from the division of labour, in which case we are likewise dependent on the State, or (3) performing unpaid and/or unrecognised labour and hence dependent on patriarchal relations for food, clothing, etcetera. In any case, our access to resources is severely limited by contemporary relations of domination. One partial solution to this problem may be to STEAL [sic].[4]

They calculated wrongly in the end, for their idea of shoplifting was already mired in a certain nostalgia, as their thoughts belonged to another era altogether when there was acknowledged authority and fear of it. They remained unaware of the brazen nature of the politics of proletarian aggression:

> Don't be put off by signs such as 'shoplifters will be prosecuted' or 'security police patrol this store'. Often this is just bluff anyway, and in any case there is no security measure that cannot be undone by a clever shoplifter or a quick talker. Do, however, keep your eye on security and be on the lookout for video surveillance cameras ...
>
> Finally, if you get caught – lie your teeth out! Never admit to premeditation. Always say that the opportunity arose, so you took it. Don't act tough or be a smart arse. Cry. Bawl. Admit a guilty conscience. Beg them not to call the cops. Tell them that CSV will take your kids off you and then weep. If the cops do arrive, it's a good idea to act scared shitless because they may assume you're a first offender and not bother to check your record. Don't antagonise the filth – it is [at] their personal discretion as to how bad you get busted.[5]

Today, we are living in disturbed times; all those in authority think so. The Prime Minister thought so when he spoke on 15 August 2011 of a 'broken society' after the summer riots. These were a 'wake-up call for our country' to remind us of the 'social problems that have been festering for decades' and that now had 'exploded in our face'. Something was wrong in the state of Britain 'about behaviour' and 'with indifference to right and wrong', and with people with a 'twisted moral code' and those who had a 'complete absence of self-restraint'. 'We', emphasised the Prime Minister, need to 'reclaim our streets'.

Yet how and with what means? On 4 January 2011, Bob Broadhurst, then Commander for Public Order and Pan London Operational Support,[6] predicted more disturbances through 'fears around unemployment' and the possibility that violence would increase. The then Metropolitan Police Commissioner, Sir Paul Stephenson, looked into his crystal ball in late 2010 and warned that 'the game had changed' and there was 'the likelihood [of] more disorder',[7] whilst in 2011 he even predicted that 'a new era of civil unrest is upon us'.[8]

On 6 November 2011, Lord John Stevens, former Head of the Metropolitan Police, returned to the subject, commenting about his concern that he could 'see that there [was] disquiet on the streets'. He predicted that 'it [was] going to be a very difficult eighteen months to two years' and added rather apocalyptically, 'I hope to God I am wrong but I do not think I am'. The cause of the problems were, in his opinion, 'youth unemployment and unemployment generally [and] signs of increasing crime', relationships between communities and the police, and the use of stop and search. The government too in their most recent strategy papers confirmed that 'we are entering an age of uncertainty' and that 'our national interest requires us to stand up for the values our country believes in – the rule of law, democracy, free speech, tolerance and human rights'.[9]

Hard times require hard men. In the wake of the student demonstrations against Conservative Campaign Headquarters, Michael Gove, the Secretary of State for Education, argued for draconian education laws which would see soldiers taken from the front line in Iraq and Afghanistan and retrained on a 'troops to teachers' plan in order to tackle class indiscipline. He said 'I can't think of anything better than getting people who know all about self-discipline, teamwork and a sense of pride' into the classroom.[10] The 'landmark' decision was laid out in a White Paper, perhaps as a threat, perhaps as a promise of authoritarian times ahead, perhaps merely as a marker of growing government intolerance towards dissent. As he gave out the news, a police van and bus stop burned in Whitehall and students were being kettled in the cold.

As early as November 2010, Sir Paul Stephenson predicted that the student attack on Conservative Campaign Headquarters (where the police had been wrong-footed and unable to control the situation, and where those protesting no longer showed the expected fear and respect for those in authority) heralded a new phase of activism and a new turn of tactics by demonstrators.[11] The economic downturn, coupled with the success of the new activism, meant that flash mobs and demonstrations were becoming bolder and less predictable. In the spring of 2011, for instance, town halls across the UK were invaded by residents angry at government cuts, especially those affecting libraries, welfare, youth services and sports facilities. Often the police were unprepared for the level of anger. As Haringey, Tower Hamlets, Lewisham, Lambeth and Islington made council cuts, protesters invaded offices and council chambers and fought police.

Indeed, the pattern of police unpreparedness for prolonged disturbance is interesting. The police were not prepared for the ferocity of the student protests and specifically the Millbank attack, an attack that could easily have been predicted by the very logic of the protest. Of these protests, Bob Broadhurst had to admit that 'we were caught out … we've accepted that. We were probably going a bit too much on the intelligence ... none of which suggested disorder'. Intelligence failed where plain logic might have succeeded. Broadhurst continued that '[the police] can't keep throwing hundreds of police at every event'.[12] Four months later and again six months after that, it was both mistakes of logic and of intelligence that saw the police having to catch up with events that had eluded them.

There is now a sense of official foreboding that did not exist in 2009 and that has only increased since the summer of 2011 when, for a few days in August, Britain's cities looked on the brink of chaos (with an enormous 3,003 arrests in London alone by November 2011, which had risen to 3,864 by March 2012). So serious were the disturbances that in November 2011, the Home Secretary, Theresa May, fearing trouble at the marches from students and trade unionists that were scheduled, 'authorised' the potential use (in a civil order emergency) of baton rounds (colloquially but erroneously called rubber bullets) at future 'violent' demonstrations. Such rounds have never been used in mainland Britain before and suggest a new level of panic amongst those in authority.

The use of baton rounds does not, however, require authorisation for use from either the Prime Minister or the Home Secretary and are actually part of the operational equipment of the police. In November 2011, Assistant Commissioner Lynne Owens authorised the doubling of the amount of trained officers in the use of baton rounds.[13] She did not have to do so with government permission.

The case for the authorisation of the use of baton rounds remains confused. It was during the emergency debate on the summer riots that Yvette Cooper, the Shadow Home Secretary, reminded the Prime Minister that it was not actually in his gift to authorise their use:

> Let me add a word of caution to the Government briefing on water cannons and baton rounds. The perception in the newspapers has been that it was only the Prime Minister's intervention that has made possible the use of water cannon and baton rounds, and the Home Secretary seemed to suggest something similar in her statement today. However, it is important to be clear that the police already had the power to use baton rounds or to ask police in Northern Ireland for the use of their water cannon. That is an operational matter for the police, not a political judgment for Ministers.[14]

Nevertheless, so difficult is the issue, especially regarding the potential wounding or death of rioters (some mere children) or bystanders, that the police would, in effect, have to get permission for their deployment. Thus, the fact that the Home Secretary could or could not 'authorise' the use of such weaponry is a moot point. The potential use of water cannons and other very visible means of crowd control has been debated endlessly by police and politicians since the student protests of November and December 2010. Less well reported was the use of CS spray on ten UK Uncut protesters at a leafleting demonstration outside Boots the Chemist in Oxford Street on 30 January 2011.

The new Commissioner of the Metropolitan Police, Bernard Hogan-Howe, appointed in 2011 but after the August riots, was taking no chances after the apparent lacklustre police performance during the first two days of rioting during the summer. Hogan-Howe is the former police chief in Merseyside, a supporter of old-fashioned robust 'have-a-go' policing and 'aggressive tactics' in riots if it is believed that life is threatened.[15] Indeed, his hand in these regards was considerably strengthened by the report of Her Majesty's Inspectorate of Constabulary in December 2011, which followed a request by the Home Secretary for clarification as to the needs of the police in public order actions following the August riots. Amongst a number of conclusions, it was felt that in certain circumstances the use of 'lethal force' might be appropriate. This was first time that such a conclusion has been reached in England since the founding of the police in 1829.[16]

No hostages were to be taken now, the message of authority fully reinforced. On 9 November 2011, during the National Campaign Against Fees and Cuts march, for instance, there were 4,000 police officers (including City of London police) to supervise what was probably no more than 5,000–7,000 student protesters (police estimates were 2,000 and those of student organisers 10,000) who had threatened to unleash a 'sea of rage' on the one-year anniversary of the beginning of the tuition fees protests.

The police would act in a more cautious and subtle manner from now on.[17] The students would not be obviously kettled; instead, the use of box barriers effectively siphoned the students along the route to London Wall and successfully away from the St Paul's 'Occupy London' anti-capitalist camp and a distance from the Stock Exchange. At the throwing of a few bottles, the police donned helmets and took up riot shields, a sensible precaution to some, but a provocation to many marchers.

Despite this, 200 militants broke away and temporarily squatted in tents in Trafalgar Square just before another unrelated demonstration by black cab drivers over infringements by illegal minicabs brought Trafalgar Square and its environs to a halt far more damaging than the student 'camp', which lasted a mere few minutes but resulted in 24 arrests, including some at London Wall. Even as that was occurring, a march through London by the electrician's union protesting against 35 per cent pay cuts was itself temporarily actually kettled, whilst at Woolwich Arsenal the emergency services practised attendance at a civil disaster.

Nowadays, in London, there are always a range of demonstrations and security risks. In the end, 19 protestors were charged: three for violent disorder and affray respectively; one for possession of an offensive weapon; three for 'going equipped'; one for a breach of Section 60aa of the Criminal Justice and Public Order Act 1994 resulting in a forceful removal of a mask; and 12 for a breach of the peace. More significantly, some saw the threat of baton rounds which had been publicised at the time as an overt warning to protestors regarding the limits of government toleration.

There was a clear decision to stop protests spreading. The attempt to protest by anti-capitalists in front of the American Embassy on 15 November 2011 was broken up by police with some arrests. Meanwhile, the Guildhall and Canary Wharf were all cordoned off by police to prevent the camps in front of St Paul's and Finsbury Circus spreading. Nevertheless, protesters at St Paul's were able to raise funds and to hold a continuous series of informal political awareness lectures, many well attended both by curious 'city types' as well as by political campers. On 15 November, the City of London Corporation gained approval to order the protestors to remove the camp within two days. This did not happen, but on 23 November 2011, the *Evening Standard* ran a controversial headline suggesting the 'St Paul's Junkies [were] a Health Hazard', including the potential of HIV being spread through abandoned needles. With little except anecdotal evidence, the headline seemed to be nothing more than an unfounded 'smear' to create a cordon sanitaire round the protesters and thus isolate them. Boris Johnson continued to vilify the demonstrators as 'hemp-smoking, fornicating hippies', an accusation that caused St Paul's to respond by offering the campers limited 'sanctuary' inside the cathedral should the camp be formally disbanded either by bailiffs or the protesters themselves, an invitation that was not taken up, even though the Corporation of London was able to send the bailiffs in at midnight on 27 February 2012, thereby ending 137 days of occupation.[18]

The row over the camp has done little to stop the capitalist excesses that the protest was concerned with. The protesters wanted 'structural change towards authentic global equality', did not 'accept that cuts are inevitable' and 'refuse[d] to pay for the banks' crisis'.[19] The camp has done much to focus the Church of England on its role in a time of crisis ('you cannot serve both God and money': Matthew 6:24) and direct discussion to questions of moral and communal significance and the idea of charity in its widest sense. Moreover, there were a surprising number of practising Christians and older people at the camp.[20]

Indeed, there have always been protesters in London against the excesses of wealth. Such was the case of William Fitz Osbert or William with the Long Beard, an educated charismatic Londoner and friend of Prince John who briefly flourished as an 'advocate of the poor' in 1196. His story is one repeated (with less violence on the steps of St Paul's today) and the 'smear' campaign against him has a distinctly modern note. William, a man of commanding presence, seemed to believe that he was the Messiah come to free the people from their poverty from 'the insolence of riches'. He preached to ever-growing crowds of the poor and conceived the idea, with a number of convinced followers, that only an armed rebellion against the wealthy would restore harmony in the kingdom:

> This William stirred and excited the common people to desire and love freedom and liberty, and blamed the excess and outrage of rich men: by such means he drew to him many great companies, and with all his power defended the poor man's cause against the rich, and accused divers to the king, shewing that, by their means, the king lost many forfeits and escheats. For this, gentlemen and men of honour maligned again him, but he ... kept on his purpose ... William, an innocent of [any] crimes ... was a defender of the poor people again extortioners and wrongdoers, was by them put wrongfully to death.[21]

The modern debate within the Church led to the resignations of the Dean of St Paul's, the Right Reverend Graeme Knowles, and Canon Chancellor Giles Fraser on moral grounds. Yet the battle over political protest camps and the sins of the wealthy goes on.

With the Olympics nearing, and wanting Parliament Square to look its best for the event, the government intends to bring in a new bylaw incorporated into the Police Reform and Social Responsibility Act 2011 banning camps in large areas of central London, not just on the central traffic island in Parliament Square. Such tented communities as the Peace Camp, Democracy Camp and Anti-capitalist Camp have over the last 11 years become a feature of the landscape, since Brian Haw and others originally squatted in front of Parliament to protest against the Iraq War.

After ten years of protest, Haw died of lung cancer on 19 June 2011, aged 62. His protest had begun against the Iraq War on 2 June 2001. Although born in Barking, Haw lived in Redditch until he set up his peace camp in Parliament Square. He ran for Parliament and was voted 'most inspiring political figure' by *Channel 4 News* in 2007. Despite the proliferation of camps, Members of Parliament, the Greater London Authority, Westminster Council, the Royal Parks and the City of London have failed to find a satisfactory solution to the perceived problem of tented cities. Indeed, as long ago as January 2010, Assistant Commissioner Lynne Owens had warned

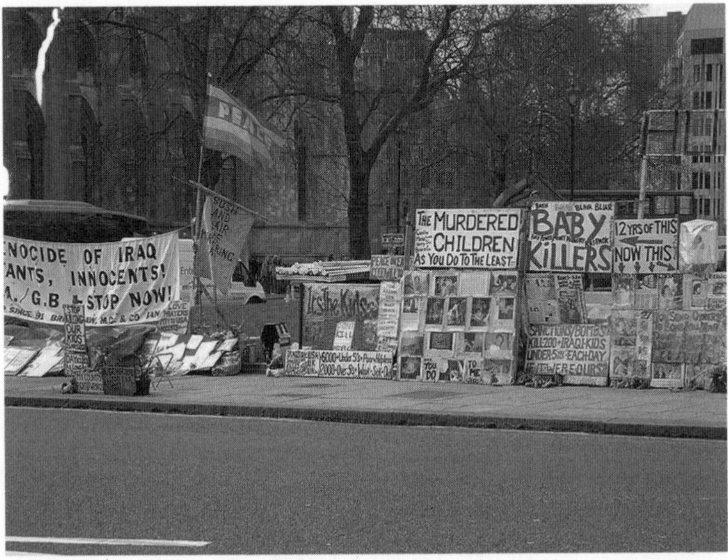

Figure 2.1 Brian Haw's peace encampment (Laura Hadden, 'Iraq Demo in London', Creative Commons Attribution)

the Commons Select Committee that the current specific legislation about Parliament Square left the decision about removal in the practical hands of the police without solid guidance from human rights law or clear government policy as to 'proportionality'. Such dithering would prove dangerous.[22]

The last months of 2010 saw a number of student political demonstrations, including the attack on Prince Charles (9 December 2010) and riots and disturbances on London's streets due to the rise in tuition fees and the withdrawal of Educational Maintenance Allowances (EMAs), whilst in the spring of 2011 there were disturbances at Fortnum & Mason in Piccadilly and at Oxford Circus following the 500,000 public sector TUC 'March for the Alternative' rally (26 March). After the 'March for the Alternative' rally, there were 145 arrests of whom ten were found guilty of aggravated trespass. One of those arrested was Ben Brailsford, who subsequently wrote a comedy called 'My Fortnum and Mason Hell', which played at the Edinburgh Fringe in 2011.

These highly publicised disturbances, mostly by young people, were followed in the summer of 2011 by riots in London in Tottenham, Enfield, Edmonton, Walthamstow, Clapham, Peckham, Hackney, Ealing, Croydon and elsewhere in or near London, which ignited so-called copycat disturbances across Britain in the worst street violence since the 1980s and in a fashion more reminiscent of the eighteenth century in its ferocity and outlook.

At the time of writing, there remained 'Occupy London' anti-capitalist camps at Finsbury Square and Mile End park, as well as a recent march by students through central London to protest against the raising of tuition fees and the 'privatisation' of higher education (9 November 2011), and a major one-day strike and demonstration by public sector workers against massive budgetary and pension cuts in the public sector, poor fiscal growth forecasts, youth unemployment at record highs and the news of huge bonuses for corporate business men and bankers (30 November 2011). The strike, which included two million workers, was peaceful except for the occupation of Panton House in the Haymarket by UK Uncut and Occupy London. A total of 5,000 police monitored approximately 20,000 marchers.

World finance and the way it is manipulated is now the single biggest issue for protest and will often unite disparate groups. In 2010 *Rolling Stone* journalist Matt Taibbi described the investment bank Goldman Sachs as being a blood-sucking 'vampire squid' in a piece which has become an article of faith for anti-capitalists campers:

> Even on its own terms the banking system is broken ... To design a banking system that is fit for purpose and able to underpin the imminent Great Transition to a new, low carbon, high well-being, and stable economy, we need to revisit the social and economic contract that banks have with society. We must take back our banks.[23]

The anti-capitalists call for a 'great transition'. Perhaps, one day, it will come and perhaps the state will collapse 'and all manner of things shall be well'.

3

2010 TO 2012: THE CONSTANT THREAT AND THE DISTANT FEAR

Until the time when all is well, the state must be vigilant and must prepare for the worst. Social breakdown, as everyone now knows, is a mere whisper away, a little cloud of dissent on the horizon.

Violent clashes between police and protesters at an illegal gipsy settlement in Dale Farm, Basildon, Essex in October 2011 (where electronic 'tasers' were used for the first time in a public order situation) and the custard pie 'terrorist' attack against Rupert Murdoch on 18 July 2011 whilst he gave evidence at a Commons committee emphasise the protean nature of modern protest. These events were merely side issues to the continuing problems of terrorist attack by Islamic fundamentalists, a revived Irish nationalist movement and a growing English Defence League (EDL) with the possibility of a violent racist incident as had occurred in Norway in 2011, not to mention the entirely new threat of a cyber-attack on vital information, all of which keep authority guessing and require absolute vigilance.

Security forces in the UK and especially in London are convinced that another attack is imminent, a situation exacerbated by the relaxing of the rules regarding border checks by the Home Secretary in July 2011 and again in September. Brodie Clarke, head of the UK Border Force, resigned over the fiasco in November 2011, accusing Theresa May of causing the situation in the first place. Regardless of the internal row, it was suggested by many observers that an unknown number of immigrants, including potential terrorists, were 'lost' in the tracking system or were not properly screened on entry. Most immigrants would pass through London before dispersing. The evidence for imminent terrorist attacks was again emphasised during December when Ronald Noble, the retiring Secretary General of Interpol, suggested that screening suspects against the international database of lost or stolen passports was too often ignored. Although Noble feared another attack might therefore be a possibility, the evidence remains sketchy and less than convincing at times, although the home security budget continues to rise whilst other areas are cut, especially front-line policing.[1]

It is also clear that despite the curtailment of the activities of Julian Assange and his associates, computer attacks on government sites and the release of unauthorised information will continue, even given the 'blockade' by various banks and governments to shut down WikiLeaks itself. Islamicist activity, although only partially diminished by the effects of the 'Arab Spring', is still fuelled by a hatred of British troops being based in Afghanistan, where they will remain in active service until at least 2015.[2] Irish nationalists are still attempting to buy arms to continue the struggle and although there may be a lack of hunger for more bloodshed in Northern Island, a maverick may just get through. Such a maverick was Michael Campbell of the Real IRA, caught in an MI5 operation when he tried to buy arms from Lithuania. Right-wing international extremism (closely associated with the style of racist policies once associated with the National Front and currently considered by many to be inherent in the British National Party) is now under a spotlight that it was not under before Anders Behring Breivik's attack in Norway in July 2011.The economic downturn may yet throw up new groups willing to go to extremes to fight their cause.

The situation is always changing, the targets always uncertain. Indeed, before the Breivik attack, it was apparently police policy to ignore the activities of the EDL except in terms of public order. Detective Superintendent Adrian Tudway, who in 2010 was National Coordinator for Domestic Extremism, claimed during November that the EDL posed no threat as it was not 'an extreme right-wing organisation'.[3] Nevertheless, after the Norwegian attack, the focus shifted to one of close surveillance. Moreover, Assistant Commissioner Tim Godwin was clear that one of the main and emerging threats to security was international right-wing extremism. So concerned were the police for public order that they arrested 170 EDL supporters on Armistice Day (11 November) 2011 based on intelligence that the protesters would go on to create trouble at the 'Occupy London' camp at St Paul's. Meanwhile, two potential national threats went head to head at the 9/11 tenth anniversary commemorations where both the EDL members and 'Muslims against Crusades' held opposing meetings near Grosvenor Square. After burning American flags and chanting 'USA Terrorists', about 100 Muslim radicals moved up the Edgware Road. Meanwhile, 60 EDL members went on a parallel march ending at the Tyburn pub. When the Muslim protesters walked past, a fight broke out in which two men were stabbed. In the end 40 people were arrested.[4]

Such tactical policy shifts in response, as are required by these sorts of clashes, need to be the result of day-to-day pragmatism rather than clear and thoughtful long-term planning. Not that such planning is ignored, but it is painted in broader rather than particular strokes, something made quite explicit in the shift of attitude from 'Cold War' politics to the emphasis on multiple potential attacks by 'non-state actors' utilising cyber technology, a position laid out in the government's strategic outlook, presented in two documents during October 2010. These were *Securing Britain in an Age of Uncertainty: The Strategic Defence and Security Review* and *A Strong Britain in an Age of Uncertainty: The National Security Strategy*, a more pertinent document for law and order.[5]

Both documents rather strangely laid out the security needs of 'Britain' rather than those of the UK, the first document emphasising the role of the armed forces and the second internal security matters. The economic depression was identified as a 'security deficit', whilst Britain's commitment to 'free trade and open markets' could not be diminished. It is this which drives many current security concerns amid much civil discontent. That is not to say that old concerns are not still present. A resurgent Irish nationalism and the continuing threat of al-Qaeda and those influenced adversely by Britain's policy in Afghanistan remained priorities, but these were accompanied by the possibility of terrorist cyber-attacks on vital resources. In 2010, the national threat level from Islamists was 'severe' (or 'highly likely') and the mainland threat to Britain from residual Irish terrorist groups was moved from 'moderate' to 'substantial' following the rise in attacks from 22 in 2009 to 37 by October 2010, one of which closed the Mall in London in May 2011.[6]

Nevertheless, and despite the fact that Osama bin Laden was assassinated by US special forces on 2 May 2011, al-Qaeda is still the greatest external threat to British security, the fear being that home-grown terrorists and outside extremists would target the 2012 Olympics. In his first annual review of the 2010 *Strategic Defence and*

Security Review, the Prime Minister highlighted the potential threat from Islamic extremists:

> The past year has seen significant changes in the threat from international terrorism. Al-Qaeda's leadership is now weaker than at any time since 9/11. But al-Qaeda continues to pose a threat and groups affiliated to al-Qaeda in countries such as Yemen and Somalia have emerged as a threat in their own right. We are implementing a revised counter-terrorism strategy to tackle the terrorist threat to the UK and our interests overseas.[7]

As early as November 2010, the Home Secretary was looking at special detention and control orders. During 2010, 101,248 people were stopped and searched by police under Section 44 of the Terrorism Act 2000, of whom only 506 were actually arrested and only 52 actually charged. Some individual threats still lingered. Thus, the family of the imprisoned Finsbury mosque preacher Abu Hamza continued to haunt the security services. One son, Yasser Kamel, was arrested at pro-Palestinian demonstrations outside the Israeli Embassy on 10 January 2010. Kamel threw sticks and missiles at police and used a stolen police shield when demonstrations turned into violent running battles down Kensington High Street and in Kensington Gore. One officer received a broken jaw as a result of a metal rivet being thrown at him. Because Kamel only arrived after most of the fighting had finished, he was given a 12-month youth detention sentence. The eldest son, Mohammed Kamel Mostafa, was imprisoned for a plot to kill British tourists. During February 2012, four men, who were inspired by al-Qaeda, stood trial at Woolwich Crown Court for conspiring to attack the London Stock Exchange, the American Embassy, Jewish leaders and the London Mayor, unleashing a 'Mumbai-style' attack with bombs. Five others faced lesser charges. All were caught after police surveillance operations that included watching the leader, Mohammed Chowdhury, visiting tourist attractions as potential targets. Nevertheless, other suspected terrorists remain at large, including Samantha Lewthwaite, the widow of Jermaine Lindsay, one of the 7/7 bombers.

At the same time, 21 terrorists were discharged from prison. New threats appeared, however, although the intelligence was sometimes faulty. For instance, Amir Ali, an Ilford-born driver for London Underground, was found not guilty of plotting 'violent jihad' in Britain and accused MI5 of 'framing' him when he wouldn't spy on colleagues for them, whereas Roshonara Choudhry was found guilty of stabbing the MP Stephen Timms at his surgery in East Ham with the intention of committing murder for his part in voting for the war in Iraq. Members of Parliament with large Muslim constituencies were also targeted by Islamic groups such as the 'Muslim Political Action Group', both Mike Gapes and Lee Scott in East London constituencies being threatened by these radicals in the run-up to the 2010 election. The security services were jittery. In September 2010, they arrested five street cleaners from Westminster in connection with an alleged plot to shoot Pope Benedict XVI. The plot proved groundless. Even more problematic has been the release of Abu Qatada in February 2012, al-Qaeda's alleged leading voice in Europe, after six-and-a-half years in jail. Currently under virtual house arrest, unable to have access to virtually any form of communication and watched 24 hours a day, he is now awaiting possible deportation to Jordan. In April 2012, legal proceedings to deport Abu Hamza and a number of his associates to stand trial in the USA as well as returning Abu Qatada to Jordan seemed to have come to a successful conclusion. All are accused of terrorist-related activities. Abu Hamza and five colleagues are currently appealing, but the Home Office seemed to have miscalculated its dates for the extradition of Qatada, who appealed to the European Court, thereby prolonging the question of deportation until the autumn of 2012.[8]

After banning the wearing of the burka (the niqab specifically) in France, the French warned of an imminent attack on Europe and the UK. In the first week of November 2010, ink cartridges filled with explosives were seized at East Midlands Airport and a plot to machine gun London shoppers in a Mumbai-style attack was foiled at Christmas when 12 men were arrested. The suicide bomber who struck in Stockholm during December 2010 was Taimour Abdulwahab Al-Abdaly, an Iraqi who lived in Luton, whilst in February 2011, Mohammed Gul of Hornchurch was jailed for five years after posting terrorist information on the Internet. He lost his subsequent appeal. At the same time, the government was paying out *ex gratia* payments to 16 men who accused M16 of aiding American 'rendition' even though it was claimed that 'waterboarding' torture prevented terrorist attacks in London. Rather than fight the cases, the government settled.[9]

Meanwhile, during the summer of 2010, universities and politicians were warned against the problem of further radicalisation and allowing speakers such as Raed Salah and Abdel Bari Atwan, editor-in-chief of the London-based *Al-Quds Al-Arabi*, whose views may have been construed as worrying by some in the gay, feminist and Jewish communities, to give lectures to students and MPs; such views compounded comments by the likes of John Galliano and were even reinforced by institutions such as the School of Oriental and African Studies at London University inviting the lawyer Jacques Verges, who has defended extremists, to speak in early January 2012. The University of Westminster elected two Islamicist students who allegedly held views of a potentially extreme nature to the Student Union in April 2011, despite the attempt to curb extreme Islamic ideologists by the government the previous year, a policy that has so far proved fruitless. In January 2011, it was suggested that Muslim and Jewish peace ambassadors should be trained to deal with both Islamophobia and anti-semitism on university campuses.[10] Nevertheless, a provocative 're-enactment' of an 'Israeli checkpoint' by the Palestinian Society of the London School of Economics during its 'Israeli Apartheid Week' was attacked with water balloons by an unidentified group of assailants in March 2012. Tensions on London campuses have, it seems, far from lessened.

The review of terror laws was nonetheless delayed because of a row over civil liberties concerning control orders. Such orders put suspects under supervision, although the suspects have not been convicted of any crime. The review conducted by the Office for Security and Counter-Terrorism recommended the ending of such orders, but was opposed by MI5. High-level terrorism may be receding, but low-level hatred continues. On Armistice Day 2011, around 20 supporters of Muslims against Crusades gathered in Kensington, burned replica poppies and shouted abuse during the annual two-minute silence. They were arrested but were only fined £50 by magistrates. In May 2011, four men were convicted of attacking teacher Gary Smith in East London for teaching the Koran but not being Muslim.

Homophobic attacks also continued into 2011, with two attacks at Charing Cross Station, an attack on Philip Sallon in Piccadilly Circus in May and Islamic posters in the East End declaring it to be a 'gay-free zone' in February. Metropolitan Police statistics for 2011 showed five homophobic attacks per month in Tower Hamlets. In February 2011, a gay man was stabbed in Camden by an armed gang. Stonewall Chief Executive Ben Summerskill was unimpressed with police responses, saying that he felt 'people were more cautious about reporting attacks' because the police did not act swiftly enough. In 2011 the Metropolitan Police recorded 1,335 homophobic offences compared to the previous year, in which 1,345 offences were recorded. Although the response appeared lukewarm, the police did swoop on 145 suspects of hate crime on 7 December 2011.[11] Nevertheless, racist hate crimes, of which there were 12,711 in 2011, represented 83 per cent of all hate crimes prosecuted. Only 565 cases of those which came to court represented other hate categories, including those perpetrated against people for their sexuality, religion or disability. This of course does not suggest that hate crimes are on the increase, merely that, Summerskill's remarks notwithstanding, the police are more vigilant with regard to certain types of crime and perhaps less vigilant to others.

To combat both internal and external threats no longer linked to the Cold War, the Coalition government set up the National Security Council, appointed a National Security Advisor and carried out a National Security Risk Assessment (NSRA) to look at the needs of the next 20 years, whilst greatly increasing the National Cyber Security Programme budget by £650 million up to 2014.[12] This strategy includes looking at how far the 'private sector' may also contribute to security against 'malicious acts' causing 'civil emergencies' by enemies of the state, whether international or home-grown.[13] In this regard, the government will continue to invest in 'covert intelligence' and give Government Communications Headquarters (GCHQ) an even greater role in cyber-surveillance. Nevertheless, counter-terrorism would be determined by 'efficiency savings' that might appear to have fatally flawed police intelligence gathering and order enforcement in recent years.

Ironically, the NSRA predicted that, given demographic shifts and a dangerously rising population, 'in some areas … poor infrastructure, political exclusion and unemployment, combined with population and resource pressures, caused in part by urbanisation, will increase the risk of instability and conflict'.[14] This extraordinary prediction, commissioned by the government itself, was neither heeded nor remembered. With all of its strategic preparation, rioting during the summer of 2011 caught the police and security forces off-guard, their training, in the end, being defeated by nothing more than violent groups of teenage looters against whom they had not thought to prepare. Furthermore, the government's report pointed out that in a civil emergency, the government should 'support small and medium-sized enterprises, which may suffer disproportionately from civil emergencies' precisely because they 'have a potentially significant contribution to make to the resilience of communities'.[15]

The government was slow to implement the policy of compensation implied in its proposed 'corporate resilience programme', little expecting the exact circumstances to arrive as it had predicted.[16]

Internet surveillance has been expensive but entirely ineffective in preventing major group disturbances, even though the plans for such disturbances were posted for easy access by followers of UK Uncut, students, squatters, anti-capitalists, environmentalists, human rights campaigners and anyone who could use a computer, the maps of suggested routes freely downloadable. The use of new media networks such as Twitter and Facebook and the ability of young people to manipulate a simple text message also baffled the Metropolitan Police to the point of government embarrassment. The resorting to police undercover agents to infiltrate various environmental groups has also proved an embarrassment. What has succeeded is the use of CCTV surveillance to convict looters, a technology that proved extremely slippery when employed to bring police officers to book for wrongdoing, as witnessed by the protracted legal wrangle over the death of Ian Tomlinson. Indeed, following the problems in the summer of 2011, where very few were arrested in the act of looting (there being no law to cover looting except the laws regarding theft), it appears that the police were more keen on arresting rioters than preventing riots.

Scrutiny of police methods and the increasing criticism to which the police are subject is hardly to be unexpected as the police stand between actual protestors and an invisible but weighty conceptual idea of the state, the democratic process and peaceful protest. At the very least, the police are paid to keep public order and to prevent disturbance which may damage property. The role of the police in the 'sandwich' between protestors and the rest of the population is often 'untenable', the police being forced to lobby for those laws and extra equipment which then provide evidence of their alleged inherent dislike of the democratic process, but 'the rule of law cannot tolerate civil disorder, nor can it act to intervene without infringing basic liberal freedoms'. It is a circle that cannot be squared.[17]

So worrying has it been regarding the position of police forces in society during the early years of the twenty-first century and especially regarding the idea of 'policing by consent', which had recently been severely damaged at various events including the G20, that the human rights group Liberty (the National Council for Civil Liberties) was invited by the Metropolitan Police (and the

Trades Union Congress) in spring 2011 to monitor the 'March for the Alternative'. This was to be held on 26 March, and Liberty was to subsequently report on its rally in Hyde Park in order to give evidence on the police handling of demonstrations against government cuts and finally report the findings in a publicly available document. The findings seemed to exonerate the police in the light of earlier less favourable conclusions. Indeed, Liberty had been set a limited remit and stuck, quite rightly, to this, but these findings were limited and faulty precisely because of this remit and were still a matter of debate, even within the police, six months later.

An estimated 500,000 marchers were expected and the police, after much criticism in the previous year, wanted to ensure their operations were transparent. The march itself went off without incident, even though it was the largest since the anti-war protests of 2003. The police had 4,500 officers watching the crowd from Blackfriars up to the finishing point at Hyde Park; Liberty had 120 observers, some working in pairs and some moving with the crowd. In addition, Liberty stationed observers with Bronze commanders in charge of vital sections of the march and placed some in the Special Operations Room with Silver and Gold command.

The report shows that the march was peaceful and the police response 'proportionate' and good hearted. In Downing Street, a large Trojan horse was observed being set alight, but there was no real trouble. Reports of kettling in Whitehall that circulated on Twitter were unfounded, although the tactic was employed later by some protesters at Fortnum & Mason against the police and then by the police themselves against demonstrators once sufficient reinforcements had arrived. The troubles that then erupted around and after the march through the Black Bloc tactics of those 2,000 or so demonstrators who had attached themselves to the main protest were reported second hand or ignored by Liberty observers and were mostly downplayed by the final report, Liberty's remit being merely to cover the TUC march. The report's conclusion did not suggest any misdoing by the police or any heavy-handedness, although it did criticise the use of kettling as a dubious tactical device likely to irritate demonstrators.

Kettling is still perhaps the best known of recent police tactics, being used to hem in protesters within a confined area and hold them there until it is deemed 'safe' to let them out. Effectively, this allows the police to collect data in order to individualise protesters,

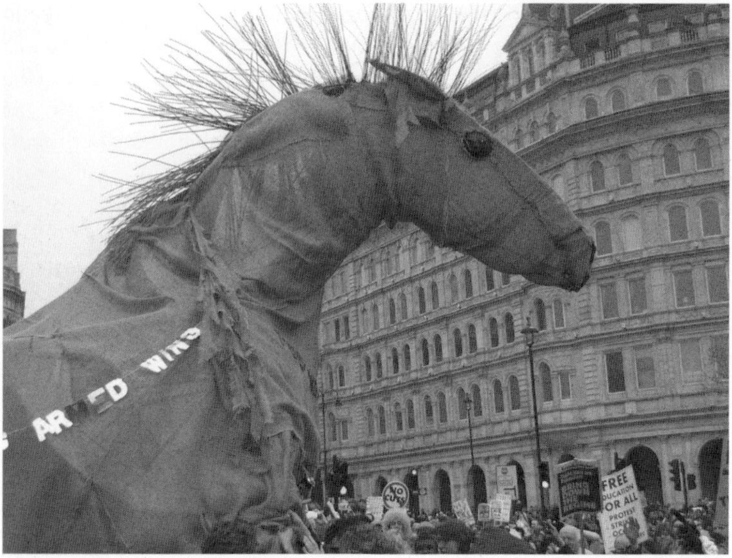

Figure 3.1 The Trojan Horse of the Armed Wing of the TUC just before being set alight (courtesy of Jonathan Bloom)

categorise, arrest and neutralise them. More than once it has been pointed out that a potential breach of human rights legislation is at stake, for during the student disturbances in late 2010, protesters were kept without food, water or toilets in freezing conditions for hours. Students point out that kettling is, effectively, a temporary form of open-air imprisonment. Indeed, 'it hands the police control over what is supposed to be a manifestation of popular, not police, will', the language of the kettle being 'force' used to turn demonstrators into a passive 'spectacle' of the 'repressed rising', now, however, bereft of power.[18]

In the 'cage' of the kettle, however, something is born. The many individuals caught by the net become a collective 'we' whom the state needs to fear. Those kettled cease to be victims and become agents or 'actors' of the sort of violence and dissent that the state cannot tolerate. As such, kettling ironically produces that radical power whose very presence is a threat to the state, which can only react by containment – a weak reaction by the state rather than one suggestive of a strongly proactive policy.[19]

The use of kettling or corralling to keep large groups under tight control and in one place began in Germany in 1986 (where it was deemed illegal), but only appeared in the UK a decade later and then actually against a disability rights demonstration in Parliament Square during October 1995. The tactic was again used without great success at a protest at Euston Station in 1999, when there were demonstrations against the World Trade Organization, but it was not perfected until 2000, when protesters at the 'Guerrilla Gardening' event were corralled by sufficient police in a tight cordon. Two protesters, believing their civil and human rights had been breached, took the police to court, but lost their case in 2005 and at appeal in 2007. Not unreasonably, Lord Hope at the Court of Appeal concluded that the 'purpose' of a kettle had to be decided before human rights law applied, a 'pragmatic approach' being paramount in all cases.

Yet a 'pragmatic approach' might be intended to mean reactive rather than proactive or aggressive, aiming to contain rioters rather than mere protesters. How can this decision be made? Thus, an attempt at kettling the crowd at the Gaza protest of 2009 went wrong, and the same attempt at the G20 protests went even more disastrously awry, leading the then Commissioner of Police, Sir Paul Stephenson, to comment on the need for 'appropriate and proportionate' policing and the High Court to rule in April 2011 that the kettle on that occasion was illegal.[20] This has not prevented the police from continuing to use the method as their tactic of choice, a simple and effective method of restricting movement and collecting data. As such, the students were contained on 24 November 2010 and again on 9 December, the method this time also restricting the movement of children left without food, water or toilets, something possibly illegal under the European Convention on Human Rights and certainly open to challenge. The Fortnum & Mason demonstrators were also kettled in a more 'responsible' way, only to be filtered out later and arrested.

The kettle is a blunt instrument, capable of achieving its aim of absolute containment only if there are sufficient police, a small enough space and a tightly packed demonstration. Without these criteria, it is impossible to impose. Since the student riots, more sophisticated tactics by demonstrators, such as 'break out' groups, better strategic forward planning, more international understanding of expected police movements and better contact via social media, have meant that fragments of demonstrations may break away and escape police supervision. The kettle is stationary, but such movement requires rapid mobile response. The students at Millbank and the rioters in Tottenham and Croydon proved how easy it is to break kettling tactics and how hard it is for the police to contain trouble without the availability of that tactic.

The police now consistently face criticism both from officially recognised bodies and from protest groups for disregarding human rights law by their incorrect or questionable actions at demonstrations, of which kettling is the most obvious. Such attitudes towards kettling suggest the need for sophistication (and critical distance) in the analyses of public disorder, such sophistication not being shown in Liberty's approach. The problems inherent in the Liberty report arose from the original remit in terms of what was allowed to be observed and reported. This has led the Metropolitan Police to claim clear transparency and fairness, but this was only really in terms of the main march, which was always going to be peaceful. The secondary disturbances after the rally were reported indirectly. Indeed, the report states that 'we did not observe events which took place after the official march had ended and therefore [we do not] comment on them'. Nevertheless, protests continued into the night, but were ignored.[21]

These findings led Assistant Commissioner Lynne Owens (now Chief Constable of Surrey) to claim that there was no problem with public order policing in London, as proved by the Liberty report.[22] This is not the case. Liberty neither observed the parallel demonstrations where there was a problem of keeping order nor the manner in which that order was kept. Indeed, the report itself also seems to have oddly confused some facts. The incident of the Trojan horse is instructive. This was a very large puppet-style model, reportedly set on fire by protesters calling themselves the 'TUC Armed Wing' outside Downing Street at 12.45 pm. Nevertheless the author witnessed the very same horse in Trafalgar Square, evidently undamaged. It was here that the head was partially set on fire and fireworks were let off. The 'TUC Armed Wing' (if it ever really existed) was, in fact, very young people, neither armed nor attached to the TUC, the title being entirely ironic.

Owens herself was in charge of operations at the marriage of Prince William and Kate Middleton on 29 April 2011. Previous to the event there had already been the feeding of disinformation (from some source: possibly the Home Office) to newspapers in order to create scare tactics. Papers such as the *Evening Standard* ran with headlines such as 'Anarchists Plot to Wreck Will's Wedding'.[23] The peace camp in Parliament Square was forcibly moved by bailiffs and a number of arrests were made, including activists Brian Haw and Barbara Tucker. On the day before the wedding, 20 people were arrested for 'conspiracy' to disrupt the wedding, seven at one squat. One of those arrested, whilst lying on a pavement, was Professor Christopher Knight, an anthropologist sacked by the University of Greenwich for his incitement to violence at the G20, and his wife Camillia Power, as well as a third man named Patrick Macroidan. Whilst being arrested, Knight told police 'you're arresting a professor of anthropology who runs a street theatre group', whilst another member of the group was arrested wearing a medieval executioner fancy dress costume.[24] The police have no sense of irony, although the mode of protest was merely intended to be in the risible tradition which goes back to the days of 'Class War' and the 'Moon Against the Monarchy' demonstration held in front of Buckingham Palace in June 2000.

Indeed, Knight and his associates belong to an alternative anthropological 'comedy' collective called 'Government of the Dead', an anti-monarchist group whose aim is to 'dance on the grave of capitalism' and who were intending to hold a 'zombie wedding' in Soho Square on the morning of the marriage followed by a 'zombie fertility rite' in Piccadilly Square and a 'heads will roll' party at Westminster. The group had previously posted an online comic invitation to a day of 'rumpy pumpy' under the 'spanking new working guillotine' with 'Hell's Grannies' invited as the cackling crones. To ensure that everybody got the joke, it also posted a disclaimer renouncing terrorism and all things 'Jacobinical'. It was not enough to allay fears of anarchist violence.

Surreal comedy is now part of protest. Aaron Barschak came to prominence as a 'comedy terrorist' on 21 June 2003, when he was able to smuggle himself into Prince William's twenty-first birthday party whilst wearing a pink dress, a false beard, a merkin and turban, looking like Osama bin Laden. He was arrested after climbing the stage where William was giving a speech, but was not prosecuted.

Jonnie Marbles (Jonathan May-Bowles) appeared to be an 'anarchist comedian' of the same ilk. Both he and Barschak seem to believe in creating 'situations' in which the action is a type of comic surrealist event which bursts the pretensions of the victim. In Marbles' case, this was a custard (or shaving foam) pie in Rupert Murdoch's face at

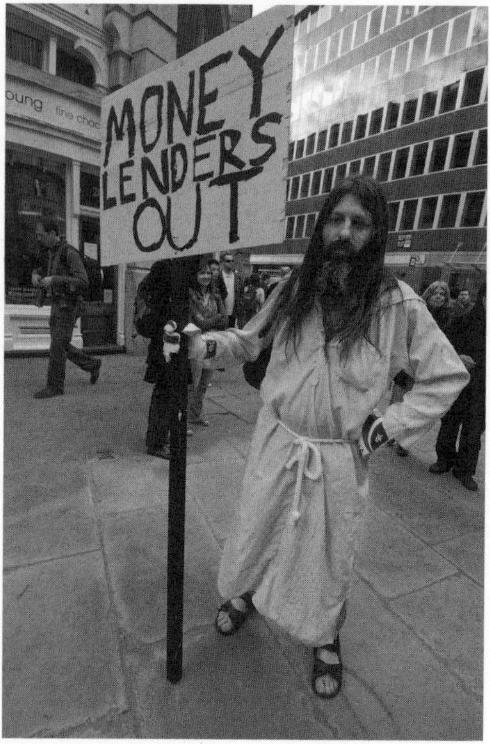

Figure 3.2 Jesus wants me for a sunbeam: the point is well made by comedy terrorist Aaron Barschak (courtesy of David Hoffman)

his meeting with a parliamentary committee on 18 July 2011 – a case of literally eating humble pie. Later, Marbles, a member of UK Uncut, reflected on his antics:

> To be honest, I had not expected to get so far, but parliamentary security, with its machine-gun toting cops and scatter X-rays, is apparently no match for a man with some shaving-foam covered plates in his bag. Then, once inside the committee room, I was helped along by some unwelcome luck. I had always intended to wait until the end of the hearings anyway before I launched my circus crusade, and as the penultimate speaker finished several people made their way out, leaving me a clear path to Murdoch. It was a horrible feeling: I had a plan, a pie and no excuses left.

> I had intended to unleash a wave of polemic as I made my move. As it turned out, the whole thing was far too weird for me to string two thoughts together, particularly as Murdoch's wife rose from the chair to prevent and avenge her husband's humiliation. As it went, I'm glad I was even able to make the accurate understatement that he was a 'naughty billionaire'.[25]

Attacking people with custard pies for political reasons really began in earnest during the second Iraq War with 'Operation Dessert Storm' (a rather witty joke), in which politicians were custard-pied instead of egged. The idea of attacking people with custard pies suggests not only that the victims need to be humbled but also that the situation leading up to the event is literally a farce. The custard pie provides a media event, which makes you smile, is not intended to wound, but is intended as a photo opportunity, highlighting both the victim and the perpetrator who wishes to promote his or her point of view. Although they have the frisson of actual violent assault, such activities are, in fact, a very British way of coping with the unbearably pompous and overweening. The police unfortunately remain unamused and have to treat such exuberance with the full power of the law.

The police have found it harder and harder to find a 'correct' yet swift way of dealing with the many types of public disorder that now exist. Liberty's findings, which were intended to exonerate police tactics, coupled with the implementation of more careful riot control procedures (learned after mistakes at both the G20 and student demonstrations) as well as other concerns regarding media revelations, may have made the police feel complacent about their tactical policies regarding street protest. By 2011, they were geared towards keeping order amongst relatively traditional protest groups using less traditional tactics. The student riots could be contained if violence broke out again.

At the very same time and unbeknownst to all, the senior Metropolitan Police leadership was under severe threat and government decisions were about to cut into front-line tactical policing. In the middle of the summer of 2011, a number of senior police officers were exposed to accusations of scandal and actual bribery, and although exonerated of all misdoing by the Independent Police Complaints Commission (IPCC), the Commissioner himself, Sir Paul Stephenson, resigned amid the scandal. Redundancies and efficiency savings in the police dominated headlines too and demoralised officers. During the summer riots of 2011, this led to strategic weaknesses in direction and evident tactical hesitancy. Such a combination of corruption and threatened layoffs paralysed the force at a crucial moment and even put the police in opposition to the government at a time when security at the Olympics in 2012 was being emphasised and when the financial downturn was at its worst and was likely to create tensions in those economically deprived areas predicted to be troublespots by governmental strategic reports.[26]

In the light of these considerations, the dependence upon the reliability of CCTV during the summer riots of 2011 suggests a recent and unspoken policy of letting situations descend into public disorder (something the police have always robustly denied). As nothing could be done about police action on the first two days of rioting, because the Prime Minister, the Home Secretary Theresa May and the Mayor, Boris Johnson, were on holiday, the practice was accepted in hindsight by the government in order to use the courts to punish protesters and rioters with exemplary sentences designed effectively to cow others into obedience (an accusation denied by the Chairman of the Magistrates' Association, John Thornhill, who said the claims that sentences were overly harsh by design were 'unreasonable and unfounded').[27]

The attack on Conservative Campaign Headquarters at Millbank in 2010 and the subsequent summer riots were apparent disasters for police intelligence, actions on the street quickly descending into situations that were on the brink of chaos. The riots in Tottenham, Hackney, Croydon and elsewhere in the country were, as we have seen, predicted as far back as the government's risk assessment of 2010, but apparently were not acted upon, which is not to say that infiltration of dissident groups (rather than inner city gangs) did not continue as before, although here too things did not go smoothly.

The police are certainly not under-equipped with intelligence officers. The National Public Order Intelligence Unit (NPOIU) and the National Domestic Extremism Tactical Coordination Unit were for many years secret organisations which employed 60–100 personnel to collect data on alleged extremist groups through the Confidential Intelligence Unit. By 2011, they had been aligned to the Metropolitan Police under the title of the National Domestic Extremism Unit. The organisation has a budget of several million pounds which has doubled since 2005/6. The NPOIU was intended to 'perform an intelligence function in relation to politically motivated disorder' through the 'exploitation and dissemination of intelligence on the extremist threat to public order'.[28] These were highly secretive organisations whose headquarters and operational head remained shrouded in secrecy, although both are located somewhere in central London. The head of operations of the National Domestic Extremism Unit reported to Detective Chief Superintendent Adrian Tudway in 2011, the national coordinator for domestic extremism working for the Association of Chief Police Officers (ACPO).

The idea of a secret police force goes back as far as the 1880s, when a number of police departments came together to combat Irish terrorism and later monitored various anarchist groups, but most of the time the detectives were obvious and were often actually greeted by those under surveillance. Since the 1960s, trade unions, Trotskyist groups, BBC applicants and the Communist Party were regularly watched, their files being passed on to MI5. The force was strengthened in its campaign against the members of the Animal Liberation Front (ALF) and other animal rights activists and lobbyists who were seen as using terror tactics to intimidate individuals and organisations working in animal experimentation, especially Huntingdon Life Sciences based in Cambridgeshire. So valuable had bio-tech business become for the UK that it had to be protected. Operations of this sort do not yet require a judge's authorisation.

Since the millennium, dissident 'fringe' groups of the environmental and anti-capitalist 'left' (the term now reaching redundancy) have been infiltrated by a number of surveillance officers from the Special Demonstration Squad, another secretive unit within Special Branch whose members were nicknamed 'the hairies' for their hippy appearance. One was PC Mark Kennedy, who grew his hair long, pierced his ears, got tattooed, donned shades and called himself Mark 'Flash' Stone to go undercover to watch green activists for several years, but actually offered to give evidence *on behalf* of six defendants accused of disturbances at the Ratcliffe-on-Soar power station in Nottinghamshire (which happened in 2009) after he went 'native' in 2011. There were 114 arrests at the event after 200 police entered the Iona school in Sneinton, Nottinghamshire. Eleven people belonging to 'Eastside Climate Action' were also arrested for chaining themselves to railings.[29]

Kennedy had been recruited into the NPOIU and worked for seven years undercover within anti-war, environmental and anti-capitalist protest groups, both in the UK and the Republic of Ireland. At the Gleneagles G8 summit, he acted as an agent provocateur, whilst at Drax Power Station he was actually assaulted by police and arrested (to maintain his cover) to disguise the fact that he had been part of an entrapment plan.[30]

Another special operations officer, Jim Boyling, using the name 'Jim Sutton', was also exposed in 2011 for giving evidence in a trial in 1997 against green activists 'Reclaim the Streets'. The practice of such infiltration is questionable, its legal limits dubious and actually considered entirely illegal by some, although it is still 'widespread' according to some observers. To maintain their cover, such officers were also open to conviction whilst still under their false names, a practice which is entirely illegal. Such officers may go into dissident groups as observers, but the nature of their work and its practical implication are that they end up as agents provocateurs in police-initiated conspiracy and entrapment operations.

Moreover, Kennedy and Boyling had affairs with female members of environmental groups whilst undercover and Kennedy appears to have visited numerous countries including Denmark where he worked undercover, seconded by the Metropolitan Police to supply intelligence (INTEL) to Danish and international police forces. Sexual liaisons are meant to be forbidden and tighter vetting will now take place. The ability of secret policemen to prevent widespread or localised public disorder by providing information seems not only compromised by their own actions and the remit of the force, but actually counterproductive.[31] By turning dissident groups into criminal gangs, the very nature of such surveillance work is damaged by the confusion of aims and objectives attributed to those involved in legitimate protest by the authorities attempting to watch them.

Thus, recent policing (always conservative with a small 'c') has been exposed as more overtly politicised in terms of its targeting, actions and results (ironically, on behalf of government policy by top officials and against government cuts and unfair practice by the rank and file and police federation officials); agreement as to direction splits according to where one is in the chain of command regarding strategy and tactics. Nevertheless, the role of law enforcement, both in terms of police neutrality and in terms of sentencing by courts, remains a matter of serious concern. The question now regarding law enforcement agencies is how far they serve the real interests of the population and how much in the name of authority and 'law and order' they have too closely aligned themselves with the government or, worse, with the abstract needs of a bureaucratic and increasingly secret state to whom they feel a greater alliance than to the rest of us.

Nowhere is this better exemplified than in the continuing fortification of Downing Street and the Palace of Westminster, once easily accessible to visitors but now hemmed in with gates, police, fences and barriers, security checks and CCTV. In 2011, it was proposed to raise the level of the railings around Westminster by 2.3–3.5 metres to deter rooftop invasions, as happened in 2009, when Greenpeace scaled the roof. As so often in recent years, the threats of public disorder and terrorism are the reasons given for restricting democratic access.

Protest in 2012 has proliferated through ever-more ingenious methods of organisation using sophisticated tactics to frustrate the police and to hold geographical space yielded to them during periods of dissent. This ground may now be held not for hours but for several months (as with the 'Occupy Wall Street' camp in Zuccotti Park) using the law and through manipulation of the media. In this way, protesters avoid policing by making their position one not of criminality (usually regarding property), but of legitimate political struggle. The fact that young people from both ends of the social spectrum have lost their fear of the authority of the police will be a major worry in the future for those trying to keep order in a disintegrating context. The likely use of more extreme measures to enforce the law may lead to the escalation of trouble rather than its defeat, especially amongst those alienated sections of society that have hitherto been ignored.

Either way, the options for riot, rebellion and revolt have never been higher. However, to defeat the power of the state is no easy business. After all, demonstrators now might choose from a medley of traditional political marches and union rallies or parallel alternative marches alongside legally agreed marches, perhaps with separate and secret intent and motivation. They might choose an occupation demonstration or 'spontaneous' squatting, creating free schools and tent cities in order to occupy prime city centre space and thereby politicise it. This happened during October 2010, when there was the temporary occupation of empty office space in Holborn for a Halloween party, followed by the attempted occupation of houses in Bishop's Avenue during January 2011 and the occupation of Guy

Ritchie's house and the Hand and Racquet pub as 'free schools' in February and March 2011. More recently, squatters occupied an empty UBS building in November 2011 and a property in Hampstead Garden Suburb belonging to the Democratic Republic of Congo, which had been empty since 2006. Of course, the acts that attract the greatest fear are spontaneous rioting and looting spread by social media networks and the unpredictability of individual protest and comedy 'assassinations', viral rioting and swamping or hacking websites, unexpectedly targeting secret information held by governments.

Nevertheless, the nature of rioting and protest has divided sharply along class lines in recent years. The anti-capitalist camp, set up in imitation of the protests on Wall Street and elsewhere in the USA and as part of a global network of protest camps around the world, was part of a well-informed and politically literate international movement. Those at the camp were a mixture of students and well educated middle-class activists, many from privileged backgrounds whose motivations were essentially moral rather than political (although the distinction is often considered moot). The Mayor, Boris Johnson, labelled them 'crusties'. One protestor was a freelance journalist at Harper's Bazaar, another was Ben Westwood, the son of the fashion designer Vivienne Westwood, whilst a number of celebrities, including Alan Bennett, have also visited the camp.[32]

The attitude towards the 'educated' protester is best summed up in Judge Michael Snow's sentencing of the Fortnum & Mason trespassers, whom he said had 'common sense' and 'decency'. He then went on to praise the morals of the protesters and to make a statement defending civil liberties. This was in contrast to the comments regarding the rioters during the summer of 2011, whom Assistant Commissioner Tim Godwin called 'a feral underclass' and whom the *Evening Standard* merely labelled 'yobs'.

It all seemed to have been so much clearer in the 1970s and 1980s, when political divides were clear-cut and obvious. Internal national security in those decades suggested that the state was besieged from left and right. There were numerous extreme fascist groups: the National Front; the British National Party; the National Party; the British Movement; the League of St George; Column 88; SS Wotan 18; the British League of Rights; and the Racial Preservation Society. From the left came mainstream Trotskyism; Militant Tendency; the Chartists (formed in 1970); the Workers Revolutionary Party;

the International Marxist Group; the Socialist Workers Party; the Communist Party of Great Britain; the Revolutionary Communist Party of Britain; and various anarchist groups. These often small and fragmented bodies did not even include the threat from the Irish (on both sides) or the growing militancy of Scottish or Welsh nationalists.[33]

Since 2000, the old ideological divisions of left and right have almost entirely broken down, as has the division between fascists and those fighting fascism. On the one hand, the EDL flies the national flag of Israel to suggest that it is not anti-semitic and that it is pro-Zionist in its stance against Muslims (although Jewish groups are justifiably concerned over the connection). Indeed, the group's leader, Stephen Lennon, once disguised himself as a Hasidic Jew to lead a rally near Aldgate Station after being banned by the courts from attending rallies within ten miles of the centre of London. On the other hand, anti-capitalist groups in favour of a Palestinian state make alliance with Muslim fundamentalists who hate gay people, disdain women's rights and have a loathing for all forms of Jewish life.

This odd coupling of opposition groups is identifiable in the singular personality of WikiLeaks founder Julian Assange, who, whilst attacking the culture of capitalism and faux democracy, apparently believes he is the victim of a conspiracy concocted by 'Jewish journalists' working for *The Guardian* newspaper.[34] There is often a hint of unspoken anti-semitism when Zionism is brought up: the canard that 'Jews' run the media and big business in favour of Israeli interests. Assange was initially backed by prominent campaigners such as Tony Benn and Bianca Jagger. However, the revelations of his alleged beliefs seemed to have dampened enthusiasm. It again seems a short journey from 'secret government' conspiracy theorist to advocate of Jewish world conspiracy.[35] Meanwhile, Assange was to be extradited to Sweden to face charges of rape after his High Court bid to avoid extradition was rejected on 2 November 2011, although he has been given leave to appeal.

Security services will have to watch both actual terrorists who pose an immediate threat to life and are trained in the use of bombs or other weapons and those extremists whose political and philosophical opposition to the system may be classified as terroristic by those whose wish it is to defend the ideological assumptions of the state. Police methods and closer collaboration with other security services, which began in earnest after 9/11, will also – it may be suspected – considerably increase the use of armed force to quell dissident opposition. Its results may already be consciously ingrained in security service protocol.

The killing of Jean Charles de Menezes in 2005, at the height of the terrorist attacks of that year, was a consequence of the technique of assured 'defensive' killing by a shot to the head which had been developed by British police and military forces after 9/11, when it was felt imperative to find a certain solution to terrorist bombers who were willing to die in an attack. The model was found in Israeli tactics.[36] The tactic was again employed on 23 November 2011 against Justice Livingstone by Transport Police, but using taser guns instead. He was seen carrying a pistol, which turned out to be a present for his son.

In summer 2012, the Olympics saw the biggest peacetime security lockdown in London's history. Between 12,000 and 14,000 police were on the streets, 23,700 security guards were needed at 32 sites, 13,500 from the army, navy and air force, but the rest supplied by security company G4S. Indeed, Tim Godwin, who had retired from the Metropolitan Police in 2011, went on to work for management consultants Accenture, a security company for the 2012 London Olympics.

Two naval warships were moored in the Thames and there was a rapid response force of 1,000 personnel and surface-to-air missiles trained on the skies, roads were closed to traffic (within a 30-minute walking distance of the venues) and areas cordoned off, the Internet was constantly monitored for cyber-attacks such as those that occurred during the Beijing Olympics, Britain's borders were presumably more tightly patrolled, vaccines against a possible anthrax attack were stockpiled and other countries flew in their own security, 1,000 officers coming from the USA alone, including 500 FBI agents – this measure supposedly due to the USA's alarm at the relaxation of terrorist laws such as the stop and search legislation repealed in Section 44 of the Terrorism Act.[37]

In anticipation of the Olympics, it was claimed by protesters at a former Midlands Bank site in the City of London that illegal squats in a number of empty bank buildings by Occupy London were closed down with 'American'-style tactics. The crackdown was part of security measures in the run-up to the Games. Both the Home Secretary and the Minister for Culture have spoken of their zero-tolerance stance on protest of any sort, such protests being seen as a 'threat' to security. It is, however, quite beyond the Home Secretary's power to determine the law and, as such, laws may be twisted and broken to enforce government policy, being answerable only later in court when challenged. Meanwhile, London Underground drivers and bus drivers were given large 'bonus' inducements to keep trains running and black cabs were allowed to raise fares.

Cyberspace too would have to be patrolled, as that is also a type of new border region. The UK now spends hundreds of millions on national cyber-security, working in partnership with private industry to police our virtual borders and hosting a major international cyber-security conference in November 2011. In doing so, and in reviewing the armed forces, the government believed that the country had an 'adaptable defence and security posture' backed by a 'transformative cyber-security programme' and new measures to 'tackle ... terrorism'. CCTV, having proved its importance after the summer riots, was improved as all parliamentary parties now demanded, no doubt, the tightening of the grip of the 'surveillance society' on the streets. Democracy was effectively suspended in London for the duration of the Games and a type of unspoken martial law was imposed – the first time in London's history. Big Brother had finally arrived dressed as an athlete. During March 2012, Occupy activists threatened the 'greatest act of disobedience' during the Olympic period, being intent on targeting the key routes or sites of the Olympics. They had already set up various small camps, one being on Leyton Marshes.[38] Meanwhile, on 7 April, protestor Trenton Oldfield disrupted the 2012 Oxford and Cambridge boat race by swimming in the way of the rowers near Chiswick Eyot in an effort to highlight 'elitism' and set out a 'manifesto for disobedience'. Despite the much-publicised cordon of land to air missiles, more likely to intimidate Londoners, there was always the threat from low-key attacks: cyber-hacking; hindering athletes and races; blocking designated roads; bomb hoaxes or unfurling protest banners and general low-level nuisance such as flash mobs or protest camps.

The police have long worked with business to deter terrorism. Project Griffin, which started in April 2004, aims to arm private business against attack by working in partnership with the police, whilst Project Argus works to ensure continuity after any major disruption by terrorists. The City of London Police not only produce regular bulletins (such as *City Security*) but have a number of police officers trained as Counter Terrorism Security Advisors (CTSAs) to help deal with such events as searches, bomb alerts and securing a building under threat.

Using these methods of control, one may create permanent change in the landscape of London. The USA propose building a new embassy at Nine Elms in 2016. The Embassy Gardens development will include 2,000 homes, restaurants, shops and a hotel around an 'impenetrable' building based within a plaza. The building, on 15 acres of land, will follow strict American guidelines on defence against terrorism 'by making a defensive area around the embassy take the form of landscape', as Boris Johnson's advisor Sir Terry Farrell pointed out. Thus, the landscape of urban development will effectively disguise the 'fortress' nature of the structure and geographical manipulation will effectively seal the Embassy from threat.

This new building would replace the USA's heavily defended current premises in Grosvenor Square where, after the riots of 1968, a number of evident defensive measures were erected to stop the Embassy being rushed by protesters. Should the new structure, in its discreet environment, go ahead, it will be the first purpose-built fortress in London since the building of the Tower of London in 1078 and it will also provide a model for the authorities to build riot-proof establishments immune to 'attack' and sealed by a friendly invisible environment of closeable entry points, roads and buildings: by the very nature of the urban landscape itself.

And free speech? The Victorians allowed free speech through mass demonstrations in Hyde Park and elsewhere, but soon tried to close such spaces down by remodelling them into parks by legislation. Even so, with so many unregulated and unlawful meetings, it was felt prudent by the government to allow some sort of unregulated 'soap box' for the expression of free speech. This it did through the Parks Regulation Act of 1872, which allowed the park authorities to decide on who was allowed to demonstrate. Thus evolved a portion of land in the north-east corner of Hyde Park now known as Speaker's Corner. There is no statutory right to speak there, although as late as 1999, in the case of *Redmond-Bate v. Director of Public Prosecutions*, Lord Justice Sedley established the right to 'offensive' free speech and the right of popular reply inside already-existing laws regarding race hatred, etc.:

> The decision upheld the freedom to express lawful matters in a way which other people might take great exception to; that the right to free speech, enshrined in Article 10 of the European Convention on Human Rights includes the right to be offensive; and a police officer has no right to call

> upon a citizen to desist from lawful conduct. That others might react unlawfully does not itself render the actions of the speaker unlawful.
>
> Free speech includes not only the inoffensive but the irritating, the contentious, the eccentric, the heretical, the unwelcome and the provocative provided it does not tend to provoke violence. Freedom only to speak inoffensively is not worth having. What Speaker's Corner ... demonstrates is the tolerance which is both extended by the law to opinion of every kind and expected by the law in the conduct of those who disagree, even strongly, with what they hear.[39]

With the need to protect the interests of the state against the interests of free speech, the security forces will also be only too aware that they have to act with greater secrecy, ironically to defend the transparent democracy we all hope to live in. Indeed, many of the liberal protest movements share with terrorists a disgust for the workings of Western democracy whilst exploiting the very framework of democratic institutions in order to undermine them. Most demonstrators would argue that they are more democratic than the secretive capitalist 'dictatorship' globalism they defy by their protests.

What is clear is that London remains the crucible in which popular 'street' politics may be gauged in Britain, and that such politics is increasing and virally proliferating and shows no signs of diminishing. Britons like to think that they are a peaceable lot and that compromise is the British way. We are not revolutionaries like the French. Londoners might like to think that, but deep down they know that London is a place where urban disturbance is becoming a norm rather than an exception and where, if the revolution might still be a distant dream, radicalism and street protest are not, and confrontation with authority will continue. London is going through one of its many periods of disturbance and dislocation, this time with a new set of episodes with new demands and different methods of expression.

In late 2010, almost without warning, the very grounds of political debate shifted; it shifted again in the summer of 2011, but this time it was the very grounds of civilised society that unexpectedly shook. The student actions of the winter of 2010 were the culmination of one traditional form of politics recognisable for many since the 1960s, but it heralded a new politics and a new space for political action: the days of rage were coming.

4

2010: THE CRISIS AND THE STUDENT RIOTS

Some 40 years ago, the American activist Huey Newton predicted that:

> As the ruling circle continue to build their technocracy, more and more of the proletariat will become unemployable, become lumpen, until they have become the popular class, the revolutionary class.[1]

For Lewis this was 'a call to revolution'. Forty years later Paul Mason in *The Guardian* had this to say:

> The financial crisis of 2008 created a generation of twenty-somethings whose projected life-arc had switched, quite suddenly, from an upward curve to a downward one. The promise was: 'Get a degree, get a job in the corporate system and eventually you'll achieve a better living standard than your parents'. This abruptly turned into: 'Tough, you'll be poorer than your parents'. The revolts of 2010–11 have shown, quite simply, what this workforce looks like when it becomes collectively disillusioned, when it realises that the whole offer of self-betterment has been withdrawn.[2]

Since the premiership of Tony Blair, mainstream politics had suffered a malaise; voters were (and many remain) disdainful of the deceitful corruption of those in power, where bribery and financial misdemeanours seemed normal and the values and beliefs of ordinary people seemed to be ignored. The excesses of those in charge of the banking industry rankled, as did the morals of those who conspired to protect those who were considered to be culpable.

It seemed a corrupt world without salvation run by people who no longer cared. It was a market-driven nightmare where globalisation seemed to imply simply global slavery.

Thus, the wave of protest at the rise in student fees was fuelled by an already deep well of animosity which only needed a government policy to unite all sections of opposition in order to create long-anticipated trouble. This was provided initially by Lord Browne's *Independent Review of Higher Education Funding and Student Finance*, published on 12 October 2010, in which removing the fee cap from universities was suggested, thus effectively privatising them. The government's decision to authorise universities to raise student fees was bound to be a catalyst for revolt, a moral revolt as much as a political one. The new student politics represented a spectrum of beliefs ranging across anti-capitalism, tax avoidance, environmentalism, the protection of public services and the punishment of those whom the system rewarded whilst others suffered. It was a rallying cry not only for those young people in education but also for their parents, whose demonstrating days lay in the rosy past of the 1960s and 1970s. Although the proposed rise in fees for higher education was the catalyst, it soon became part of a wider political philosophy.

The immediate cause of the problem was the need to finance universal higher education, an idea that had developed since the late 1980s and became a mantra of government in the 1990s, but which could no longer be maintained in the current economic circumstances. The Labour government of Tony Blair had been the first to reverse the policy accepted since the Second World War that free education at all levels was the only way to beat the poverty trap. By the 1960s, this had turned into a cornerstone of socialist-modified capitalism and the welfare state. It had succeeded in many of its aims of bettering prospects, especially for the lower middle classes, for instance, and was now considered a right rather than a privilege of the few, although, ironically, the idea of true mass higher education only really took off in the 1980s under Margaret Thatcher. Such educational rights were, however, already under threat from a state which could no longer run the system without either raising general taxation or charging fees. The problem was ignored until the Labour government could ignore it no longer. The creation of American-style tuition fees up to £3,000 per annum was, perhaps, necessary, but it was seen by many as a betrayal of old Labour values and a return to the politics of the haves and have-nots traditionally exemplified by Tory politics. The Labour Party was also considering raising fees when it lost the General Election in 2010.

Before the disastrous downturn in the economy, the Liberal wing of the Coalition government, headed by Nick Clegg, promised to return education to the status quo ante. It was something promised by the Liberal Democrat manifesto, a traditional cornerstone of the Liberal belief in equality of opportunity and was itself an important component of the promised new politics of David Cameron's 'Big Society', where community, not personal greed would be paramount and where moral veracity would again be important. After the Election, this attitude would no longer hold against economic realities. It was a bitter realisation. Many voters were soon disappointed with the same old double-speak. The world was in recession and economic difficulties would necessitate a rethink of manifesto promises. Liberal promises could not be kept and much soul searching went on as the Liberals, and Clegg in particular, tried to square their consciences with their promise.

The rising cost of higher education, coupled with the continuing refusal to give up the egalitarian dream of every young person's right to attend a university, meant that the government had no choice but to overhaul the system. Rather than have the strength of mind to cull poorly performing institutions, it decided both to squeeze money immediately, in order to force universities to cull themselves, thus leaving blood on someone else's hands, whilst at the same time proposing to raise tuition fees to a new high. Such proposals would infuriate not only those who were already in education and feeling the pinch but also their parents, who enjoyed free higher education in the past, and their brothers and sisters still in school, for whom the rise in fees would be a coming reality.

The reality of a rise from £3,000 to a proposed ceiling of £9,000 to pay for a year's tuition suggested higher debt levels in a shrinking jobs market, but was also compounded by the shrinkage of the university sector and poorer 'value for money' for higher costs. At the same time, the Educational Maintenance Allowance (EMA), which was designed to help the most economically deprived from the poorest areas stay in full-time education, was to be abolished. The calculations suggested that students would be frozen out of a university education for the first time since the War, a belief that, however erroneous, was important in the 'myth' of educational rights for all, regardless of class or parental income. Debt levels for a student studying for three years at £6,000 were calculated by protesters at around £30,000 (although given without explanation, but probably including cost of living expenses), whilst a student in London might find his or her bill to have risen by a further £10,000, the London university vice chancellors suggesting that they would embrace the higher levels of fee.

Thus, the students argued:

> Within the perverse horizon of capitalist realism and its imperative of reducing the deficit by cutting universities ... higher fees have been as a panacea. Higher education can expect a cut of 40% in funding (excluding research funding) down from £7.1 to £4.2bn, while further education is to be cut by 25%, 1.1bn down from 4.3bn by 2012–14. More concretely, this will mean the disappearance of between 75% and 95% of all teaching funding. In practice this will mean the total or near total withdrawal of state funding from the social sciences, the humanities and arts. The University and College Union (UCU) has warned that a third of all English universities could close.[3]

It was an apocalyptic scenario, set against what appeared to be a world crisis in capitalism itself and coincidentally the democratic and spontaneous uprisings across the Arab world. Revolution was in the air. Students would have their own 'Days of Rage', but not before the Conservative Party Conference in Birmingham. On 6 October 2010, David Cameron addressed the party with a joke borrowed from Monty Python:

> I want to tell you today, in the clearest terms I can, what we must do together. And what we can achieve together. But first we should remember where we've come from. Three defeats. Thirteen party conferences. 4,757 days in the wilderness. Remember what they said about us? They even called us a dead parrot. They said we had ceased to be. That we were an ex-party. But it turns out we really were actually only resting. And here we are. Back serving our country.

It was a speech with more than a little hint of the resurrected. And what was Lazarus to achieve but a new caring form of Conservatism, based on community and benevolence and hard work. There would be no more of Thatcher's deadly market-driven individualism, nor of her 'laissez-faire' attitudes.

Instead, the Big Society was a vision of communal cooperation within real society (the word 'society' deliberately recuperated from

Mrs Thatcher's notorious dismissal of the term even as Cameron wished her a happy birthday); voluntary activism was Cameron's claim on modern Conservatism, a deliberate snub to the old style of Conservative individualism summed up by Thatcher's phrase that 'there [was] no such thing as society':

> We need to change the way we think about ourselves, and our role in society. Your country needs you. And today I want to tell you about the part we've all got to play, and the spirit that will take us through. It's the spirit that I saw in a group of NHS maternity nurses in my own constituency, increasingly frustrated by the way they were managed and handled, who wanted to set up a co-op to use their own expertise, their ideas, their contacts to provide a better service for the mums in their area. It's the spirit you see just down the road from this conference in Balsall Heath, where local residents were fed up with the pimps and the prostitutes and the gangs and the drug dealers. So they set up street patrols to clear them out of the area and turn what was a no-go zone into a desirable place to live. It's the spirit that just today has seen some of our leading social organisations come together to set up a new Citizen's University, to help give people the skills they need to play a bigger part in our society. It's the spirit of activism, dynamism, people taking the initiative, working together to get things done.

The thrust of the speech was not only to cast the Conservatives as 'radicals', but also to suggest that old-fashioned leftism as well as New Labour were finished.[4] 'We are the radicals now', exclaimed Cameron, 'breaking apart the old system with a massive transfer of power, from the state to citizens, politicians to people, government to society. That is the power shift this country needs today.'[5]

This was a one-nation rallying cry for middle Britain, with its rhetoric borrowed from Churchill, Disraeli and even Lord Kitchener's famous poster: one nation whole again after bankruptcy and failed bureaucractic-welfarism, pulling together within the warm bosom of the Big Society. The TUC remained hostile, the Labour Party dithered and the 'marginalised' were momentarily silent, but the students had already left by the back door. They answered Cameron's pleas for unity with the following manifesto:

> The protest movement … is directed at the totality of the government's economic policy and therefore engages with the state's management of democracy and power … Market fundamentalism is losing political legitimacy, a profound shift that opens up a space for far reaching

> challenges … One of the drivers of the crisis has been capitalism's capacity for productive transformation … Social networking is already transforming the way social decisions are being taken, which is itself a definition of politics. A politics without a culture is merely technocratic. But we are at the forefront of an immense cultural transformation … a complex confrontation is underway. This applies especially to what it means to be educated and therefore cultured … The principles of the Enlightenment, from human rights to the influence of religious belief, are in play. The Westminster system has entered an endgame ... There is little meaningful democracy, the 'sovereignty of parliament' is a joke, reliable checks and balances have ceased to exist in the UK: the executive rules and the constitution is broken. Hence the need to riot.[6]

There would be no escaping trouble and trouble there would be. It started on 10 November 2010, when coachloads of students from all over Britain arrived in London to protest against the rise in tuition fees. Between 24,000 and 30,000 (the *Daily Mail* even put the figures as high as 50,000) protesters arrived in bitterly cold conditions to march against the proposed change, but also to protest against Lib Dem capitulation, the party having pledged to oppose the rise whilst in opposition. Some students were annoyed and frustrated with their own stupidity. One student from Goldsmiths College complained that he had 'voted Lib-Dem' and now felt like a 'right mug'.[7] As they gathered at around noon, Harriet Harman and Nick Clegg argued the point in Westminster while students prepared to march down Whitehall. If he had been listening, Clegg would have heard the faint echo of a chant: 'Nick Clegg/We know you/You're a fucking Tory too', more imaginative perhaps than 'Tory Scum' scrawled on the side of 30 Millbank next to a large erect penis later that day.[8]

Yet things soon got out of hand when at around 1.45 pm, a section of students and A-level pupils broke away from the march to besiege Conservative Campaign Headquarters at 30 Millbank, which had been left virtually unguarded by police even though it was near the route of the protest. For many, this was their first protest and they had expected it to be peaceful, but now adrenalin kicked in. Five minutes after arriving, windows were being smashed and the building was stormed by 300 protesters. The police were outnumbered and outgunned. For once, authority was not able to cow protest into submission. It was a decisive moment in the modern protest movement itself. At one point, 20 police were left to cope with up to 2,000 protesters. As the windows broke, those present saw a unique opportunity both unplanned for and unimaginable – the opportunity to storm the stronghold of Toryism. It was something too good to miss (one pupil recalled, 'I may as well') and between 50 and 80 protesters surged through the doors and up to the roof, whilst others fought police and tried to steal their caps.[9]

Although the protesters were not, in the end, able to gain access to Conservative Party offices, they battled with police reinforcements (which finally arrived at 2.20 pm) for four hours, with injuries going evenly to both sides and 50 arrests, including one student, Edward Woollard, who came to epitomise the 'wanton' nature of the violence when he threw a fire extinguisher from the roof. The building was finally entered by police at around 5 pm and order was restored at 6.30 pm. It later transpired that the police had deployed only 225 officers to marshal a demonstration of tens of thousands: a costly mistake. The day had been a disaster for both the police and the National Union of Students (NUS), both organisations having lost control of events. The *Evening Standard* smelt the sulphurous whiff of 'professional' trouble-makers, the NUS saw 'rogue elements', whilst the police could only apologise for the 'embarrassment to London'.[10]

The public's reaction was one of astonishment, but not necessarily one of outrage. After all, many people had reason to want to 'have a go' at the Tories and their perceived backers: the wealthy, the privileged and the bankers (the so-called 'one per cent'). Many felt worried about uncaring general reforms to welfare and the NHS, others feared for their children's future and still others felt that the Lib Dem offices should have been the target; many people watched their televisions with memories of the G20 and the death of Ian Tomlinson, and found vicarious pleasure in the drubbing taken by the police. This was political revenge by proxy against a government for which no one had voted. As Nick Clegg stood up to speak the day after during Prime Minister's Questions, a street artist friend of Banksy called 'Cartrain' sat in the Strangers' Gallery and smoked a joint before jumping out of his seat and demanding the legalisation of cannabis![11] Something wicked and disturbing was heading towards Westminster; 'this is just the beginning' was the message both from students and police.

On Wednesday 24 November ('Day X'), the students were joined by many schoolchildren fearful of their own futures and the end of the EMA. The demonstration would wind its way from the

University of London in Malet Street, form a carnival of resistance as it moved towards Leicester Square, rally at Trafalgar Square and end after marching down Whitehall at the Lib Dem headquarters at 4 Cowley Street. Protesters were in good spirits, the initial feelings of anger that had precipitated the attack on Millbank had cooled and the opportunity for some mischief was going to be lessened anyway by greater police alertness. It was not, however, to be a peaceful demonstration after all: rioting and kettling were the order of the day, and mayhem the result.

Nevertheless, the image that lingered was not that of mob violence or anarchist outrage, but of a police van which had been following the march apparently being hastily abandoned by police who feared for their safety in the midst of the action. The van was covered with graffiti, a wreck amidst chaos. Pictures showed schoolchildren defending the van against 'hooligans' and 'yobs'. The image seemed to prove the government correct that these protests were no longer legitimate.

Something seemed not to be right with the police story. The van was clearly shown on *Sky News* as parked and empty, the police standing around and protesters nonchalantly passing by.[12] Was this the same vehicle? It appeared to be so, even though its number plates mysteriously disappeared later. Therefore, was the vehicle 'bait', a trap planted and waiting for trouble (as many students claimed) so that an official media narrative could be created after the event? Did the abandonment of the vehicle signal a new police tactic which left the streets to rioters who could not be effectively policed with existing resources, thereby leaving the 'policing' until after the event so that punishment might be swifter and harsher? The police denied any such complicity in the troubles that day and there is no proof of any misdoing, but a suspicion lingers of an unwritten strategic attitude that would abandon the streets on the day to return harder and faster later on. There was certainly much obfuscation in the answers that the Police Minister, Nick Herbert, gave to *The Guardian* about the incident.[13] If this is a police mistake as opposed to conspiracy theory, it still bears a remarkable and coincidental resemblance to policing at the beginning of the August 2011 riots.

By the end of the day, many students and schoolchildren were freezing and hungry within the police cordon, which lasted six hours. The 'game has changed', insisted the police, whose 'bullish' tactics prevented an attack on Cowley Street but did not prevent clashes all along Whitehall and Parliament Square.[14] Two days after the riot, and without irony, the Prime Minister unveiled his 'happiness index', which attempted to measure the country's 'wellbeing'.

On a snowy Tuesday, a week later, students and schoolchildren marched again to increase pressure on MPs to abstain or vote against the proposed legislation to raise fees. The freezing temperatures did not stop 200 schoolchildren climbing Nelson's Column at around noon and making a bonfire out of the Socialist Workers Party (SWP) placards with which everyone had been issued. Indeed, the SWP was doing a fine job of claiming the event as its own, swamping the area with its own brand of revolution, so appealing to the young. At 12.10 pm, students trying to get down Whitehall to join other protesters were blocked by police and so began moving towards Buckingham Palace. This would have been a prime target, undefended by police, but the protesters chose instead to surge away down Horse Guards Parade and back towards Parliament as reggae blared from a large mobile sound system. It was a moment missed for the time being.

At the same time police rushed across the open space of Horse Guards Parade, aware of the danger. The statues and memorials to the fallen of many wars which line one side of the parade ground were carefully avoided out of respect by students, as was the Cenotaph with its memorial wreaths, something later forgotten by both sides. At 12.42 pm, the police cordon opened to allow an apparently unaware Lord Winston to drive his jaguar to the House of Lords. His car was left unmolested too. At exactly that moment, the police mobilised six police vans to protect Buckingham Palace.

Police fought running battles with students, who, refusing to stick to an agreed march route, let off flares in Regent Street and were determined not to be kettled. There was much damage in Trafalgar Square with graffiti on the lions and on Nelson's Column, and shops attacked or vandalised. Interestingly, photographs show that it was only at this protest that students started to 'mask up' due to fear of reprisals, something not considered before, *V-masks* being noticeably absent from these demonstrations. In all, there had actually been few arrests over the events so far, with just over 150 people being apprehended and only one or two being charged with a serious crime.

As Nick Clegg fought both for his intellectual integrity and his political future, David Cameron went on the offensive. In a full-page article in the *Evening Standard* on 23 November 2010, he laid out the 'full facts' of the government's position to avoid 'misconceptions'.

The changes were, he said, 'unavoidable' given the parlous state of government finances and could not be ignored. There was still a subsidy of £5 billion on English higher education (such education was subsidised in both Wales and Scotland by the Westminster government so that Welsh and Scots higher education was free for indigenous inhabitants) and no more could or should be found as 'taxpayers' should not foot a bill for things that did not directly benefit them. (This is, of course, is a disingenuous argument, given that students are also future taxpayers and many things are paid for without direct benefit to the public.)

Nevertheless, in order to maintain a 'world class higher education system', it would be necessary to adjust higher education finances so that direct payment of student fees would 'drive up the quality of teaching' because 'universities [would] be pressured to up their game in order to attract more students'. It was a way of enshrining market-led customer demand, a trend that went back to the 1980s. The Prime Minister reiterated that no one would pay back anything if they earned less than £21,000, but this is perhaps, in some student's opinions, so low a wage as to make going to university counterproductive in the first place, the time spent learning dictating higher expectations later. Part-time students would supposedly benefit too under the new arrangements, but by 2010 almost all students were de facto part time, earning a few bob on the side to stay at university. With further promises on outreach and widening access for poorer families, Cameron concluded that his 'plans [were] fair' and that 'hard decisions were in the national interest'. Students did not agree.

The day of the actual vote on the fees was 9 December and there was much preparation on both sides and much anticipation throughout the country as to how the Lib Dems would finally vote. There were threats of an invasion of London Underground by students dressed as monkeys and bears, and King's College, University College London (UCL) and the London School of Economics (LSE) were all occupied. The police were preparing for more than mere monkeying about with a cordon around Westminster, something virtually unheard of before. The NUS was preparing a vigil outside Parliament with glow sticks (something that was planned but may never have actually happened – candles being against health and safety!). In the end only 200 joined the NUS protest, being forced to watch from the sidelines as battle commenced.

As the debate and vote came to its fateful conclusion, things accelerated outside Parliament. At 11 am students gathered at the protest start point in Malet Street outside UCL. Another group started to gather outside Parliament as Clegg and his Lib Dem ministerial colleagues attended a meeting at Downing Street before heading to the House of Commons where Vince Cable, the Business Secretary, began the debate. At 1.30 pm, a breakaway group of students headed towards Buckingham Palace and a half an hour later there was a full-scale riot in Parliament Square, where workmen's barriers left in the road were used as weapons. An hour later, the order was given to kettle the protesters as flares and fireworks were thrown at police.

At 5.41 pm, the vote was cast: 323 for and 302 against, and the motion passed. It was the signal for an outbreak of activity amongst students who attacked anything they could reach, including starting a fire and defacing Winston Churchill's statue. Tempers had risen inside the Commons as well as outside. Three ministerial aides had resigned, but 27 Lib Dem MPs who pledged not to vote in favour finally did so. The *Daily Mail* crowed the next day that 'Nick Clegg had [signed] the Liberal Democrat's death warrant'.[15] Nevertheless, not everyone was in the kettle and not everyone wanted to be in Parliament Square.

Most exhilarating for those who had escaped the police bottleneck and most shocking for television viewers was how near the students came to humiliating the royal family, an unexpected *coup de theatre* at the end of a long day of disturbance and a case of 'Off with their Heads' if ever there was one. Somewhere between 7.15 and 7.30 pm, Prince Charles and the Duchess of Cornwall were being driven down Regent Street on their way to the Royal Variety Performance held that night at the London Palladium. Unfortunately, their route took them on a collision course with the demonstration, which was now moving from Oxford Circus and mixing with late-night shoppers.

At first, it was clear that there was only the desire to attack a 'nob's car', but this soon turned into the realisation that the protesters had royalty in their grasp. A cheer went up as this understanding sank in and the car was blocked in by a bin and attacked with paint and a volley of kicks and punches; a large handprint outlined in white decorated the front window. 'That put rocket boosters under the whole story', quipped a senior police spokesman.[16] Hardly surprisingly, both Charles and Camilla were rattled and held each other's hands as they waited to escape. Police were momentarily caught off-guard, as were the security services, who scrambled to restore order. The rear security vehicle was also isolated and attacked, the attendant motorbike police being unable to help. Indeed, the security men showed a reluctance to leave their vehicles. Finally, police aided by a helicopter searchlight came to the rescue as the cavalcade sped away.

The police had apparently been warned by a street cleaner 15 minutes before the attack that a group of protesters were on their way and a squad of riot police standing around Argyll Street (next to the Palladium) had been redeployed moments earlier even after police intelligence had recced the area. Of course, the police were aware of the gala event and the route that the royal couple were taking, but they had apparently failed to pass between themselves intelligence as to where the crowds were gathering and their possible direction. Indeed, the police had known about breakaway groups targeting Oxford Street as early as 9.30 am. It was, as the *Sunday Times* suggested, yet another 'police blunder' and a further humiliation for the Met.

The debacle was more than a little embarrassing for the police, and the Commissioner, Sir Paul Stephenson, offered first an apology (on the day after the incident) and then his resignation, a resignation he knew full well would not be accepted according to sources at the *Sunday Times*.[17] Yet Sir Paul was not long for this world. He actually resigned on 18 July 2011 after allegations of improper behaviour in relation to the *News of the World* phone-hacking scandal.

However, most shocking of all was the involvement of schoolchildren in all the demonstrations. Thousands of school pupils across the country were seen playing truant and playing politics with their older brothers and sisters. Chris Knight saw the schoolchildren as part of a 'revolutionary situation', leaving school despite threats from head teachers. Fearful of their future and in any case enjoying a taste of freedom and licensed wickedness, schoolchildren flocked to Trafalgar Square on 24 November 2010 and occupied Nelson's Column. Nevertheless, as the effects of kettling made themselves felt, and with no toilets and no way home, anxieties rose. It was bad publicity for the police and the Met tried every means to scare parents into preventing their children from joining in. This was reasonable enough, since the police wanted to avoid injuring young people in a 'sea of violence and disorder', as Commander Bob Broadhurst rather colourfully put it:

> Schoolchildren have as much right as anyone else to protest but young people are more vulnerable and likely to be injured if violence breaks

> out. We would ask parents to talk to their children and make sure they're aware of the potential dangers, as there is only so much police officers can do once they are in a crowd of thousands.[18]

There was much soul-searching regarding the participation of children in the protests. Graham Stuart, chairman of the Commons Education Committee, thought allowing children to go to London for rallies was 'despicable', whilst Nick Seaton, chair of the Campaign for Real Education, thought it 'crazy'; however, Russell Hobby of the National Association of Head Teachers was actually broadly supportive, understanding the anger of those denied the potential support of EMAs.[19] One teacher, Sue Caldwell, was suspended by Barnet Council and charged with 'gross misconduct' for encouraging her pupils to demonstrate in the November actions.[20]

Further peaceful demonstrations also occurred on 20 January 2011 as Parliament debated EMAs and the opposition tried to force Michael Gove, the Education Secretary, to rethink his policy. Nevertheless, the policy was upheld by 317 votes to 258. Even so, protest by London schoolchildren with their teachers forced a reinstatement of the 'School Sports Partnership' in the run-up to the Olympics.

This was not, however, the first time schoolchildren had had enough. They have gone AWOL before and usually during periods of economic crisis. They struck in 1889, closing many schools across Britain, as they did in 1911, 1914, 1929, 1938, 1968 and again in 2003 during the Stop the War Coalition marches. During the 1889 incidents, banners were emblazoned with 'NO CANE' and other libertarian slogans, and schoolchildren had worn red 'liberty' caps and had 'flown the red flag'. Moral outrage followed, with the educational press in apoplexy: 'schoolboy strikers ... are simply rebels. Obedience is the first rule of school life ... School strikes are therefore not merely acts of disobedience, but a reversal of the primary purpose of schools. They are on a par with a strike in the army or navy ... They are manifestations of a serious deterioration in the moral fibre of the rising generation ... They will prove dangerous centres of moral contamination'.[21] *Plus ça change...*

Scapegoats had to be found and demonstrators punished. First was Edward Woollard, the 18 year old who had thrown the fire extinguisher from the roof of 30 Millbank (not Millbank Tower as

Plate 1 'That Beastly Rabble' (Hudibras): Temple Bar, the centre of London unrest during the seventeenth and eighteenth centuries; bonfires blaze, guys are hanged and heads are stuck on pikes (author's collection)

Plate 2 Bomb!: police recreate an anarchist bomb after the Walsall Anarchist Bomb Plot trial of 1892 (author's collection)

Plate 3 Suffragettes flaunt the purple, white and green flags of the movement. Johnny Cyprus, 'Suffragettes demonstrating outside the Police Court' (Creative Commons Attribution)

The Daily Mirror

THE MORNING JOURNAL WITH THE SECOND LARGEST NET SALE.

No. 1,641. SATURDAY, JANUARY 30, 1909. One Halfpenny.

POLICE CONSTABLE TYLER, WHO WAS MURDERED BY ALIEN TERRORISTS AT TOTTENHAM, GIVEN A HERO'S FUNERAL.

Plate 4 Police funeral after the 'Tottenham Outrage': the twentieth century's first terrorist attack (author's collection)

Plate 5 2010 memorial to the four policemen killed in Houndsditch during a bungled robbery by revolutionaries in 1911 (author's collection)

Plate 6 Oswald Mosley before a capacity crowd preaches the fascist gospel (courtesy of the Mary Evans Picture Library)

Plate 7 1968: Grosvenor Square riots (courtesy of the Mary Evans Picture Library)

Plate 8 National Front march (courtesy of the Mary Evans Picture Library)

Plate 9 Blair Peach, who died during an anti-fascist demonstration in Southall. Unknown, 'Blair Peach' (Creative Commons Attribution)

Plate 10 Guerrilla Gardening in Parliament Square, 2000 (courtesy of the David Hoffman Photo Library)

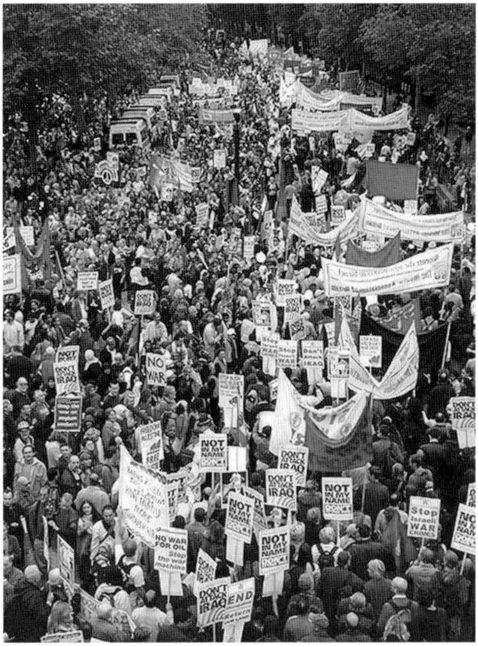

Plate 11 2003: 'Not in my Name' march against the Iraq War. Users AK7, William M. Connelly on Wikipedia, 'London anti-war protest banners' (Creative Commons Attribution)

Plate 12 Defended against the people: the gateway to 10 Downing Street (author's collection)

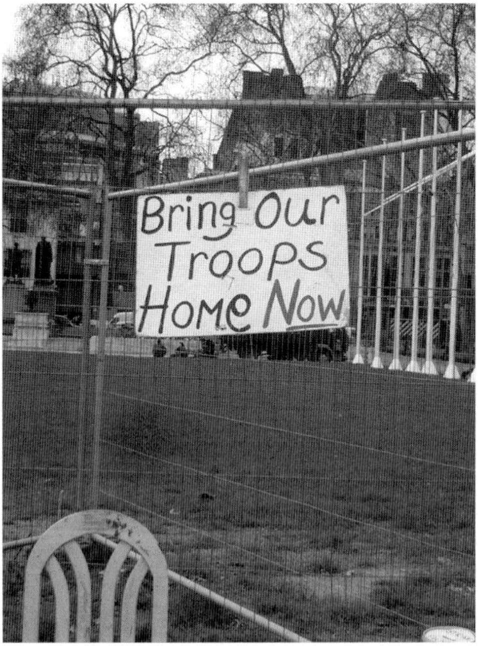

Plate 13 Iraq and Afghanistan war protest camp in Parliament Square (author's collection)

Plate 14 The mounting international anti-war propaganda in Parliament Square (author's collection)

Plate 15 'Eat the Bankers': French revolutionary tactics of hanging effigies from lampposts, this time from convenient traffic lights (courtesy of Jonathan Bloom)

Plate 16 To hell in a handcart: bankers, the enemy personified (courtesy of Jonathan Bloom)

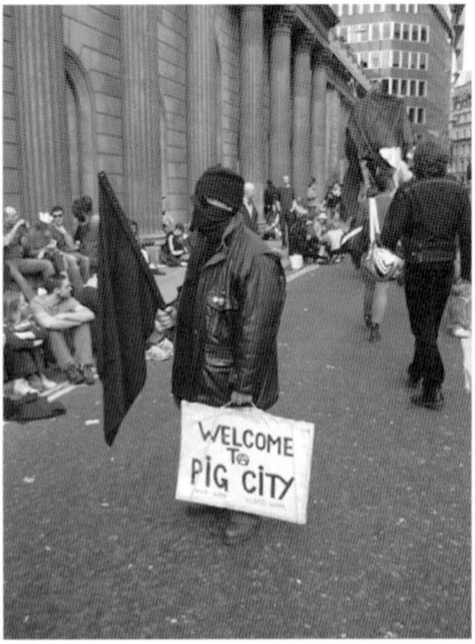

Plate 17 Black flag of revolution at the G20 protests (author's collection)

Plate 18 Militant gardening: a tank dumped in a garden off the Old Kent Road and now a focus for protest (author's collection)

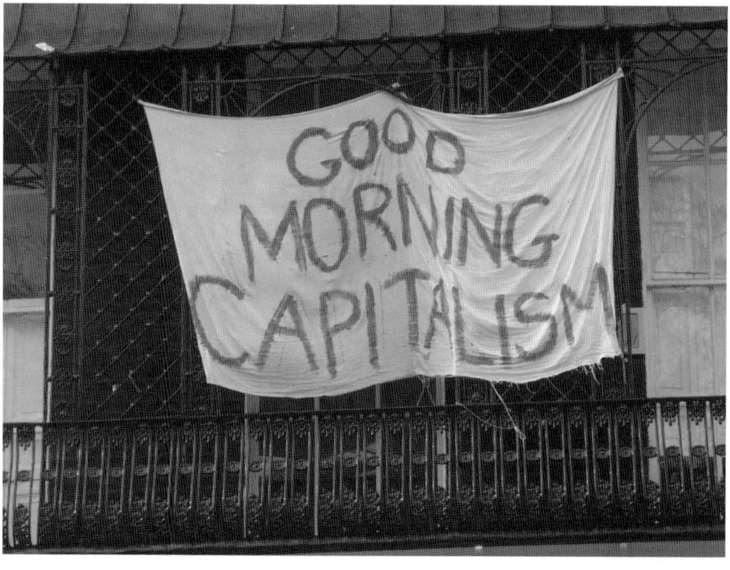

Plate 19 Temporary occupation of empty offices in Bedford Square (courtesy of Lesley Bloom)

Plate 20 Graffiti is still at the heart of revolutionary politics (author's collection)

Plate 21 Che forever: the embodiment of radical thought and action seen in an underpass in Cambridge in 2012 (author's collection)

Plate 22 G20 protests in Oxford Street (courtesy of the David Hoffman Photo Library)

Plate 23 Always the same tune: student protest (courtesy of the David Hoffman Photo Library)

Plate 24 Police lines; students protest. Bobby D'Marca, 'Student protests – Parliament Square, London 2010' (Creative Commons Attribution)

Plate 25 A cold wind in December: students keep warm by burning banners. Bobby D'Marca, 'Burning – student protests – Parliament Square, London 2010' (Creative Commons Attribution)

Plate 26 The kids are alright: pupil protest at the student demonstrations (courtesy of Jonathan Bloom)

Plate 27 Margaret Thatcher, still the ghost in the machine on the 'March for the Alternative' rally (courtesy of Jonathan Bloom)

Plate 28 The symbol of unrest: anarchism has replaced Marxist-Leninism as the protest ideology of choice (courtesy of Jonathan Bloom)

Plate 29 War!: the summer riots 2011. Hughe Paul, 'Police push back rioters in Camden, 2011' (Creative Commons Attribution)

Plate 30 The new look of the bobby on the beat? The summer riots 2011. Eric Hossinger, 'London Met Police riot gear' (Creative Commons Attribution)

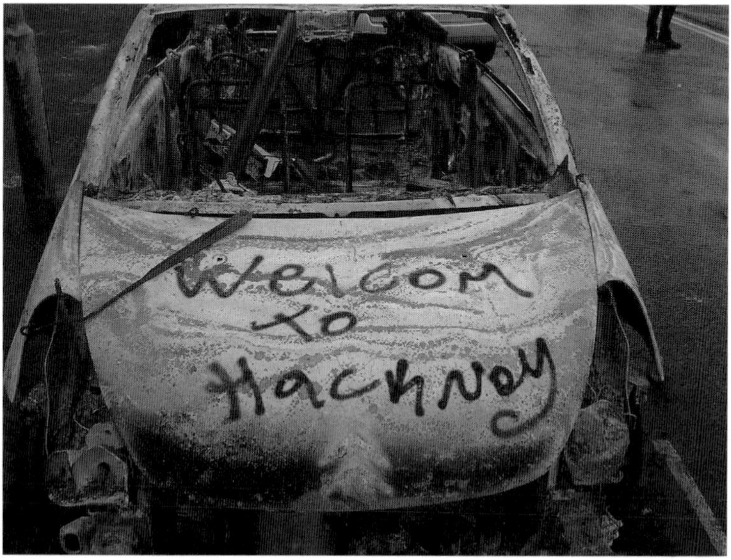

Plate 31 Not a good place to park: Hackney during the summer riots 2011. Alastair, 'Welcome to Hackney, 2011 riots' (Creative Commons Attribution)

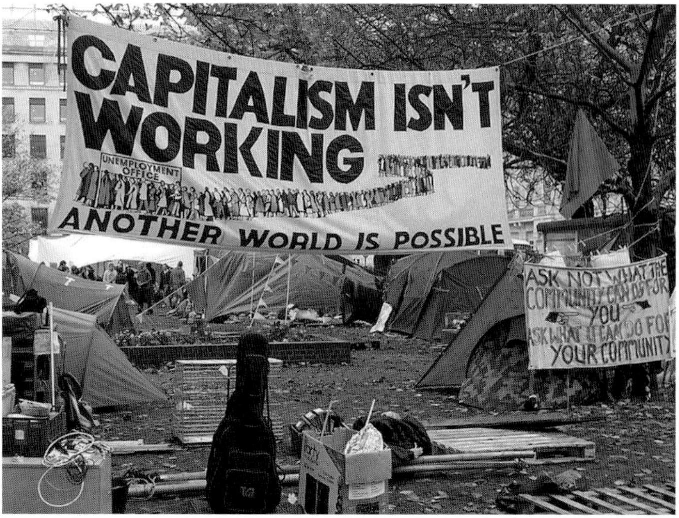

Plate 32 Occupy anti-capitalism camp at St Paul's Cathedral: the most successful post millennium-protest movement. Alan Denney, 'Occupy London – Finsbury Square' (Creative Commons Attribution)

Plate 33 Is 'capitalism really in crisis'? Occupy London think so. Neil Cummings, 'Occupy London banner' (Creative Commons Attribution)

Plate 34 Confrontation: police and rioters amid coloured flares in the West End of London (courtesy of Arthur Prior)

Plate 35 Fortnum & Mason riot in March 2011 (courtesy of Arthur

Plate 36 Everything has to be on camera. Filming riots provides narrative structure to memory (courtesy of Arthur Prior)

Plate 37 The last hurrah: 'Occupy' leave a calling card in Bishopsgate during the February 2012 eviction at St Paul's Cathedral (courtesy of Jonathan Bloom)

Figure 4.1 'No Cane': the wave of schoolboy strikes in 1889 (courtesy of the Mary Evans Picture Library)

repeatedly reported in much of the press) and whose reckless, but wholly spontaneous, actions had come to epitomise the riots themselves. Woollard was one of 50 arrests, but his actions alone suggested a custodial sentence. He was eventually sentenced to two years and eight months. The discharging of a toxic halon fire extinguisher by a police medical officer into the faces of demonstrators on 24 November was, however, hardly mentioned by the press and was soon forgotten.[22] Such devices are banned for civilian use but are allowed to be used by the police. The Metropolitan Police investigation concluded that:

> These [extinguishers] are approved and issued to public order officers so they can instantly extinguish flames on people that are burning. During the protests there had been incidents of protestors spraying aerosols once they had ignited them. The LAS reported treating people who had received burns to their faces as a result of this behaviour.
>
> Given this information, it is correct operational procedure that officers would have the fire extinguisher in their hands ready for immediate use if presented with this situation. The pin is always removed so that its use is instantaneous. By design these fire extinguishers are

> extremely sensitive and can easily be discharged by sudden movement or pressure.[23]

This was really no answer to the original accusation, but instead a description of when such appliances should be used. Nor was much heard of the alleged attempt by three policemen of the Forward Intelligence Team to 'frame' a demonstrator on 9 December 2010 by arresting him on false grounds and then assaulting him, even though the case was serious enough to be referred to the IPCC and passed on to the Criminal Prosecution Service (CPS).[24]

Perhaps the greatest gift to middle-brow and middle-England outrage was the action of Charlie Gilmour, who, in full view of the media and, perhaps, the full knowledge of what he was doing, attacked the Cenotaph and pulled down a Union Flag. This was a horrible mistake of tactics and one no doubt caused by an overflow of adrenalin, but attacking the national memorial to the war dead was not going to be easily forgotten. Gilmour and his iconic picture (hanging in his black coat from the flag) would become, for a short time, the story of the riots that day. Gilmour was the stepson of Pink Floyd guitarist David Gilmour (worth £78 million: something not easily forgotten when recriminations are handed out), the actual son of Heathcote Williams and Polly Samson, but adopted on the couple's divorce. He was also a history student at Girton College, Cambridge.

With his long hair and his middle-class, privileged rock kid background, 'Champagne' Charlie fitted a mould for certain 'posh' protesters that first came to the public's notice with the arrest of Otis Ferry during the Fox Hunting Riot of 2004. Gilmour was tracked down through Operation Malone a week later as part of investigations into a number of incidents, including urinating on the statue of Winston Churchill, breaking the windows of the Treasury, throwing balls and flares at police and attacking the car containing Prince Charles and the Duchess of Cornwall. One of 177 people arrested after 10 November and branded with others as a common 'criminal' by Superintendent Julia Pendry, Gilmour had little option but to plead stupidity, 'writhing in embarrassment' and 'wishing to curl up and die', although his attitude had previously been somewhat different, having apparently quoted Byron and Keats at the police arresting him.[25] It all seemed to be public schoolboy braggadocio, exactly the sort of misbehaviour expected of drunken bankers. *The Times* saw something in Gilmour that was more than mere vandalism and suggested a 'clash of values' against those in authority who censored, dissimulated or concealed:

> It is tempting to argue that Charlie Gilmour swinging on the Cenotaph flag symbolised nothing other than idiocy. But the pattern of event[s] surrounding the student protests does point to a burgeoning generational divide.[26]

By the time he had got to court, Gilmour had cut his hair and donned a suit. Surrounded by bodyguards, he arrived at Kingston Crown Court to be chastised and possibly punished. What was missed, despite the apology and the return to middle-of-the-road courtroom fashion, was that the privileges of birth don't stop people from having a social or moral conscience or an ideological outlook, however poorly expressed. Gilmour was eventually sentenced to 16 months in Wandsworth for 'violent disorder', a sentence considered by many, including those in the legal and prison system, as over-harsh and as setting an example to others. In a bout of nostalgic bravado, Otis Ferry thought that prison was a doddle compared to public school.[27] Sir Elton John and Julian Assange sent Gilmour books to pass the time![28] He was actually released after four months, but was forced to wear an electronic tag.

The revolution would also turn on its own for sacrifice. Aaron Porter, the President of the NUS, fell on his sword and refused to seek re-election after his softly, softly approach to negotiations failed catastrophically, leaving him without a constituency, as students mutinied *en masse* and went on the offensive independent of their official union. Recriminations were bloody. Branded everything from a 'careerist sell out' to a 'Tory Jew' (he is neither Jewish nor a Tory), Porter found himself barracked and attacked by his own side, actually having to be escorted away by police at a rally in Manchester.

However, Porter's success on behalf of the student movement was clear. He had negotiated with the Liberal Democrats to pledge not to raise education fees before the General Election. His failure was his inability to hold them to their promise, to then condemn the violence at Millbank and not to support the occupations at LSE, UCL and King's.[29] Instead of Porter and an impotent NUS, another body came into existence created out of the London Student Assembly, which met in the autumn of 2010. This non-hierarchic body was more akin to a leaderless 'parliament'; the collective called itself the 'National Campaign Against Fees and Cuts' (NCAFC) and took its inspiration from the collaborative actions of the world anti-globalisation movement and the climate camps, targeting as it did tax avoidance and the abolition of EMAs as much as the problems in higher education.

Victims were many and varied, but none so worrying as the cases of Jody McIntyre and Alfie Meadows. McIntyre was a well-known activist, easily identified as he was wheelchair-bound. Yet on 9 December, he was dragged from his wheelchair twice by police and struck by a police baton, before being manhandled behind police lines and unceremoniously dumped on the ground until his brother could reach him with his abandoned wheelchair. Half an hour later, on his own and reunited with his chair, McIntyre was again noticed by police, who told him to move on. When he refused, he was pulled from his chair and dragged along the road by his arms. The incident was so serious that it was later investigated by the IPCC.

On the same day, Alfie Meadows and his mum decided to have an outing in London. Like many others that day, the two of them were protesting against the proposed rise in student fees. Alfie was in his first year studying philosophy at Middlesex University and saw an immediate connection between the closure of the department and the current crisis. It was sufficient to motivate a quiet lad into action.

The police began kettling the crowd at the bottom of Whitehall and the two of them became separated at some point in the early evening. At approximately 5.30 pm, Alfie's mother received the news that her son had been struck on the head. In the ambulance, Alfie suffered a stroke. On arrival at the hospital, there was confusion, but an immediate operation and 52 staples in the head saved his life. That evening, Alfie had his 15 minutes of fame as a casualty, but his mother Susan was about to have hers as a rather modest human rights campaigner forced to speak for others from the immediacy of personal experience. Alfie currently stands accused of 'violent public disorder' at the protests in London on 9 December 2010. His first trial at Kingston Crown Court ended in a hung jury and he is set to go for retrial in October 2012.

Susan Matthews, Alfie's mother, was a senior lecturer at Roehampton University teaching English literature, a position she had held for 20 years. Educated at Oxford, where she had excelled, she nevertheless remained a believer in education for all, especially for those who come from familes where they are the first generation at university. She was an opponent of elitism. For Susan, those educated in English and the humanities had the potential to gain a voice in the 'public debate', which was central to the democratic process.

The family had been involved in the 'big society' for years. Married to a husband who had worked in the community and taught art to those in prison, Susan was not a natural protester or a trouble-maker and admitted that she was a comfortably brought-up middle-class girl with a nice middle-class education, who 'didn't get' what 'other people did' about Vietnam and the class struggle.

Iraq politicised Susan for the first time. For her, an 'absolute disjunction' suddenly opened up between what was being said and the reality on the ground. There was no 'logic to going to war' and so, with millions of others, she took to the streets, taking one of Alfie's sisters along for the ride. The abject failure of the Iraq protests threw her into the arms of the Lib Dems, for whom she voted for the first time in the last General Election, only to find another 'betrayal' and policies effectively neutered. Ed Miliband's rebranded Labour Party was, for her, 'unbelievably feeble' in the face of welfare cuts. On the fees demonstration, she was shocked by the 'scorn' of the police and was told by one officer that 'protest never works'.

Alfie's particular circumstances were subject to yet another IPCC inquiry. Susan felt no guilt about her son's injuries, just a newly awakened sense of activism motivated by the need to right a wrong. She found herself in a tradition of radical libertarianism and street democracy that stretched back to John Lilburne in the seventeenth century and came right up to recent times with Brian Haw. It is this sense of a wrong needing righting that infuriates and motivates liberal middle England. The perception of the corruption of power also makes for unlikely but articulate advocates of liberty, and Susan Matthews is articulate.

Susan is modest in her aims, campaigning with many others to get kettling outlawed under European human rights legislation, but she also has no real sense of how to solve the current higher education crisis. She still believes in the 1960s ideal of 'communal responsibility' and feels education is a form of communal 'insurance'. As for how it is all to be paid for, she hesitates and is unsure; she advocates the cancellation of Trident, of course, but she also argues for a greater sense of debate over the issues.

In the last few years, there has been new and growing distrust of the state and state institutions. Yet it is a deeper anxiety than that. It is a fear that what should have been addressed by the older generation was ignored and that somehow they let the mess happen and now it may be too late to help their children. Not since the Poll Tax riots has middle England been so rattled. It is small things that motivate the middle classes: fairness, even-handedness, reasonableness. There is now a feeling of injustice and moral outrage that has gone far beyond *The Guardian* readers of Islington and Crouch End.

The betrayal of the trusting and supportive middle classes, of those who believed until relatively recently that election promises were made to be kept, that policing was by consent, that education was a right and not a privilege and that English, Philosophy and History counted for something in the civilising process may be the biggest betrayal of all.

The last hoorah (at least for now) of student ire and Black Bloc tactics happened after the TUC-organised 'March for the Alternative' rally on 26 March 2011, which would end in Hyde Park, where there would be speeches from Ed Milliband and Ken Livingstone. The police had expected trouble from demonstrators and had already warned shop-keepers and hotels as early as 22 March to clear fronts and secure premises. The police, led by Assistant Commissioner Lynne Owens, who was in charge of public order, had intelligence that 'a number of groups [were] planning trouble'.[30] Indeed they were, and they had broadcast the fact and their routes and targets on the Internet for anyone to see. Nevertheless, no shops or hotels in Piccadilly were closed or guarded.

As the TUC march crossed Piccadilly on its way to Hyde Park, shoppers in Fortnum & Mason looked on and those staying in the Ritz waved from balconies. There was almost no police presence. It therefore comes as no surprise that the police were unable to deal with the alternative 'civil disobedience' demonstrations by UK Uncut, anti-capitalists and dissident groups when they descended on Oxford Circus as a flash mob of around 150 and attacked HSBC, McDonald's and Top Shop (owned by the alleged 'tax avoider' Philip Green). Others targeted both the 'fat cats' in the Ritz and a Porsche showroom with flares, ammonia-filled light bulbs, paint and metal road signs (which had not been removed!) and occupied Fortnum & Mason with around 200 protesters (a figure exaggerated to 1,000 in the *Daily Mail* the next day) who invaded the store.

The papers saw nothing but 'mobs' and 'masked thugs' whose coordinated attacks across the centre of London evaded the 4,500 officers policing the TUC event. 'It was pretty scary at times', said Karen Underwood, speaking to the *Sunday Telegraph*, 'paint was being thrown and large groups of men were charging through the streets'.

Ed Milliband, whose speech coincided with the disturbances, 'unequivocably condemn[ed] those who [had] committed acts of violence', and Brendan Barber, the TUC general secretary, 'bitterly regretted the events'. The reaction was, as ever couched in predictable clichés: mindless thugs, acting in mobs with the intention of ruining everyone's day.[31]

One protester, used to shopping with his parents in the store, chose not to loot or do anything crass, but rather to drink a bottle of champagne whilst inside, a most civilised and almost old-fashionedly Tory form of revolt.[32] The series of events were part of anti-tax avoidance demonstrations that accused the shop's owners of not paying their taxes, an accusation that also led to the occupation of Vodafone, Boots and BHS.

Protests turned nastier as the night progressed, with bins being set alight near Charing Cross Station and barriers being used as weapons. Simon Hardy, a spokesman for the NCAFC, suggested that the fault lay with the government's policy of 'political vandalism', the Olympics countdown clock being daubed with paint and 'Tory Scum' being scribed across Trafalgar Square.[33] It was an answer of sorts to those who accused the agitators of being 'parasites' and 'hooligans', as Shadow Defence spokesman Jim Murphy called them.[34]

The whole affair had been preventable, but was not. The Ritz and Fortnum & Mason (both representative of conspicuous consumption and unnecessary luxury) stayed open whilst evidently at risk and police intelligence was obviously faulty. Assistant Commissioner Owens could not even recall the route of the march some four months later and accused protestors of ignoring agreed procedures; hardly surprisingly, she defended the 'robust' response of the police. Of more interest is the treatment of the Fortnum protesters, who were told by police 'that you can leave now if [you] want, and you will not be detained'.[35] None of this was true. Forty protesters were arrested and charged.

Nonetheless, the events had greater significance for the unquestioned enforcement of law and order at the forthcoming royal wedding. Indeed, the idea of 'safeguarding' the royal couple was paramount, anarchists given fair warning that 'deliberate targeting' would not be tolerated and would be a legitimate reason for a pre-wedding round-up of opposition. The Mayor, Boris Johnson, would also not tolerate problems and issued a warning that 'it would be extremely unwise of anyone to try to spoil a happy day of national celebration', whilst MP Keith Vaz saw the spectre of 'terrorism' in the disruption at Fortnum & Mason.[36]

Those in authority convinced themselves that they saw only the signs of incipient hooliganism and rowdy behaviour in the attacks on royalty and posh grocers in Piccadilly, but the students saw something else, something they suspected in their theoretical discussions, although they could hardly have dreamt of any of it coming true. The spirit of revolution was already intoxicating and infectious. The students, however, merely dreamed of 'running wild in the streets'. Even if they did have a theoretical grasp of a 'social curve', they could only fantasise about a visceral violence actually quite alien to their own protests. And yet the students did foresee the future, if only in a glass darkly and as something that would tie student protest to

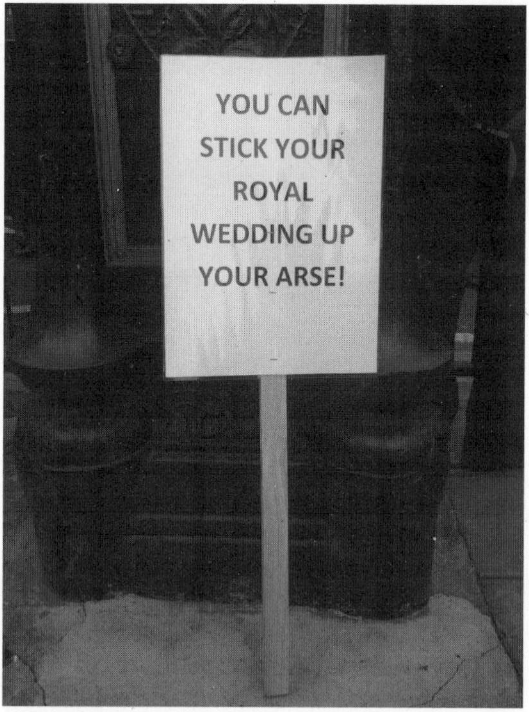

Figure 4.2 Disapproval of the royal wedding at the 'March for the Alternative' (courtesy of Jonathan Bloom)

the charge of a 'colonised' and disinherited 'subaltern' underclass. Theory foretold all:

> In a colony, forms of punishment are inseparable from forms of productive labour. Confined, immobilised. Commanded. The colonies come home. Low waged labour, precarious, without progression and with debt beyond hope of repayment. The ASBO and the kettle both match the labour to be performed. Workfare, zero hour contracts and temp work: these are the punishments of the excluded. [37]

Finally, student 'outrage' metamorphosed into that 'universal emotional condition' which they had hoped for, yet quite different from their actual expectations and with apparently quite different roots. It looked like it would turn into a nightmare scenario of students on the barricades at war with the 'theatre of baton charges, horse charges and late night imprisonment'. Instead, it metamorphosed into the warped reality of another social class at war, one the students had little or no contact with and one that raided shops rather than talked about it. On 29 November 2010, Paul Noon, General Secretary of the civil service union Prospect, accused the Chancellor of the Exchequer of 'ratcheting up the class war'. He might not have realised how the full truth of his words would be demonstrated.[38]

5

2011: THE SUMMER RIOTS – A COLD WIND IN AUGUST

Chaos theory predicates that a minor event in one place may have catastrophic consequences in another. The death of Mark Duggan was hardly minor for his family and friends, but he was little known outside his community and those involved in his killing could not predict the national carnage that was to follow. They may, nevertheless, had paused to think about the circumstances and location of his death – Tottenham, the scene of the Broadwater Farm riots in 1985, sparked by the death of a Black woman, Cynthia Jarrett, and ending with the murder of police constable Keith Blakelock and the arrest and imprisonment of three innocent men. Pause for thought enough, perhaps.

Duggan was born and lived on the Broadwater Farm estate in Tottenham. On 4 August 2011, he was shot in the chest by a police marksman whilst he sat in a stationary minicab. It was either at 6.13 or 6.15 pm. He was 29 years old. He had been the subject of police surveillance and was believed by them to be carrying a gun which he was thought to have fired, and in the ensuing exchange of bullets was hit and died. This was not so. Although a gun was recovered from the body, it was not the gun that had fired the shots. Those had come from a police Heckler & Koch MP5 semi-automatic carbine, the bullet wedged in the police radio (of which much was made at the time), the effect of a ricochet at close range. The police gunman, who had apparently feared for his own safety, was part of the Specialist Firearms Command (CO19) working within Operation Trident, which targets Black on Black crime. There were problems from the start. The IPCC investigation which started soon afterwards was criticised for its poor methods. David Lammy, the MP for Tottenham, called for further answers, while some community workers even refused to cooperate with an investigation they considered 'shoddy'.[1]

Duggan's history remained a mystery. Was he, as the police suggested, a 'major player' in the drugs trade who, some claimed, 'caused grief … by the gun' or was he a good father and family man trying to avoid a spell in jail?[2] What was established was that Duggan was related to a criminal in Manchester called Desmond Noonan who had been killed in 2009, but this proved nothing, nor did the idea that he was planning a revenge attack for the death of his cousin, Kelvin Easton. The family claimed that painting him as a notorious gang member was planted disinformation. The very circumstances of his death remained mysterious, with the IPCC having to correct stories appearing in the newspapers and then having to correct its own press releases (about shots being fired at the police). On 9 August, the IPCC press release claimed that the gun owned by Duggan was illegal, had been used elsewhere and had a cartridge ready to fire, but that there were unsubstantiated rumours of the gun being thrown into the minicab from *outside*. On 5 August, a post-mortem was carried out, but in mid-August the family were calling for a second autopsy to establish whether or not there was an exchange of fire (apparently Duggan had a firearm hidden in a sock).[3] A month later, Duggan's mother was still accusing the police of murder and a cover-up.[4] A second post-mortem was held on 12 December 2011.

The death of Mark Duggan proved to be a slow-burning fuse. The day after the shooting, David Lammy released a press statement that attempted to calm the situation down after the *Evening Standard* had published an inflammatory article suggesting that Duggan had been deliberately shot whilst lying on the ground.[5] In the afternoon, the police, suspecting trouble, set up Operation Atemoya to manage tensions that were considered 'above normal', a reasonable conclusion as a march was planned on Tottenham Police Station on the Saturday, an event that had sparked disorder in the past.

Around 100 marchers arrived at around 5.30 pm and by 6 pm the local police were requesting reinforcements. Things may have remained calm, but it appears that riot officers may have pushed a friend of Duggan, a 16-year-old girl, down on the pavement after she was seen throwing a bottle at police. The girl was allegedly hit by batons and apparently cut in the face before being dragged away by others. The incident looked suspicious enough to be posted on YouTube almost immediately. By 7 pm, the police station was under attack from bottles and bricks and the ground floor had to be evacuated. Information came in that the station might even be firebombed. Duggan's family (but not Duggan's mother) had arrived, but this only seemed to increase tension. Bottles and bricks were now being thrown at police vehicles, several of which were burning, the local fire station actually being blocked by the burning cars. By 9.09 pm, police reserves had been rushed to the scene to quell the general looting and chaos, with banks, shops and other commercial premises being attacked and broken into.

It was now that serious looting started to occur. At around midnight, youths, apparently armed with knives and bats, were hijacking cars and blocking roads with burning vehicles and bollards. In nearby Wood Green, approximately 100 young men masked up and ran rampage through the local shopping centre. At the same time, about 200 people started to attack shops in Tottenham Hale Retail Park, where there were no police. They stole electrical goods and nonchalantly wheeled them away. At around 3 am on Sunday morning, young men were being reported as carrying guns in the street and further unconfirmed reports were of passers-by held up at gunpoint. At 6 am on Sunday morning, the police had mustered 825 officers, complete with horses, dogs and firearm experts, to deal with the disorder. By the early morning, the violence had subsided, 42 people had been arrested and 10 police officers had been injured.

However, the problems hadn't ceased, and at lunchtime on Sunday (7 August) the police received the worrying news that gangs were preparing to meet at 4 pm to start riots in Tottenham, Enfield, Walthamstow and Hackney. By 3.20 pm, there were youths on the streets of Enfield and gangs appeared in East Croydon. More information suggested that south London gang rivalry had been put aside in order to have a showdown with the police and undertake more organised looting in both Enfield and Croydon. Young people now started to gather in numbers at Enfield railway station and in the town. Neither buses nor trains were disrupted, despite gangs entering the town on public transport. Unbelievably, there were only seven police in Enfield to keep order, and these officers called for urgent back-up units. From 5 pm, serious trouble erupted in Enfield town centre when 100 or so youths damaged and looted shops and destroyed vehicles. Ordinary police, fearing for their safety, retreated and were replaced by units trained in civil disturbance with dogs, helmets and riot gear. The groups of youths were all hooded and masked, and tried to block roads with debris. A dispersal command was broadcast by loudspeaker, but to no effect.

Between 7.30 pm and 9 pm, gangs tried to break into a bank and a man was reportedly stabbed. In Ponders End and Enfield there were now about 600 rioters, many walking down the road in masks, hoods and bandanas armed with 'petrol bombs', knives and other weapons. Some were on BMX bikes and some actually used bikes to smash shop windows. At 9 pm, the train station was still not secured and the trains were still running rioters into the Enfield area, where police were trying to sort the situation out through the use of dogs. By this time disorder has broken out in Wood Green and Hackney, with electrical shops being targeted. At two minutes past midnight, it was reported that a group of 500 had set fire to the Sony Building in Enfield's industrial park. Meanwhile, in south London, a group of 100 had been effectively dispersed in Brixton after looting for a while, finally stopped by the use of lights and helicopters. Trouble seemed to be spontaneously breaking out all around London. The next target was Croydon, a virtual suburb of south London A reasonably large police presence in the area did not deter gangs of around 100 smashing into shops, looting and setting buildings on fire. There seemed to be too many incidents of an almost random nature and too few police to deal with all the things that were occurring.

On the morning of Monday 8 August, with adverse headlines in the newspapers already asking about 'police blunders', the Greater Manchester and Nottingham police forces started to work on contingency plans in case of trouble, whilst police from Essex, the Thames Valley, Kent, Cambridgeshire, Northamptonshire, Suffolk, Surrey and Sussex were hurriedly deployed to London, Oxford Street being guarded by police from as far away as Wales.[6] By mid-morning on Monday, the police had learned that Croydon was again to be a target in the evening, easy prey, perhaps, for predatory looters. Section 60 (stop and search legislation) was now authorised across London boroughs. Croydon was not the only target, as extreme and uncontrollable violence and looting broke out in Hackney.

At 5 pm on Monday, fears in other parts of England were realised as youths started gathering in Birmingham. The rioters in Croydon, armed with bottles of bleach and other makeshift weapons and uncaring of any intervention, had fought apparently unprepared and ill-equipped police (they had no riot shields) into a corner. Fires burned everywhere. The rioting in Hackney was still not under control either. By 6.18 pm, police received information relating to attacks in Ealing. The streets had to all intents and purposes been abandoned for lack of deployed resources. The *Evening Standard* that evening ran page after page of rioting news under the headline 'Lawless London'.[7]

At 7 pm, Croydon was under siege from around 200 to 300 people, the town centre being filled with looters throwing petrol bombs and missiles at police and onlookers. The police again found themselves wrong-footed when a shield charge went wrong and three officers were left isolated to confront 30 rioters. A vehicle was also driven straight at police in order to force them to fall back. There was now some urgency to get vehicles with 'stinger equipment' deployed so as to protect police lines from such attacks and prevent loss of life.[8] It looked to be too late to prevent major destruction. Between 9.05 pm and 9.17 pm, Trevor Ellis was discovered in a car in Warrington Road, Croydon with gunshot wounds, from which he later died. He had apparently got into an altercation with a group of men who were possible looters. He was not. Yet another angry crowd gathered as vehicles were pushed towards police lines by around 100 youths and the fire brigade was attacked. Five people were actually injured with burns that night as a loud, unidentified explosion was heard.

Indeed, Croydon was virtually abandoned to the mob when general fires were started and department stores looted. Many of the trouble-makers were still able to enter the town by minibus and train! A man caught up in the street violence was stabbed with a broken bottle, whilst another across London in Uxbridge was seen carrying a gun to steal a cash machine from a supermarket. At 9 pm, a crowd estimated at between 200 and 300 was rampaging through Woolwich, setting fire to the Great Harry pub, which burned to the ground.

In Croydon town centre, tram lines were set ablaze and cars were still being driven at police lines. Perhaps realising the opportunity brought about by the police being overstretched, gangs of 200 to 300 began a rampage in Clapham Junction and Battersea at around 8 pm, as did smaller groups in Ealing, where much destruction was caused, the police being left with almost no resources and thus unable to intervene. The situation shown live on television news was almost surreal, especially when, at some time in the evening, the House of Reeves furniture store in Croydon and the block of buildings around it were set ablaze and began collapsing onto the tram lines. There were only around 50 actual rioters in the High Street when the blaze began. Perhaps these were the most terrifying scenes of all during the whole of the riots, suggesting growing lawlessness and chaos. Emergency vehicles were withheld for fear of attack and police were nowhere to be seen. This above all else created a sense of public fear as well as outrage. The police meanwhile had no time to ponder events as they were dealing with potential disorder at nearby Thornton Heath.

Figure 5.1 London burns: the summer riots 2011 (Andy Ryans, 'Shop fire during London riots, 2011', Creative Commons Attribution)

As that long warm Monday evening progressed, the first hints of trouble began to emerge outside London when gangs started to gather in Liverpool, Birmingham and Manchester. In all three locations looting and violence soon followed. Yet the disturbances in these towns seemed slightly different, reflecting ethnic tension and hatred for police as well as mere opportunism. In Birmingham, Holyhead Road Police Station was set on fire and Staveley House Police Station was firebombed. In Nottingham, a bus, petrol station and police station were set on fire and barricades were built as armed groups looted at will. As the night progressed, the situation in other British towns and cities looked ominous. Many people feared a general breakdown in law and order across the country. At approximately 11.20 pm in Ealing in West London, an unnamed 68-year-old man was assaulted and later died from his injuries, the police and emergency services battling unsuccessfully to get assistance to him.

With English cities apparently burning and mob rule on the streets, the Prime Minister, the Home Secretary and the London Mayor all hurried home on 8 August after breaking off their summer holidays. There was much press vilification of this delay, such as that in the *Daily Mirror*, which had a headline shot of David Cameron against a burning building and asked 'Where is the PM? Posing with a waitress on holiday in Italy', which gave added urgency to the return to all three prodigals.[9] Both Cameron and Johnson were soon seeing the destruction for themselves, although only Johnson was brave enough to confront angry residents in Clapham, where he was heckled; the Prime Minister preferred to meet emergency workers away from the public's gaze.

There was to be no let-up. The *Evening Standard* grimly warned 'Stay Off the Streets'.[10] In the early hours of Tuesday 9 August, more shops and buildings were looted and set on fire in Lavender Hill, Peckham and in West Ealing. Nevertheless, Birmingham city centre had, at least for the moment, been brought under control. Elsewhere things were no better. In Croydon, Manchester, Nottingham and later Wolverhampton, virtual 'mob' rule continued. In the afternoon, violence broke out in Salford in Greater Manchester, in Wolverhampton and yet again in Birmingham. In Manchester city centre, between 5 pm and approximately 7 pm, 300 young people descended on the shopping mall and began unhindered looting, as was the case in Salford. The riots here seemed to be undertaken with more venom than in London, rioters making use of homemade petrol bombs and street signs to break into shops. The Greater Manchester Police, out-manoeuvred and under-resourced, called for urgent back-up from the Police National Information Co-ordination Centre. Such panic was obvious to all and *The Times* wanted to know why the streets had been surrendered to 'mob rule'.[11] It was the question on everyone's lips.

The violence seemed to be spreading, for at 9 pm that night, reports arrived that there was looting in Huddersfield, Coventry and West Bromwich. To make things worse, there now seemed to be a cyber-attack against the West Midlands Police website. In Manchester, supermarkets were being looted by groups allegedly armed with petrol bombs; the police, unable to properly control the looters, simply dispersed them with shield advances, which pushed rioters elsewhere in the city. At 8 pm, Birmingham police reported aimed gunfire at their lines. At midnight, with disorder mainly unchecked across England, emergency calls peaked.

The worst was not quite over. Between midnight and 1 am on Wednesday 10 August, there were gunshots reported at Winson Green in Birmingham, attacks on police vehicles and on the police station at Smethwick. Yet at 1.10 am, the worst incident was to occur when three men were struck by a speeding car which failed to stop. The three men later died. It was a turning point. By the afternoon, 390 police support units, numbering 9,750 officers, backed by forces from as far away as Scotland were being deployed. Indeed, forces had been increased as rapidly as possible once the disorder continued. On Saturday 6 August, there were approximately 3,000 officers across London, with over 380 public order officers deployed to Haringey. By Sunday 7 August, there were 4,275 officers across London, including 1,275 trained in public order. By Monday 8 August, there were 6,000 officers across London, including 1,900 trained in public order and, by Tuesday 9 August, these had increased to 16,000 officers deployed across London, including 3,750 trained in public order. It was enough to quell the disturbances.

Although disorder continued in Manchester and Birmingham, it now began to subside so that by Wednesday afternoon, Manchester city centre could again be declared safe, although further trouble seemed on the horizon as a train full of EDL supporters was on its way to Birmingham. And with that, all Section 60 and 60aa (enforced removal of disguises) requirements were rescinded and things simply returned to normal, ending not with a bang but a whimper. No one quite realised this at the time. Journalists at the *Daily Telegraph* were still worried enough over the possibility of more violence that they led with the alarming information that 'anarchy spreads [across England]' when, in point of fact, it was all but over.[12]

As rioting died down in London, residents, victims and sympathisers turned out on the streets to clear up the damage. Every newspaper ran stories about the depth of public-spiritedness and the community spirit of those affected. The media concentrated on the punishment of those who rioted ('payback time' as the *Metro* called it) and the bulldog spirit of those whose homes and livelihoods were affected.[13] Television reports concentrated on the clear-up by local volunteers armed with mops and brooms, the local shop-keepers who were starting again, the number of spontaneous donations, the visit of the Duchess of Cornwall to Tottenham to meet those residents burnt out of their homes and the visit of the Duke and Duchess of Cambridge to Birmingham, one of the worst-hit areas. The Duchess of Cambridge, it seemed, with rather more bravado than tact, wore a suit costing £2,000 on this visit. Some of the following Saturday's football fixtures were cancelled, but the Notting Hill Carnival, which was to be held soon after the riots, was not and went ahead peacefully.

The general image during and after the disturbances was one of 'broom armies' pitching in to fight back against mob rule with domestic cleaning equipment in a 'Blitz Spirit'.[14] The *Daily Express*, catering to a certain alarmism, invoked the war spirit by claiming that the 'terror is [the] worst since the Blitz'.[15] The *Weekly Gleaner* ran straplines that talked of 'one of the world's most respected capital city [sic] [becoming] a war zone'.[16] *The Sun* ran with a double-page spread of broom-armed volunteers in Lavender Hill and Hackney, featuring Hayley Miller, whose t-shirt was emblazoned with the motto 'Looters are Scum', while the *Daily Express* ran the headline 'Sweep Scum Off Our Streets'.[17]

These sentiments seemed to sum up what the general public felt. Indeed, *The Sun* ran a YouGov poll which suggested that 90 per cent of readers favoured the use of water cannons, 78 per cent wanted tear gas, 77 per cent wanted the army on the streets and at least 33 per cent favoured the use of live ammunition! The public reaction was hardly surprising and even ministers seemed infected with alarm and revulsion, for as late as October, when the heat had left the debate, the Community Secretary Eric Pickles (himself raised on a council estate) was still harping on about the 'uneducated, unemployed sub-class' that had started the riots. It would be his job to help the 120,000 problem families targeted as at risk by the government after the riots (with 'benefit conditions' attached, however).[18]

Attention soon turned to the victims of the events, with shopkeepers, those burnt out of their homes and those injured being found and interviewed, a process that revealed yet again the multicultural sense of London's population. Here were Asian newsagents in Clapham, Turkish and Kurdish grocers in Dalston, Greek and Cypriot residents of rented accommodation in Peckham and Tottenham, Aaron Biber, a Jewish barber of 89 in Tottenham, the owner of a reggae shop in Lavender Hill, the owners of a furniture store in Croydon, Sikhs wielding ceremonial swords defending their temple in Southall and a mosque in Ilford, and Jews and Muslims defending a synagogue in Stamford Hill against possible attack.[19]

Londoners may have been heartened by multi-faith and multicultural co operation, but such cooperation had its reverse side: apparent multi-ethnic antagonism. The multicultural nature of the perpetrators and their victims took a sombre turn when mere thuggishness turned to violence and murder, as it did in Hackney and Birmingham. In Barking, CCTV footage showed an injured Malaysian student Asyraf (or Ashraf) Haziq Rossli apparently being helped by Black youths only to be brutally mugged for his backpack and wallet,[20] while in Birmingham, Haroon Jahan, Shahzad Ali and Abdul Musavir were apparently run down by a speeding car driven by rioters. Tariq Jahan, the father of Haroon, actually found his son dying in the street.

For a moment, tempers in Birmingham were at breaking point and race riots threatened to follow, but were dampened by the increased police presence and community good sense. Violence seemed endemic. A scooter rider in Camberwell Green was randomly forced from his bike and beaten. In Ealing, Richard Mannington Bowes, the previously unnamed pensioner, lay critically injured. Darrell Desuze was 16 years old when he committed the attack. Bowes was fatally injured after he tried to put out a fire in a bin and was punched. He died three days later. Desuze's mother Lavinia destroyed her son's clothes to hide the evidence, but both were caught and prosecuted. Desuze later changed his plea to that of 'manslaughter'. Many of these violent incidents were captured on mobile phone cameras and posted on YouTube before finding their way to the police investigating the crimes. There was also continuous television footage of people jumping from burning buildings and flats in Hackney, Croydon and Tottenham.

The shadow of murder and of race war signalled by the events in Birmingham was something other than mere robbery, and the appearance of the EDL acting as vigilante patrols in Edmonton, Enfield, Eltham, Ponders End (singing football chants as they did so) and elsewhere in London aroused concerns that were only assuaged by a swift end to the riots, the dignity of the families of the dead men in Birmingham, the good humour of the victims in Hackney and the swift movement of the police in containing the actions of the EDL. Local newspapers across London praised their residents' resolution, while national newspapers such as the *Daily Express* rallied readers and started celebrity-backed 'crusades to raise funds for the victims' and funds to 'Reclaim our Streets', over 40 people in Tottenham alone having been rendered homeless.[21] One victim, Charlene Munro, who was burnt out of her flat, was helped out by Sue Duncan, a pensioner touched by the plight of the young woman and who decided to do 'something to help'.[22]

Parliament, which had remained quiet at the start of the riots, now had to be seen to act, and it was recalled the day after the Prime Minister's return. MPs could not afford to be absent during the debate. Heidi Alexander, the MP for Lewisham East, even returned from her honeymoon.[23] The atmosphere was one of crisis and the approach one of unmitigated panic. Cameron had called special meetings of Cobra on 9 and 10 August, whilst on the morning of 11 August he had hurried to Westminster; at 11.35 am both Houses of Parliament were packed for the debates.

Cameron began with a statement covering the events in Tottenham following the death of Mark Duggan and the three deaths that had followed in Birmingham, but he prefaced it with the comment that 'keeping people safe is the first duty of Government'. The first line of that duty lay with the police. As was to be expected, he also condemned the violence, which he blamed on 'thugs in gangs', the riots being 'not about race [but] about crime', a message reinforced by the new Commissioner of Police, Bernard Hogan-Howe, and his own war on gangs in 14 of London's boroughs, which he conducted in December 2011.[24]

Nevertheless, it was the subject of keeping order that was to prove the most contentious that day:

> But what became increasingly clear earlier this week was that there were simply far too few police deployed on to our streets, and the tactics that they were using were not working. Police chiefs have been frank with me about why this happened. Initially, the police treated the situation too much as a public order issue, rather than essentially one of crime.[25]

These comments and the remark that during the Cobra meeting 'we [but who exactly?] have taken the decisive action to help ensure more robust and more effective policing' suggested that the Prime Minister's return was decisive in turning the corner and that previous police tactics had contained serious errors not corrected until his intervention.[26] The police saw such comments as a slur and continue to hotly disputed them, comments indeed exacerbated in no little part by the Prime Minister's decision to employ Bill Bratton, the former Commissioner of Police in New York and Los Angeles, to advise on controlling British gang culture.

Dismissing those who were concerned for 'phoney human rights', the Prime Minister went on to praise the use of CCTV and the courts, and, whilst dismissing the need for baton rounds, water cannons or the military, nevertheless came down in favour of 'curfews' and 'gang injunctions'. Much of the statement was taken up with the idea of the nation as a whole as a 'broken society' (although no disturbances took place in Wales or Scotland and the BBC was instructed to refer only to 'English rioting') brought about by a 'gang culture' which threatened the vision of the Big Society laid down in his speech on 6 October 2010 to the Conservative Party Conference:[27]

> This is not about poverty; it is about culture – a culture that glorifies violence, shows disrespect to authority and says everything about rights but nothing about responsibilities.[28]

Against this lawlessness, Cameron invoked the war with the idea that 'the fight back has well and truly begun'.[29] This was not only the 'Blitz' spirit but a spirit of revenge and retribution:

> In the past few days, we have seen a range of emotions sweep this country: anger, fear, frustration, despair, sadness and, finally, a determined resolve that we will not let a violent few beat us. We saw that resolve in the people who gathered in Clapham, Manchester and Wolverhampton with brooms to clean up our streets. We saw it in those who patrolled the roads in Enfield through the night to deter rioters. We saw it in the hundreds of people who stood guard outside the Southall temple, protecting it from vandalism. This is a time for our country to pull together.
>
> To the law-abiding people who play by the rules and who are the overwhelming majority in this country, I say, 'the fight back has begun. We will protect you. If you've had your livelihood and property damaged,

> we will compensate you. We are on your side'. To the lawless minority, the criminals who have taken what they can get, I say: we will track you down, we will find you, we will charge you, we will punish you. You will pay for what you have done.[30]

There was nothing in the speech about why the riots took hold apart from some comments on 'social media' and the refusal to see a causal link between the death of Mark Duggan and the riots themselves.[31] Later in the debate, however, in a reply to Andrew Smith, the Labour MP for Oxford East, Cameron elaborated on future social policy:

> Let me give the right hon. Gentleman just one area where we have already made progress but I want to see further progress: discipline in schools. We have got to make sure that schools are able to confiscate things from children and to exclude children without being overruled by appeals panels. All those steps add to responsibility. We must also make sure that every single tax and benefit is pro-family, pro-commitment and pro-fathers who stick around. Part of the problem is that fathers have left too many of these communities, and that is why young people look towards the gang.[32]

Ed Milliband, replying for the Opposition, was more concerned with the underlying issues:

> To seek to explain is not to seek to excuse. Of course these are acts of individual criminality, but we all have a duty to ask ourselves why there are people who feel they have nothing to lose and everything to gain from wanton vandalism and looting. We cannot afford to let this pass and calm the situation down, only to find ourselves in the same position again in the future.
>
> These issues cannot be laid at the door of a single cause or a single Government. The causes are complex. Simplistic solutions will not provide the answer. We can tackle the solutions only by hearing from our communities.[33]

Yet, as might be expected, there were the usual calls for draconian punishments. Sir Peter Tapsell, the Conservative MP for Louth and Horncastle, was almost incandescent:

> Why have our police been dispersing these hoods so that they can riot in other vicinities, instead of rounding them up? Does the Prime Minister remember that in 1971, at the peak of the opposition to the

> Vietnam war in the United States, the US Government brought 16,000 troops into Washington, in addition to the police, who rounded up and arrested the riots and put 40,000 of them in the DC stadium in one morning? Has he any plans to make Wembley Stadium available for similar use?[34]

The Speaker, desperate for order and brevity with so many standing, let the floor to David Lammy, the Labour MP for Tottenham, who gave one of a number of impassioned speeches on behalf of his constituents:

> I welcome what the Prime Minister has said about the death of Mark Duggan and about compensation for victims. In Tottenham, 45 people have lost their homes, which were burnt to the ground. They were running out of their homes carrying their children in their arms, And their cry is, 'Where were the police?' We can have this debate today, but it is no replacement for hearing from the people themselves. Will the Prime Minister come to Tottenham and speak with those victims and the independent shopkeepers, hairdressers and jewellers who businesses are lying in cinders? Will he also commit to a public inquiry to consider why initial skirmishes were allowed to lead to a situation in which the great Roman road, Tottenham High Road, now lies in cinders?[35]

The Prime Minister, increasingly tired and overwrought no doubt, even detected sedition in the chamber, so that when Robert Flello, the Labour MP for Stoke-on-Trent South, rose to speak in his shirt sleeves, the answer was by way of a tetchy sarcastic remark:

> I do not know whether we need an inquiry into safety in the House, Mr Speaker, but someone seems to have stolen the hon. Gentleman's jacket.

The comments were rebuked by the Speaker:

> I am grateful for the Prime Minister's concern, but I assure the House that nothing disorderly has happened. The hon. Member for Stoke-on-Trent South [Robert Flello] was perfectly in order. He was focusing not on sartorial matters but on violence, and he was perfectly in order. We will leave it at that. I ask the House to try to rise to the level of events.[36]

By 2.20 in the afternoon, the Prime Minister had answered questions for 165 minutes and had been questioned by 160 colleagues, who took turns lamenting the situation, complimenting the dignity of those affected, supporting the police, vilifying the culprits and calling for more CCTV surveillance.[37] At 6 pm, argument was still going strong and the debate was not finally adjourned until 8 pm.

Meanwhile, in the other chamber and after the usual prayers by the Lord Bishop of Birmingham, the Lords heard the Prime Minister's statement read again by Baroness Anelay of St John's. Although there was much debate which simply mirrored the other chamber and the 'Blitz spirit' was actually invoked by Baroness Royall of Blaisdon when referring to the so-called 'broom armies' of clear-up volunteers, the debate was somewhat more contemplative. The Archbishop of Canterbury was first to express concern over civic breakdown and to see this partially in economic terms:[38]

> Over the past few decades, many would agree that our educational philosophy at every level has been more and more dominated by an instrumentalist model that is less and less concerned with the building of virtue, character and citizenship – civic excellence, as we might say. A good educational system in a healthy society is one that builds character and virtue … not consumers or cogs in an economic system but citizens?[39]

Baroness Hussein-Ece, who lived in Hackney and Islington, was able to put the case for not 'demonising black young people' whilst recognising gang crime and its causes:

> We know that in London, for example, there are more than 250 active gangs. The police know who they are and who the leaders are. These gangs have been allowed to grow and to take a hold for more than a decade – for 10 or 15 years. They draw in young people who are out on the streets and they spread criminality. When I was a councillor, mothers would come to my surgery begging me to get them transferred because they were so terrified of living on these estates and because of the way in which their families and their children were intimidated if they tried to resist joining these gangs.
>
> These social problems did not happen overnight in our inner cities, where there were huge inequalities and a big social divide. We have to acknowledge that. We have a disconnection in a section of our society, an underclass of young people who have poor education and no skills and who come from dysfunctional families. They feel that they have nothing to lose. They have no fear of authority. Who are their role

models? Millionaire footballers and rock stars. They want the latest gadgets, trainers or mobiles. This is what they aspire to.[40]

Revenge was in the air. Magistrates were instructed to sit literally through the night to deal with offenders and were 'encouraged' by politicians to hand out exemplary sentences. A government e-petition received 100,000 signatures overnight calling for looters to lose their benefits, while Nottingham, Salford, Greenwich and Westminster Councils were actively considering applying the measure. Arrests were swift and initial punishment was tough.[41] Moreover, Wandsworth Council was the first to start evicting looters or their families from council property. The tabloids published 'wanted' pictures and parents were urged to shop their children. 'Shop a Moron' shouted *The Sun* on 10 August and 'Shop Another Moron' the next day.[42]

The rioters, however, proved at first to be a surprisingly mixed bunch: there were teenage hooligans of both sexes and all races, but there were older people, a school assistant who sipped stolen beer and was thus deemed to have 'supported the civil disorder',[43] mothers on shopping sprees, children as young as nine, religious zealots jeering police in Stamford Hill, Olympic ambassadors such as Chelsea Ives, who was handed in by her mother who saw her on the television throwing bricks in Enfield, graduates such as Natasha Reid who looted a store in Enfield and who voluntarily handed herself in to police at Chingford and the wealthy middle-class Laura Johnson tagged for theft in Charlton. There were many more and there were no clear answers provided by their motives, class or ethnic origins.

The police continued to hunt the perpetrators into December 2011 and beyond: a mother and daughter, Clarice Ali and Chantelle Dixon-Ali, were caught on camera in Dalston and convicted of violent disorder and burglary, whilst a mere child in Romford admitted to burglary, theft and disorder as he helped his father rifle a fruit machine of its contents from a local pub. The final arrest total was predicted to come close to 5,000 and, by the end of the year, Chief Superintendent Chris Greany had bagged 3,269 offenders, suggesting the arrests were like an never-ending 'production line'. Police teams spent time watching 250,000 hours of CCTV footage.[44]

Cameron vowed to wage 'an all-out war on gangs', end the 'human rights culture', make benefits tougher, ban the use of masks, deport foreign rioters, interdict social media and bring in 'citizen service for sixteen year olds'.[45] It was fighting talk and the message (so far unprovable) seemed, at least on the surface, to have translated into the practical sentencing of magistrates and judges. Judges were said to be left incredulous as to how many younger offenders were actually on the streets. 'Where were the parents?', they asked. District Judge Elizabeth Roscoe concluded that 'the parents don't seem to care'.[46] Harsh sentences, such as that for six months' imprisonment for a student in South London who looted a case of bottled water from a supermarket, were to be the norm. Prisons, then at crisis point because they were at near-full capacity, filled with young offenders caught by CCTV and by continuous police raids such as those conducted by 200 officers in Haringey on 13 August following letters sent to known gang members to give up their gang connections. There was much heat and correspondents to *The Times* demanded greater action and more civil discipline.[47]

Magistrates appeared to be given instructions from senior justice clerks to make custodial sentencing harsh: Novello Noades, Chairman of the Bench at Camberwell Magistrates' Court, felt that very harsh sentencing was appropriate because 'what was happening ... was anarchy. The very fabric of society was at risk', while the *Daily Mail* assured readers that 'rioters and looters [and] thugs' were 'at last learning to fear the law'.[48] Such sentencing should, however, be placed against the cases of Lord Taylor of Warwick, who was convicted on six charges of false accounting in respect of £11,277, and Lord Hanningfield, former leader of Essex County Council, who falsely claimed £14,000. Both only served a quarter of their sentence, something that was not uncommon or irregular, but, given the timing and circumstances, something hardly conducive to public trust in the fairness of the system. Was there, after all, one law for the rich and one for the poor? Even solid middle-class blue rinses had to question the system.

The hysteria amongst politicians and magistrates over sentencing could not last and as early as the second and third weeks of August, some of those convicted had had their conviction overturned on appeal.[49] It began with the case of Ursula Nevin, convicted of receiving some clothing (whilst apparently asleep in her bed), whose custodial sentence was commuted to 75 hours of community service after she had spent six days in prison. David Atoh, who stole two shirts in Hackney, was sentenced on 11 August, but was released in the same week as he had already spent two days in jail in custody, which was considered punishment enough. Many rioters were leaving court without custodial sentences at all and with virtually no significant punishment, despite the calls by parliamentarians for sentencing that met the severity of the crime. A number of offenders were released immediately on 'referral' orders because they were too young to be sentenced to imprisonment or community service. Indeed, a number of youngsters, many of whom showed no signs of understanding the gravity of their actions, effectively walked away from the court unpunished.[50] Nevertheless, for some the law was harsh. Nicholas Robinson was sentenced to six months in prison on 11 August for stealing bottled water from a supermarket. The bottles of water were valued at £3.50.

The MP Peter Davies saw this not as justice but as the decision of 'lily livered, wet lettuces in the judiciary', an attitude supported by over 80 per cent of those polled by YouGov.[51] The comment was part of a general bewilderment as to who to blame. Whose fault was it that so many young people were outside of normal social boundaries and beyond civilised argument? It was easy for the moment simply to blame the liberal chattering classes and the feral unwashed. It would be an explanation that would not stand up and everyone knew it.

What had caused the catastrophe? As the riots abated in London but continued elsewhere, the *Financial Times* published one of many attempts by the media to understand what was happening as it happened. The article was the first to put emphasis on economic hardship, community breakdown, gang culture and issues of 'public esteem'. Under the heading 'Economics Not Racism Riles the Nando's Generation', it commented that the similarities with riots some 30 years previously, such as the Broadwater Farm riots in Tottenham, were merely superficial as:

> underneath, the circumstances [were] quite different ... not of police racism, but of communities facing external economic pressures that ... have exacerbated internal divisions ... these are events devoid of political intent ... These are riots marked out by the looting of Foot Locker and Nando's – the shopping places of Britain's new underclass. Those who have grown [up] in a world where social identity comes from consumption find themselves barred in times of economic hardship, except by theft.[52]

There was still the question of the case of the killing of Mark Duggan and the subsequent police tactics. Stung by the ferocity of the criticism they received from the Prime Minister, Duggan's family, the public, the media and Greater Manchester's Chief Constable, Peter Fahy (who complained that lack of decisiveness in London allowed the rioting to spread), the Metropolitan Police issued a briefing report preliminary to an interim report in November and a final report in December 2011.

Understandably, the report attempted to:

> Develop a detailed understanding of the MPS [Metropolitan Police Service] response to significant public disorder in London between Thursday 4th August and Friday 19th August 2011 in order to inform future policing operations, by ensuring organisational learning is recognised and developed for the future.[53]

The report itself was an attempt to make sense of the disorder in terms of strategy and tactics. It needed first to take into account the scale of the disturbances, the biggest in over 30 years. In this respect, the police identified four areas of escalation which they linked in an explanatory narrative:

> The changing nature and sheer scale of events between Saturday 6 and Tuesday 9 August [which] made it very different from anything we had seen in the capital before. Over a short space of time on Saturday it changed from a peaceful protest in response to the tragic death of Mark Duggan into significant spontaneous disorder in Tottenham. The following night (Sunday) the disorder and criminality spread to other boroughs (Haringey again, plus Enfield, Lambeth, Waltham Forest and Hackney) and on Monday night it was the sheer number and size of simultaneous incidents, touching almost every borough which was so significant. In fact by Monday night, serious disorder – that is individual crimes or a concentration of crimes took place in 22 of London's 32 boroughs. We have never seen such levels of multi-site disorder in the capital before. At its peak we were receiving more than one piece of information per second. The number of 999 calls to the MPS increased by 400% in a 24-hr period to over 20,000. The Fire Brigade received over 1,700 calls to reports of fires.[54]

Even so, the briefing accepted that the level of escalation outstripped resources, which led to operational frustrations as officers struggled to protect other emergency services, tried to prevent further disorder and simply waited for reinforcements. One drawback was the fact that there were a maximum of 770 Level 1 trained officers and 3,500 Level 2 trained officers available, too few apparently to quell the violence. Senior officers were, however, specifically exonerated from the accusation of dithering. At this stage the review had found nothing to suggest that senior commanders briefed local commanders on the ground to hold back from making proactive arrests where appropriate; in fact, the contrary appeared to be the case. The public watching on the streets, out of the windows of their barricaded homes and on television in real time, were not convinced.

The briefing in effect was a preliminary 'review' and, as such, it made recommendations which effectively argued for greater inter-police cooperation or 'mutual aid', greater numbers of officers trained to cope with disorder, greater development of counter-surveillance technology, greater numbers of police trained to investigate public disorder and, perhaps most important of all, the call for the creation of a more integrated criminal investigation and judicial system; all this in the name of efficiency. Interestingly, the police considered deploying baton rounds and water cannons four months before 'official' authorisation by the Home Secretary and in the wake of the student disturbances:

> A range of tactics were used by police over the period of disorder; other tactical options including the possible use of water cannon and baton rounds are being considered within the review. The use of water cannon requires a precise environment. It works most effectively against large, static crowds that are (for example) throwing missiles at police or other communities. As such it does have its tactical limitations; however, if available it could have been considered as a tactical option during this disorder. The review will fully cost the options of making water cannon available to the MPS. Baton rounds are discriminate weapons that are fired at individuals who pose a violent threat where life is at risk. As a contingency, baton rounds were made available throughout the disorder.[55]

However, due to the fast-moving nature of the disorder and the availability of other tactical options, they were discounted, although the idea of using water cannons, tear gas and tasers as potential 'weapons' to quell disorder was being debated as late as March 2012. The summer riots acted, in effect, as a gigantic rehearsal for the 2012 Olympics, where the lessons learned by the police might be put into effect. How many baton rounds did the Metropolitan Police possess?

On 1 December 2009, 6,423; on 1 December 2010, 1,361; on 1 July 2011, 700; whilst on 1 December 2011, six months after the riots, there were 10,024 stockpiled. Aware of public concerns, the police explained in a cautious statement put out on 3 May 2012 that:

> Baton rounds are one of a number of operational tactics available to police and they are only considered in the most extreme situations to reduce the threat posed by specific individuals in order to protect life, to prevent serious injury or prevent significant damage to property during serious public disorder. To put this into context baton rounds have been placed on stand by on a number of occasions in London but have never actually been used. We are not eager to use baton rounds in London but they are an essential tool to protect members of the public to help prevent loss of life. Last summer we were criticised for not having sufficient numbers of specialist trained and equipped officers to make this tactical option available. Training has increased over recent months as a sensible precaution to ensure that we can make this happen. Before an event they require the authority of an assistant commissioner, and during an event they require the authority of at least a commander. We have more than 300 specially trained officers who are authorised in the use of baton rounds and receive regular refresher courses in line with national guidelines. Baton rounds are bought once per year so numbers do rise dramatically at the time of ordering. Stock is allowed to run down before re-ordering due to the high cost of the rounds and the limited shelf life of the product.

The new Metropolitan Police Commissioner, Bernard Hogan-Howe, in a bid for transparency and an attempt to stop commentators revisiting the canard of police ethnic bias, issued the following statistics after the riots regarding general levels of criminality. Of the 7,956 people taken to court for robbery during the period from March 2010 to October 2011, 55 per cent were Black, 33 per cent were White and 11 per cent were Asian; of those crimes involving robbery with a knife, of which there were 1,613 incidents, Black young men made up 60 per cent of those arrested. Although Black people are disproportionally stopped by police, it was clear that such disproportionality was warranted in some areas. In Lambeth and Lewisham 75 per cent of those in court were Black, the figure in Southwark being 69 per cent. Of course, where there are fewer Black people, there was less Black crime, as in Westminster where only 37 per cent were Black. Indeed, the statistics suggested not that Black people are unfairly targeted or are not guilty of the crimes they are charged with, but that White criminality is more likely to be 'overlooked'.[56]

The police were also quick to release data on those specifically arrested during the riots. Operation Withern resulted in over nearly 4,000 arrests in London by November 2011. There were 3,713 offences (resulting in charges and summonses) between 6 August and 17 October (actually all related to the riots), of which 35 per cent were burglaries and 28 per cent were criminal damage offences, of which 166 were arson-related and 12 per cent were simple burglaries. These showed that out of 2,897 arrested by October, 946 people or 33 per cent were White, 1,600 people or 56 per cent were Black, 230 or 8 per cent were Asian and 103 or 4 per cent were considered 'other'. Further statistics on age groups, etc. were consistent with the divisions suggested by arrest patterns. Of those arrested, 69 per cent were between 15 and 24 years old.[57] At least 25 per cent of those arrested already had a criminal record (often with ten offences or more), but, equally, nearly 29 per cent of rioters in London found themselves in court for the first time.

Many might have expected that with the end of the rioting and the subsequent rounding up of suspects, there would have been a disruption to gang culture and to the criminal activities associated with gang crime, especially teenager-on-teenager knifings. With so many gang members being hunted or already off the street, it should have followed that knife crime would quickly diminish in significance. This seemed not to be the case. Almost immediately after the riots, two teenagers (and an adult) were stabbed in Enfield and Edmonton in gang-related or gang-style violence, bringing the number of teenage deaths during the year up to that point to 11. One, Leroy James, a boy of 14, was stabbed in a recreation ground in Enfield, while the other, Steven Grisales, was stabbed to death over a conker in Edmonton.[58] Earlier in the year, a gang feud in south London resulted in the death of Nicholas Pearton. After sentencing at the Old Bailey, the gang members even began a fight in the courtroom.[59] In October, two boys began a knife fight on an Underground train, which left both badly injured, whilst a gang fight in Canning Town in December left teenager Danny O'Shea dead. Meanwhile, in south London, Shevonne Legister was convicted of hiding a MAC-10 gun in baby clothes to facilitate an alleged gang attack on Larry Malone at his house in Norwood. Malone died in the attack.[60] Legister's own brother had been gunned down years before in Jamaica.

This cycle of violence did not end with the riots or with the later round-ups of suspects or with the many convictions. Indeed, the problem may not have been touched upon, despite promises from politicians and the police. As a consequence, gang violence, especially amongst black youths, continues to become bolder. During the Boxing Day sales in Oxford Street on 26 December 2011, an 18 year old called Seydou Diarrassouba was killed in front of Foot Locker by a single knife wound in broad daylight and in front of shoppers, and another man was knifed in front of Nike at around the same time. Both attacks were similar and both revolved around alleged shoplifting or revenge activities by rival gangs. In all, 28 people were arrested in south and west London from rival groups. Police Commander Mak Chishty in charge of investigations was sure that 'gangs were certainly part of [the] events' and blamed 'gang issues' for the incidents.[61] The worst incident of gang violence was the wounding of a little girl, Thusha Kamaleswaran, in Stockwell during a gunfight between rival gangs. Nathaniel Grant (21), Kazeem Kolawole (19) and Anthony McCalla (20) of the Brixton GAS gang were all given life sentences at the Old Bailey on 19 April 2012. Thusha was left paralysed by the attack.

Indeed, there was actually a rise in knife-related crime during the period before and after the riots, possibly indicative of a rise in opportunism. Muggings increased by 18 per cent and in Lambeth the rate went up by 22 per cent between April and 31 July 2011 from 288 to 352 (a few months before the riots), Merton saw a 95 per cent increase, Southwark a 67 per cent increase to 355 and Westminster 64 per cent to 220 during the same period. A total of 2,076 Londoners aged between 13 and 24 were cut or stabbed, and more than half were teenagers. The total number of young people stabbed went up by 30 per cent, despite the attempts by the Mayor and others to reduce the figure. Knife crime had actually risen in almost all London boroughs.

The apparently overwhelming evidence suggested that certain ethnic groups are more prone to violence must nevertheless be resisted. These figures, despite appearances, do not actually suggest a systemic fault in Black British society, although from what could be seen by right-wing commentators on their television sets, the race issue was bound to come to light eventually. The historian David Starkey provided the script on BBC's *Newsnight* on 12 August. In the programme, Starkey not only referenced Enoch Powell's 'rivers of blood' speech, which he saw as 'absolutely right in one sense', but also came to the conclusion that:

> What's happened is that a substantial section of the Chavs [white unemployed youngsters] ... have become black. The whites have become

> black. A particular sort of violent, destructive, nihilistic, gangster [sic: gangsta] culture has become the fashion. And black and white, boy and girl, operate in this language together, this language which is wholly false, which is this Jamaican patois that's been intruded in[to] England, and this is why so many of us have this sense of literally a foreign country.[62]

The comments drew ire from left-wing politicians as well as 100 fellow historians who sent an open letter to *The Times Higher Education* magazine on 25 August, criticising his position as one of ignorance and snobbery. Yet, despite the 'racist' terms of his comments, Starkey's central accusation that the operation of a certain type of language identifies a certain cultural attitude may be valid, although the point has very little to do with ethnicity or Black people in particular. It is the fact that anyone at the bottom of society might act this way. There is nothing inherently problematic about Black culture, and white 'chavs' who adapt the patois do so because it is the patois of the disengaged and, like slang before it, it talks to a community fundamentally alienated and one which deliberately excludes, through its language, those it feels act oppressively (teachers, parents, police, etc.). Such language gives the community solidarity (just as Latin once did to the educated). Starkey's comments were, in the end, simply gut outrage, not racist but simply wrong.

Meanwhile, Wandsworth Council leader Paul Ellis accused the long-term unemployed of going shopping instead of working, some council estates looking 'like the Oxford Street sales', the able-bodied 'popping out to the shops' instead of finding employment.[63] At City Hall, the Mayor's advisor Ray Lewis was planning to set up more of his 'tough love' supplementary 'boot camps' around London to teach 'civic responsibility and moral leadership'.[64] Whilst the right vilified those involved on moral grounds, the left was virtually silent, dumb witnesses to the clear breakdown of social programmes and Labour welfare put in place to prevent such things happening in the first place.

6

1668, 1780 AND 1981: CONTEXTS AND EXPLANATIONS

After the wrangles came the reckoning. Compensation claims would be handled by the Metropolitan Police Authority, which:

> Received over 3,844 claims. 70 per cent of the claims [were] checked to remove duplicates and to place the compensation amount requested by the claimant onto the IT system. Liabilities [were] currently estimated [in early 2012] to be between £200m & £300m, the MPA [Metropolitan Police Authority] continue to look to fully recover all costs from the Home Office via special grant. Significant MPA/MPS resources have been committed to this work to ensure the MPA are in a position to make early decisions regarding individual claims.[1]

Yet things did not go smoothly. By March 2012, only 181 uninsured claims had been dealt with under the Riot Damages Act 1886. Nevertheless, 161 still remained unresolved. The plight of claimants was highlighted that month by the *Evening Standard*, which told the story of one disappointed Croydon resident, Carla Rees.[2] Indeed, it appeared that 9 out of 10 people claiming some sort of compensation had not been dealt with by March. Embarrassed by delays in payments, David Cameron pledged to 'chase up' any outstanding monies, complaining in the House of Commons that the Riot Damages Act was antiquated.[3]

The evident breakdown in various communities in England during the disturbances showed up the chronic drip of social decay. The riots were caused not by immediate government cuts, but by an accelerating economic and moral decline within communities that had been unable to restore their social balance since the violence of 30 years earlier. The events of 1981 in Brixton, Birmingham and Toxteth or those in 1985 at Broadwater Farm were not far from people's memories, nor were the circumstances of the death of Jean Charles de Menezes in the aftermath of 7/7.

The *New Statesman* warned against glib comparisons, despite some 'remarkable similarities', and considered that the context of the 2011 riots was 'suggestive of a far more complex and profound sense of alienation' than during the 1980s.[4] At all events, the violence of the week's looting had, it seemed, left people in such a state of shock that 'the analytical moment seems to [be] postponed indefinitely'. This was not to be the case, in fact, as endless semi-official reports, television programmes and newspapers attempted to analyse the problem. Was it analysis or mere picking at a wound that would not heal?

The Guardian teamed up with researchers at LSE to conduct an immediate social survey of the rioting and its causes. They interviewed 270 people who claimed to have been part of the week's troubles. The interviewers identified 'distrust and antipathy' to the police as central, but also opportunism as well. The overwhelming comment by rioters was that these were not 'race riots', but the following were considered as triggers to the events: poverty; policing; government policy; unemployment; the shooting of Mark Duggan; the use of social media; media coverage; greed; inequality; boredom; criminality; moral decline; racial tensions; poor parenting; and gang culture. It is obvious that some of the comments by those interviewed followed a narrative script of 'expected' answers and that others seem to be a 'too sophisticated' backdated rationale for spontaneous actions. Researchers also concluded that as there had been an apparent 'truce' between gangs and that therefore the riots were not gang-related and that gangs played only a peripheral part in the looting, a rather contentious and perverse reading of events which actually followed the official police conclusions. It all suggested that gang crime in this sense is invisible to middle-class educated investigators (60 academics, journalists, etc., or even the police) who too readily swallow what they are told and what those investigated know that the researchers want to hear, gang crime being too contentious an issue to deal with directly. The question of gang culture seems mired in difficulties and contradictions.

To find out more, the author contacted the Ministry of Justice in January 2012 using the Freedom of Information Act for the following data regarding those given a custodial sentence after the riots: levels of literacy of those sentenced; any information regarding family background and parenthood; any information regarding whether those sentenced were or had previously been in employment; any information regarding the continuance of gang activities within prison (for example, gang fights, knife or other crimes); and any information as to the names of the gangs that prisoners belonged to and the geographical location of those gangs.

The Ministry replied that such data was either going to be too costly to access or was held by individual prisons (which it is not). Thus, the Ministry either had the information, which is too sensitive to release, or had not collected it. By a fluke, Dr Susan Harvey, a forensic psychologist, did collect some sample data from those arrested whilst working at Lewisham Police Station during the rioting. Although the sample was too small to extrapolate any meaningful results from, it seemed to suggest a distinct rise in those suffering from Attention Deficit Hyperactivity Disorder (ADHD), which went up from 28 per cent before the riots to 38 per cent during the riots. However, such findings are controversial and open to different interpretation, and Dr Harvey is quite rightly concerned that they will be seized upon as proof of mental health issues which may not exist.

The riots were, of course not simply a matter of so-called feral kids running about in gangs. Many rioters were not gang members. Nevertheless, it was gang crime that focused attention. Belonging to a gang is not illegal anywhere in the UK. When David Cameron declared 'war' on gangs, it was, effectively, meaningless, which is not to say that there is not a problem or that gangs do not exist. Instead, it is to say that only when gangs break the law are they legally culpable. According to police figures, there are 250 active gangs in London which have a membership of around 4,500. Of these gangs, 60 are considered dangerous, with 22 per cent of crimes in London being gang-related according to Commander Steve Rodhouse when he reported to the Greater London Authority's Police and Crime Committee on 26 January 2012. New attempts in London to tackle gang-related crime started in the Borough of Waltham Forest and will expand to cover 19 boroughs during 2012. The campaign, led by the Trident Gang Crime Command, began in February 2012 with raids on 150 homes by 1,000 officers. In the first six months of the

2011/12 financial year there were 3,763 victims of youth crime, an increase of 9.5 per cent over the same period in the previous year.

According to the children's campaigner Camila Batmanghelidjh in an interview for the *Evening Standard* on 31 January 2012, gangs were strengthening in numbers and becoming more sophisticated in operation, using properties advertised in estate agents and Google Earth to decide on areas to target and increasing their involvement in the drug trade. She suggested there was a real nihilism amongst the young, and children who would once have run away from the police now turn and shoot at them instead. Despite arguments to the contrary, Batmanghelidjh saw poverty as the main cause of gang culture exploited by adult criminals who were aware of the need for father figures amongst poorer alienated young men. The situation seemed out of control and the small number of rioters appeared to suggest much wider problems in society. Bereft of logical explanations, there was much talk amongst the chattering classes of wholesale degeneracy and social breakdown at the lower levels of society and of communities abandoned by 'the system', which needed to be reconnected to the greater society. David Lammy, the MP for Tottenham, immediately went into print and others soon followed in an attempt both to explain events and to offer solutions.

So urgent seemed the need for answers and so rotten appeared the 'moral' state of the country that the Independent Riots Communities and Victims Panel was formed in August 2011 to 'examine and understand why the riots took place'. Thus, a 'tribunal' would sift the evidence and come to conclusions that were independent of government and therefore 'impartial', the final report to be presented to the Prime Minister, the Deputy Prime Minister and the Leader of the Opposition.

The Panel's interim report was entitled '5 Days in August' and was published on 28 November 2011, following an inquiry that began in September. The final report, 'After the Riots', was then published on 28 March 2012, with another report published on the same day summarizing the recommendations for action. The summary report began by stating that although there should be appropriate punishment for those who participated in the riots, nevertheless 'we must give everyone a stake in society'.[5]

This might be achieved through focusing on a number of areas such as 'children and parents … personal resilience, hopes and dreams, riots and the brands, the usual suspects and the police and the public'.[6] In so doing, the Panel concentrated on improvements in public services, respect for others, opportunities for the young, values and skills, police, law and order and community cohesion and a better criminal justice system, but not on the actual and specific social fabric of poorer communities, their relationship with the police or on the level of income and expectation; this was mostly implied.

The Panel also concentrated on the visibility of the '120,000 most challenged families', which seemed to stand in proxy for a further 380,000 'forgotten families who [sic] bump along the bottom'.[7] It recognised that there was no straightforward correlation between such families and the riots, but still argued as if there was. Elsewhere, it called for 'corporate social responsibility' and 'responsible capitalism'.[8] The biggest recommendation, however, was attached to personal behaviour. Although there were clear recommendations concerning social services, the major conclusions concerning male parenting and personality were neither social nor communal, but familial and individual. What needed building up was 'personal resilience' or 'character', which should be built and monitored at school. The whole thing had the smell of the Boy Scouts and an Edwardian ethos that was once the province of the public school.

'Many young people … expressed a sense of hopelessness' to the Panel, but others did not. The interviewees seemed to stress the importance of 'character' and concluded that 'young people who develop character will be best placed to make the most of their lives'.[9] Character was built through 'self-discipline, application, the ability to defer gratification and resilience in recovering from setbacks', attributes that hardly now seem to serve the type of 'lottery-based' consumer society in which we now live. After all, 32 million lottery tickets are sold every week so that individuals can escape exactly the values described as character building.[10]

The Panel recommended actual and measurable schooling in character:

> *We propose that there should be new requirements for schools to develop and publish their policies on building character.* This would raise the profile of this issue and ensure that schools engage in a review of their approaches to nurturing character attributes among their pupils. *We also recommend that Ofsted undertake a thematic review of character building in schools.* To inform interventions tailored to individual pupils' needs the *Panel recommends primary and secondary schools should undertake regular assessments of pupils' strength of character.*[11]

How would such a quotient be measured and by what criteria? The report and its final 63 recommendations (many of which would evidently be consigned to the bin of good intentions for a number of reasons, not the least of which might be a lack of funds and a lack of determination) were the subject of much debate in the days following the report's publication. Some saw the report as a recipe not to tackle riot and disorder, but to re-engineer Cameron's own social vision of a society respectful of the individual and of individuals with real self-respect; 'neighbourhood volunteering' was to be at the heart of 'community engagement, involvement and cohesion' (recommendation 63). Yet to achieve such a society would require tools of social engineering that were long out of date because they had largely been dismantled and were also deeply disliked by the actual advocates of socially responsible Conservatism.

Newspapers were full of letters discussing the issues, but many were critical both of the Panel's data and of its recommendations based on that data. Professor Ruth Levitas of the University of Leeds, for instance, pointed out the misuse of the 120,000 'troubled families' data which had originated from a 2007 Cabinet Office analysis of the 2004 Families and Children Study and which now returned to confuse the government's Troubled Families Programme.

Levitas pointed out that the number of families was originally based upon a number of characteristics. These were: no parent in the family was in work; the family lived in overcrowded housing; the parents had no qualifications; the mother had 'mental' health issues and/or one parent had long-standing health or disability issues; and the family could not afford basic food, heating and goods; and its income was below 60 per cent of the median. It was clear that 120,000 families did not riot and therefore had reasonable 'strength of character' as noted by the Panel. Levitas concluded her letter with the suggestion that 'none of these circumstances necessarily requires government intervention to stop reoffending' or were clearly attached to offending at all. Indeed, the problem was clear. The report had confused troubled families with families that cause trouble.[12]

Others saw the Panel as taking too little account of police 'inaction' in the first few days of the riots, ignoring income levels and not taking proper account of alienation and general societal hedonism. Most thought that greed and corruption higher up the social ladder were equally to blame. One letter-writer cynically concluded that schools might actually look for those signs of success which are so admired nowadays in the character of their socially more successful pupils such as 'greed and arrogance' and might make an effort to discourage them![13]

Whatever else was required, the restoration of authority was paramount. The first 'gangbo' was enforced in February 2012 against Dylan Martin of Enfield. He had breached movement restriction orders four times and was sentenced to 15 months. His mother accused both police and council of victimisation.[14] During February 2012, ten members of the 'Get Money' gang were 'invited' to attend an American-style 'gang call-in' at Wood Green Crown Court. Under heavy guard and behind bulletproof glass, the gang members were told by a series of police officers, victims' parents and former gang members to mend their ways or face severe consequences. Just before the hearing, a teenager was actually stabbed outside the Court. During the same period, police numbers fell by 3.8 per cent from 32,900 down to 31,657, thus making self-enforcement a priority.[15] This initiative was started in Glasgow in 2008, where violent crime amongst 170 gangs in the Strathclyde area was out of control. The problem was tackled as a health issue more than one of crime (much data was gathered at dentists after teeth were knocked out) and led to significant reductions in violence among a test group. Nevertheless, some senior Strathclyde police officers told the author that they were worried that youths in their area were too downtrodden, defeated and apathetic even to riot!

Curiously, Islam in both its religious and political forms has been effective in changing attitudes, as has the work of the Eastside Young Leader's Academy in Newham created by Ray Lewis to offer extra-curricular activities for black school pupils in danger of exclusion. The idea is based on American practice and concentrates on boys at risk. Here the model is one of working within the community and inside its mores. The Academy creates that sense of belonging and 'protection' afforded by the gangs and substitutes teachers for father figures who offer adult validation. The boot camp discipline gives boys a sense of self-worth usually provided by gaining a reputation as a 'bad boy' or 'gangsta', as well as a sense of future prospects and deferred gratification rather than the immediate hunt for money. It also aims to control the anger felt on the 'road' (the urban street battlefield) where other gangs and the police are a constant threat to self-respect and where it is all too easy to become a victim of one's emotions. The Academy also arranges scholarships with public schools, but recognises that there is little space for social mobility and that to move across the social divide requires a boy to 'give up' his old self-identity in order to take on a newly won identity and enter an alien world of privilege and complacency, one quite different from the social background of his family. Unlike psychiatric findings, the reports of ADHD amongst pupils at the Academy are more often the consequence of being a child in a difficult home with little money, drug problems and the other multiple distractions of simply being impoverished. This is not to diminish ADHD, but simply to give it a social dimension that is often ignored. Good diet and restored discipline often 'cure' the problem. It is also recognised by the Academy that many parents are so exhausted by everyday struggles that they will willingly acquiesce in their children's anti-social behaviour if it earns extra money and brings relief to difficult circumstances. The Academy aims to return a sense of self-motivated agency and direction to pupils. None of the Academy's pupils rioted.

Whatever the truth about gang involvement, it appears that economics has replaced racism as the main factor in those very geographical areas which most people thought had been sorted out after the disturbances of the 1980s. Yet, instead of real social improvement, there had been only the apparent action of remedial social reform where underlying resentments had been left intact. The very same places exploded as they had in 1981 and 1985. The final verdict by all concerned was that there was 'no single cause for the riots'.[16] The *Irish Times* opened its weekend review with the headlines 'The Week Two Englands Clashed', stating that the problem was that one of those 'Englands' took it upon itself to interview the other, a situation fraught with the possibility of preconceptions, misconceptions and misreadings.[17]

There seemed precious few concrete answers indeed, although everybody saw a comparison with what others were doing at the top of society. Thus: 'The looting was, on one level, pure nihilism; on another, it was a crude attempt ... to mimic the conspicuous consumption exercised by the affluent and credit-rich.'[18]

The Spectator saw the fault as much with the government's mixed messages about prison and police cuts as with the rioters. Not unexpectedly, it called for greater deterrents and stronger political will from the Conservatives to cut the 'benefit culture', to strengthen police, to maintain sentencing and to continue with educational reform. Its conclusion, if any, was that the mood of the country was more conservative than that of the actual Conservative Party.[19]

The symptoms may have been different from the 1980s, as indeed were some of the causes, but at least some of the underlying troubles remained the same – perhaps not the overt racism of authority this time, but the self-same entrapment in poverty and lack of self-worth because of lack of improvement. Rioters interviewed after the Brixton riots in 1981 told interviewers that in ghettoised communities: 'Violence is a way of life – boredom has something to do with it – the police have always been seen … as the army of repression.'[20]

The Brixton rioters saw themselves as a multitude rising up spontaneously against years of repression. They also identified the problem. It was others, from the police and the middle classes, who were the real enemy. Middle-class onlookers observed the rioting and believed the participants were somehow a 'social problem' that needed to be dealt with. This was exacerbated by the media, which portrayed certain 'faces' as 'self-styled leaders' when there were no leaders. Yet, at the same time, television was not seen as the cause of 'copycat' rioting. Instead, around the country, those in agreement with what was happening in Brixton merely had their prejudices confirmed as they watched television. Groups not mixed up in the original cause of the trouble were merely spurred on by televisual imagery and acted rather 'spontaneously' to defend their interests against the same repression that they recognised around the country: 'we were desperate, fed up, and tired of being harassed – who were we supposed to be copying?'.[21] Moreover, they also saw that the terror the rioting induced amongst television viewers and the press was caused by manipulation and editing rather than by unbiased reporting. Media reports on the television showed black rioters and implied that the problem might be attached to immigration, but 'the kids on the street were black and white', not from traditionally 'immigrant' areas at all.[22]

What had been added to the mix since Brixton and Toxteth was the alienation of a universal consumer society, where having the right clothes and mobile phone represents 'real' self-esteem. These things were, it appeared, the exact opposite, in fact, of what caused the student riots, where those children had the luxury to reject the cultural advantages of their (mostly) well-educated and privileged middle-class parents.

There was obviously the adrenalin rush of confronting the police and effectively 'winning' the encounter after years of stop and search, there was also the simple fun to be had through destruction and there was an element of recreational rioting and shopping with endless imaginary 'credit'. Who might resist such temptation? The answer was almost everyone in the areas affected. Indeed, very few people took over the streets, despite the large numbers of arrests; at a generous estimate, perhaps between 5,000 and 6,000 took part in London overall. This was no mass movement or large demonstration of disaffection youth, but a relatively contained and determined few who took part.

There was much soul-searching as events progressed. Were the young of these poorer areas the product of governmental neglect or of familial neglect, inbred immorality, feral attitudes and criminal propensities, brought on by years of incorrect parenting and the breakdown of community cohesion? Were they part of that generation who Cameron years before said we should embrace in his 'Hug a Hoodie' speech of 2006?[23] However, the looters, many of them without both jobs and family support (except for the gangs they belonged to), understood their plight in their bones and actions. Many questioned afterwards spouted a retrospective rhetoric of economic woe and the corruption in high places, but this had been a learned script. More pertinently, an authentic voice began to emerge which spoke of police harassment (especially against boys), lack of money, exclusion from opportunity and many young black people complaining that they attacked shops in the high street where they had applied to for jobs but had been ignored by.

What the looters took – clothes, electrical goods including the latest TVs and phones, trainers and food – represented the very things they would shop for normally in the shops that wouldn't give them jobs but would take their money. This was the 'raw' message of rioting and, for many, the police were letting it happen. This was the revenge of the invisible class with no jobs or prospects of jobs, those at the very 'bottom' of society. Of course, the riots were expressed in material terms, for that is how the rioters live out their lives, the owned objects coming to represent a type of disguised politics which has no other expression. This was payback big time and it felt good.

There was also debate regarding the nature of the summer riots, but such rioting was actually not so new after all. It was so old in fact that it had been forgotten. These riots may have been believed to have been the worst disturbances since the 1980s, but in their ferocity and mode of operation they bore more resemblance to those of the seventeenth and eighteenth centuries. They represented something historically very interesting as well as something disturbingly atavistic. They certainly harked back to a pre-police past. The *Irish Times* commented that:

> The current aspirational rioting, where young people go to their favourite shops, choose the latest street-cred goods and scarper are little different from the numerous apprentice riots of the eighteenth century which were also the domain of young, single men, out to cause trouble, to steal goods, to break windows and to set light to the houses of those that they didn't like, in the knowledge that there was no authority bar the army which could disturb them. These apprentices also came from the deprived area of town and spilled into the city centres, called together not by BlackBerrys but by fire beacons, the ringing of church bells or the simple act of fly posting. You do not need modern technology for social networking.[24]

It must be repeated that no two riots are ever the same, but we must go as far back as the Bawdy House Riots of the 1660s to start to see even vague parallels. In the seventeenth century, apprentices and servants were mostly educated and literate and had money for drinks with their politics. They also liked to demonstrate their grievances and usually had licence to do so by the authorities, provided that the demonstrations were not a direct attack on their rulers. In June 1667, during a nasty turn in the Dutch War, apprentices took to the street crying that the country was being betrayed to the papists and the French. The relaxation of laws against dissenting preachers after the Great Fire of London also saw an increase in accusations of 'Babylon' against the court from nonconformist pulpits. It therefore took little to ignite trouble across the traditional holiday season of protest. On Easter Monday, 23 March 1668, bawdy houses (traditional targets of apprentice anger) were attacked in Poplar. The attacks spread to Holborn, East Smithfield, Shoreditch and Moorfields, where approximately 40,000 rioters were on the move. Two days later, apprentices from Southwark crossed the river and joined in. One group was led by a Peter Messenger who gave his surname to the riots.

The Messenger riots or Bawdy House Riots continued for some days, finally being suppressed by the army under Lord Craven. The rioters themselves seem to have treated the event as part political protest (they marched under green Leveller banners) and part carnival of misrule. Either way, they became too dangerous, demanding 'liberty of conscience' and threatening to 'pull White-hall down'. To the gaoler of Finsbury Prison they were reported to have said 'we have been servants, but we will be masters now'.[25]

The Gordon Riots (against Catholic relief laws) of 1780 were even more ferocious and unstoppable. This involved a vast crowd of 60,000 people gathered from Westminster and Southwark and a major contingent from Scotland led by pipers (a banned symbol of independence). There were flags and banners and the singing of hymns and psalms as the rebel Lord George Gordon arrived in triumph ready to lead the march. Singing more hymns and waving blue banners, the people's army, marching in ranked disciplined files and led by a protester carrying the roll of 100,000 signatures, proceeded in deadly (if still peaceful) earnest towards Westminster. 'The whole city was amazed, the house-tops were covered with spectators and every person awaited the event with anxious expectation', wrote Gordon's biographer, Robert Watson, in his memoirs of 1795.

Gordon's army represented two types of protester. On the one hand, there were the middle orders, tradesmen, aldermen and merchants who marched direct to Westminster over the new toll bridge (they could afford the fee). On the other hand, there were artisans and apprentices who took the long route via London Bridge and proceeded to march through the East End back towards Westminster. The dramatist Frederick Reynolds, then a schoolchild, reported:

> Then we witnessed the most novel and extraordinary proceedings ... The mob, shortly receiving the addition of many thousands of disorderly persons, occupied every avenue to the Houses of Parliament, the whole of Westminster Bridge [the tolls being unworkable], and extended nearly to the northern end of Parliament Street, the greatest part of it, however was composed of persons decently dressed. The situation soon degenerated when the crowds arrived at Westminster itself. Lords identified as 'enemies' of the people were jostled, abused or attacked, barricading themselves against attack once inside Parliament.[26]

As the lobby of the House of Commons filled with protesters, Gordon could be seen shunting back and forth between the clamour of the crowd and the debate inside, whipping attitudes up by reporting that Lord North (the Prime Minister) considered the lobbyists a mere 'mob'. Alarm was now spreading amongst middle-class

Londoners. Sarah Hoare, wife of the Quaker banker Samuel Hoare, wrote to her mother:

> Everyone is anxious to hear the conclusion of an affair, which has made great noise in the city all this day. Thou hast most probably heard of the meeting which was advertised to be held in St George's Fields, to proceed from thence in procession to the House of Commons to deliver a petition from the Protestants. Accordingly 50,000 men, divided into companys [sic] of 8000 each, with Lord George Gordon at their head, assembled at the hour appointed and marched through the city. The Guards were ordered out, and many feared that would produce great confusion. What reception they met with on their arrival I have not heard. I must own I have seldom felt my fears equally awakened.[27]

Poor Sarah had little time to wait. Rioting began when troops tried to free the members of the House of Commons. The crowds parted, and then surrounded the soldiers and began pelting them with stones and faggots, but the worst violence was to fall upon Catholic mass-houses (chapels), one especially drawing attention in Lincoln's Inn Fields. As with so many anti-Catholic disturbances, the crowd first turned on the chapels of foreign diplomats. The Sardinian Chapel was systematically and comprehensively demolished, its attackers being both organised and disciplined. Soldiers finally arrived and arrested, apparently rather indiscriminately, anyone caught near the action. So terrified was one lady, Mrs Mary O'Donald, that she 'fell into fits which occasioned for her death'! The crowd moved on to Golden Square and destroyed the house of the Bavarian Ambassador, Count Hasling, long considered a 'fence' for all sorts of contraband goods. Finally exhausting foreign targets, the crowd made for the Irish population of Moorfields. Meanwhile, the army headed in the opposite direction for the squares of the West End in order to protect aristocratic property.

By the evening of 3 June, a crowd had marched to Rope Maker's Alley, Moorfields, to attack the chapel there. This was near to Mr Malo's silk business, where 200 looms kept 2,000 men at work. Malo, believing (correctly as it turned out) that disaster was at hand, hastened to see Lord Mayor Kennet. The Mayor did nothing, avoided contact and refused to authorise immediate action to read the Riot Act or bring out the military. It is certainly possible that he was in cahoots with the aims of the protesters (and the cause of Protestantism) or was simply unwilling to protect rival Catholic or Irish merchants.

By 5 June, various parts of London were under siege, with gossip providing regular updates of the destruction:

> We have just received intelligence which gives us equal concern and surprise, that there is actually a riotous meeting at Moorfields, and that a great number of seditious persons are employed in demolishing different dwelling-houses, and all this is done in broad day without the least interposition of the civil magistrate.[28]

From Wapping to Leicester Fields, various mobs, often led by well-dressed and 'mysterious' gentlemen, were attacking Catholic homes and businesses and building bonfires with the contents. Groups of soldiers gathered to protect property found themselves hampered by the irresolution of the magistrates, who were disinclined to protect Catholic citizens. Things had clearly gotten out of hand.

The situation had degenerated further by 6 June, with houses being destroyed without any judicial or military intervention. Charles Jenkinson (then Secretary at War and later First Earl of Liverpool) now sent the following to Lord Stormont:

> I have now the honour to enclose to your Lordship the copy of a letter and report transmitted to me by Major-General Wynyard of what happened in the course of yesterday and last night, and must beg in the most serious manner to call your Lordship's attention to some parts of that letter and report wherein it appears that in one instance the Civil Magistrate having called for the Troops was not ready to attend them; that in another instance the Troops having been called out were left by the Magistrate exposed to the fury of the Populace when the Party were insulted in a most extraordinary manner, and that in two other instances after the Troops had marched to the places appointed for them, several of the Magistrates refused to act. It is the duty of the Troops, my Lord, to act only under the Authority and by direction, of the Civil Magistrate. For this reason they are under greater restraints than any other of His Majesty's subjects, and when insulted are obliged to be more cautious even in defending themselves. If, therefore, the Civil Magistrate after having called upon them is not ready to attend them, or abandons them before they return to their quarters, or after they arrive at the places to which they have been ordered, refuses to act, I leave it to your Lordship to judge in how defenseless and how disgraceful a situation the military are left, and how much such conduct as this tends even to encourage Riots, and how much the public service as well as the Troops must suffer by it.[29]

Legal opinion was that the military could only intervene if called upon by the civil authority (a magistrate) and although this ruling was later challenged, it meant that on 6 June any soldier killing a civilian was liable to be indicted for murder. The military was therefore impotent. Mr Malo was soon to feel the opprobrium of the mob:

> On Tuesday morning he removed some of his valuable stock of silks, but the utensils of his trade and the furniture of his house he had not time to shift. At noon several large bands of rioters came to his house, from different avenues about Moorfields, at almost the same time, assembling at back and front. They knocked and threatened to murder the people inside if the door was not opened immediately. Two of Mr Malo's servants made their escape over the leads of the house. Mr Malo, his wife and daughters fled, but the eldest son fainted the instant the mob rushed into the house and was for many days so affected that both his life and his intellects were in danger. The mob demolished everything in the house; they tore down the wainscot, broke all the furniture, threw it out of the window and made a bonfire of it. Among the things they heaped on the bonfire were some canary birds with their cages. Passers by wished to deliver them from their fate and offered to purchase them but the mob said they were Popish birds and should burn with the rest of the Popish goods. Some of the birds were rescued, but the rest were kept screaming on the fire until they were consumed.[30]

So helpless was the military that one 'charge' only succeeded in knocking down a number of rioters who 'lay in the most ludicrous manner ... Like a pack of cards'. Far from being intimidated, the incident was treated as a huge joke by the crowd, many of whom were milling about Parliament attempting to scare the two Houses. The two Houses, which had finally resolved to stand up to the mob, would also have to decide on the nature of the disturbances, for riot was apparently turning into rebellion.

By now Leicester Fields was ablaze, as was Covent Garden and Bloomsbury Square. St Martin's Lane was filled with rubble when the violence seemed to take on a different and more deadly nature: to religious outrage was now added a revolutionary and quasi-republican libertarianism generated from the passion of the moment. Waving a black and red flag, a man called James Jackson, possibly a discharged or retired seaman (or a weaver disguised as one), rallied those with him by shouting: 'A hoy for Newgate.' On the way the crowd collected all sorts of bystanders, of whom one was the 22-year-old William Blake, not yet a mystical revolutionary. As the crowd passed Sir John Fielding's police offices at Bow Street, the building was effectively flattened in retaliation for the imprisonment there of some of the rioters. Newgate Prison was next:

> The mob came to Newgate and Publickly declared they would release the confined rioters. When they arrived at the door of the prison, they demanded of Mr Akerman, the keeper, to have their comrades immediately delivered up to them; and upon his persisting to do his duty, by refusing, they began some to break his windows, some to batter the doors and entrances into the cells with pick-axes and sledge-hammers, others with ladders to climb the vast walls, while others collected firebrands, and whatever combustibles they could find, and flung [them] into his dwelling house. What contributed more than anything to the spreading of the flames was the great quantity of household furniture belonging to Mr Akerman which they threw out of the windows, piled up against the doors, and set fire to; ... A party of constables, to the amount of a hundred, came to the assistance of the keeper; these the mob made a lane for, and suffered to pass till they were entirely encircled, when they attacked them with great fury, broke their staffs, and converted them into brands, which they hurled about wherever the fire ... had not caught ... all the prisoners, to the amount of three hundred, among whom were four ordered for execution on the Thursday following, were released ... they dragged out the prisoners by the hair of the head, by legs or arms, or whatever part they could lay hold of ... so well planned were all the manoeuvres of these desperate ruffians, that they had placed centinels [sic] at the avenues to prevent any of the prisoners from being conveyed to other jails. Thus was the strongest and most durable prison in England ... demolished ... in the space of a few hours.[31]

Frederick Reynolds reported in somewhat more purple prose:

> The mob fired the jail in many places before they were enabled to force their way through the massive bars and gates, which guarded its entrance. The wild gestures of the mob without, and the shrieks of the prisoners within, expecting an instantaneous death from the flames, the thundering descent of huge pieces of building, the deafening clangor of red hot iron bars, striking in terrible concussion the pavement below, and the loud triumphant yells and shouts of the demoniac assailants on each new success, formed an awful and terrific scene.[32]

These events, of which the attack on Newgate and every other London prison presented exemplary instances, suggested nothing less than armed revolutionary insurrection, a rehearsal for the demolition of the Paris Bastille and the destruction of the French monarchy. American libertarian republicanism suddenly seemed too close to home. It was for one witness 'as if the city had been taken by an enemy'.

By now, the troubles had lasted four days. The authorities might tolerate a riot, they might have a hand in helping one along, they might stand by as merchants were roughed up, but Lord Mansfield's town house was ablaze and prisons from Southwark to Clerkenwell were blackened, empty shells. It was now or never to reimpose order and it was now time for magistrates to toe the line as military reinforcements began to muster on London's outskirts and as rumours of the imposition of martial law began to circulate. When it came

The Burning & Plundering of Newgate & Setting the Felons at Liberty by the Mob.

Figure 6.1 The Gordon Riots 1780: the burning of Newgate – a prelude to the storming of the Bastille (courtesy of the Mary Evans Picture Library)

to manning the barricades, both the leading 'revolutionary' politician John Wilkes and George Gordon offered their services and their rifles to the government, and both were prepared to defend the institutions of the City.

The massive destruction around Holborn and Barnard's Inn produced perhaps the longest-lasting of all images from the riots and the definitive image of mob rampage for later generations. This centred on the explosion at Thomas Langdale's gin distillery at the Black Swan. Langdale had attempted to placate his tormentors with gin and cash, but his premises were going to be a target with or without bribery. The scenes that followed impressed upon contemporaries more than anything else a belief that the lower orders were essentially unthinking and demonic brutes if not kept under control:

> By nine the buildings were enveloped in smoke and flame, while there flowed down the kennel of the street torrents of unrectified and flaming spirit gushing from casks drawn in endless succession from the vaults. Men and children, followed by women with infants in arms, emerged from courts, lanes and alleys and hastened to the latest outrage. From the windows of burning houses men tossed furniture into the all-devouring flames below. Ardent spirits, now running to pools and wholly unfit for human consumption, were swallowed by insatiate fiends, who, with shrieking gibes and curses, reeled and perished in the flames, whilst others, alight from head to foot, were dragged from burning cellars. On a sudden, in an atmosphere hot to suffocation, flames leapt upwards from Langdale's other houses on Holborn Hill. The vats had ignited, and columns of fire became visible for thirty miles round London.[33]

As the distillery burned, the military organised and the civil magistrates braced themselves. The first major bloodshed occurred as crowds attempted to destroy the newly installed tollgates on Blackfriars and found themselves under fire from defending troops. Troops had already tried to disperse crowds at Newgate, leaving 100 dead. At Blackfriars the dead were piled up and thrown into the Thames. One observer recollected:

> We were informed that a considerable number of rioters had been killed on Blackfriars Bridge, which was occupied by troops. On approaching it we beheld the King's Bench Prison completely wrapped in flames. It exhibited a sublime sight – we stood at a central point from whence London offered on every side, before as well as behind us, the picture of a city sacked and abandoned to a ferocious enemy.[34]

The new ferocity of the action, combined with the determination of the crowds to destroy the symbols of City power (Mansion House and the Bank), lent urgency and hysteria to both sides. Colonel Twistleton, who commanded the Bank detachment, was confronted not with a mere mob of apprentices but by 'many decently dressed people' who urged on the poorer sectors of the crowd but pretended not to be involved when challenged. At least one leader was identified as a sailor or weaver, who waved his cutlass in defiance. The troops fired, killing eight or nine, including at least one innocent bystander, and continued firing as the threat seemed to continue. It was here that Wilkes and Gordon offered their services to the military. Civilians on both sides were now arming, some of the rioters having weapons despite all gunsmiths being required by law to shut up shop and secure their goods.

As the riots subsided, militia volunteers (vigilantes) found themselves pursuing their prey deeper and deeper into the rookeries of London, coming face to face for the first time with the real slum conditions of the city and their complex criminal complexion:

> Attended by peace-officers, one of our detachments visited Chick Lane, Field Lane and Black Boy Alley. From Chick Lane we escorted several persons to Prison. These places constitute a separate town calculated for the reception of the darkest and most dangerous enemies to society, in which when pursued for the commission of crimes they easily conceal themselves. The houses are divided from top to bottom into many compartments, with doors of communication in each and also with the adjacent houses, some having two to four doors opening into different alleys. In many of the rooms I saw six, seven, eight to ten men in bed, in others as many women ... Into one apartment we crept through a trap door, our bayonets and pistols in our hands ... The peace-officers and the keepers of these houses appeared to be well-acquainted with each other, and on terms which rather shocked us.[35]

As cinders cooled and the riots subsided in the face of determined and overwhelming force, the inquest began. Who had really been rioting rather than protesting? Many pointed to unruly apprentices and girl prostitutes, while others pointed to religious fanatics tanked up on brandy and obsessed with violent disorder in the name of Protestantism, but some also noticed the well-dressed agitators and speculated on who these mystery men were. Charles Stuart, writing to his father, recollected a strange incident at the massacre at the Bank:

> A very well dressed man was killed whose face they [the rioters] took great pains to hide, but after most of them dispersed a curious watchman looked at the body, expressed some surprise, and said he knew the Person. Upon which they seized the watchman and dragged him to Moorfields, where they swore him in the most sacred way to secrecy. As they also took off the body, nothing has been discovered.[36]

Hearsay and rumour turned the anecdotal reminiscences into hardened facts:

> Many had no doubt that they were agents paid by the Opposition to bring down the Government with accusations of anarchy. 'Depend on it', Richard Cumberland wrote to his brother, 'the rioters were encouraged and supported by that abandoned Party who have long been diffusing the Seeds of Insurrection'. Many others were certain that the French and Americans were to blame. 'I am convinced', Lord Mountstuart wrote to his brother, 'that tho' the beginning of the tumults was entirely owing to the Fanaticks [sic], yet they had no notion of the outrages being carried so far, and that the American emissaries took the advantage of the mobbery once begun to carry their diabolical purposes to the great extent they did'.[37]

It is convenient to see the burning of Langdale's distillery as the last scene of a first act, the second act being that of a revolutionary march on the Bank of England. However, the image would be incorrect, as confusingly complex acts of disorder were happening simultaneously across London, none of which had greater or lesser precedence. Thus, the riotous uprising of feeling against Catholics was never abandoned in favour of a revolutionary programme of jail breaking, and the systematic demolition or firing of houses and buildings whose occupants represented authority was carried out alongside wholesale looting and petty theft. At no time throughout the disturbances did the rioters unite as a coherent body and directly threaten the destruction of Parliament or the monarch, even if proto-revolutionary voices seem occasionally to have been heard to direct the action of various sections of the milling crowds. More tellingly, no contemporary talks of the revolutionary interest of the crowds, but all talk of the religious element. The rioters lacked the foundation of independence to be found in the American colonists. Not only was the entire ideological and legal basis of the American cause lacking but so was its driving force, the mercantile-legal professionals who led it and the rational egalitarian philosophy that backed it. Inatiez Sanchez lamented that the 'government is sunk in lethargic stupor – anarchy reigns'.

Part of the rising (and radical) middle class, Sanchez feared the uncontrollable (and revolutionary) potential of the labouring orders ('there is more at the bottom of this business than merely the repeal of an act'). His London neighbour Hester Thrale, owner of one of the great breweries of London (and a patron of Dr Johnson), had deeper hatreds that saw people like Sanchez (the black nouveau riche) actually in an unholy alliance with the mob itself – here was the soul of anarchy:

> Well! I am really haunted by black shadows. Men of colour in the rank of gentlemen; a black lady covered with finery, in the Pit at the Opera, and tawny children playing in the Squares, – in the gardens of the Squares I mean, – with their Nurses, afford ample proofs of Hannah More and Mr. Wilberforce's success in breaking down the wall of separation. Oh! how it falls on every side! and spreads its tumbling ruins on the world! leaving all ranks, all custom, all colours, all religions, jumbled together.[38]

Mrs Thrale's apocalyptic racist nightmare of a multi-ethnic, multicultural and truly democratic London was the most dreadful and wondrous vision of all.

The cost of the Gordon Riots was enormous. By 1783, after years of petitions, new legislation and lawsuits, the bill for the various parts of the City came to almost £42,000, for Middlesex almost £21,500 and for Surrey £7,000. Damage to prisons added £30,000; in all, it was the equivalent of several billion today. Property damage apart from attacks on chapels and prisons amounted to approximately 150 houses and shops, with damage to all sorts of goods, including clothing, furniture, money, valuables, books and pictures. Approximately 50 homes had to be demolished. Most of the victims were either prosperous gentry or manufacturers, although many were small but comfortable tradespeople living in areas such as Bethnal Green, Spitalfields or Bermondsey. Property owners were potential targets and Catholic or Irish property owners were likely targets throughout the disturbances.

The insurance companies were soon scrutinising their policies in order to avoid paying their clients. The Sun Fire Office included a clause excluding damage by rioting or 'civil commotion' and other companies tried to avoid fire-damage payments to those who furniture had first been removed from their properties, thus voiding the claim. That said, the insurance companies found themselves pursued for thousands in compensation, which they slowly but duly paid out. To cover any shortfalls, and in accordance with provision under the Riot Act of 1715, local parishes could levy a riot tax to pay for local damage. This they accordingly did.

Compensation, however, was the last thing on John Eliot's mind when at ten at night he wrote in haste to his wife, whom he had sent to friends for safety from their home in Bartholomew Close. With soldiers flooding London and rioters on the street, he could only wish for the safety of 'the ladies' and hope that the Lord would stop the rioters' 'monstrous wickedness'. Something else would need to be done to restore the peace of mind of Eliot's wife and daughters.

Troops and militia were now visibly on the streets 24 hours a day. Horse patrols could be found in the area from Guildhall to Moorfields and across from Bishopgate Street, over London Bridge as well as at Shadwell and Wapping, and from the Royal Exchange to Old Street. Patrols of troopers were also concentrated in the West End, at Green Park, St James's Park, Grosvenor Square, Pall Mall, Soho Square and around the palaces. Grenadier Guards marched in Piccadilly, Curzon Street, Chesterfield Street, Hanover Square and at various other locations, whilst hourly patrols of the 3rd Dragoon Guards kept a watch around the Artillery Ground, through Barbican, Moorfields, Broadstreet and all streets in between until three each morning. The 4th Dragoons were in Bermondsey and on Westminster Bridge, the 16th Light Dragoons were in Holborn and at Newgate, St Paul's and Cornhill, and Colonel Twistleton's Detachment were at Royal Exchange, Threadneedle Street and Tower. These forces were supplemented by Light Horse volunteers, Foot Guards and Northampton militia, which were stationed at Lambeth, Vauxhall, Bloomsbury Square and 'Gray's Inngate [sic]'.

Thus, seventeenth- and eighteenth-century disturbances bear an uncanny similarity to those in the twenty-first century. But there is an interesting twist: such pre-industrial rioting is also post-industrial, a peculiar pastiche of consuming and shopping driven by the very mechanisms of the consumer industries the looters abused both now and in the past. In both the Bawdy House Riots and the Gordon Riots, inward moral attitudes and long-held prejudices were expressed as outward social action in geographical space. The fantasy of liberty of conscience was expressed only in outward action as liberty of action.

There was, it might be suggested, a fundamental shift in the ideology of mental space at the end of the eighteenth century which remained largely unnoticed and operates even today. In the eighteenth century, as indeed before then, to think something which remained unexpressed in social action was a 'psychological' condition not developed until the Romantic revolution in human sensibility which followed the French Revolution and specifically the apocalyptic message of the French Terror. To act was to think.

Even (and especially) in the seventeenth and eighteenth centuries, it was the outward appearance of people that determined their social status and that almost alone. In the nineteenth century, a true psychology was developed which insisted on the inward nature of mental activity (and sometimes contradictory position in terms of social activity) and this became the bourgeois model of thought – inward and silent and self-affirming. Its failure to be expressed as social action resulted in that hypocrisy explored in Victorian novels. What was ignored was the continued presence of another older way of understanding the self which, rather than abating over time, has considerably increased in power alongside the rise in consumer goods and a universal culture of images in the period following the 1980s. Post-modern mentality harks backwards rather than forwards. As such, for the summer rioters, the self was no longer an inward attribute, but was worn on the outside like an exoskeleton. This is of importance, because the more middle-class educators look to re-affirm inward values, the more the 'underclass' affirm external values. The values of environmentalism, non-exploitation and global sustainability (essentially and primarily inward moral values) are eschewed by a generation fed on the contrary values of overconsumption, external extravagance ('bling') and extravagant waste.

How then might we characterise the behavior of those who rioted in the summer of 2012? It is always a question of a psycho-social nature, as much a question of individual self-motivation as of class position and economic insecurity. Rioting makes active what was passive, allows (for a short time) power to the powerless and makes 'well' what was painful because there was no outlet for relief. It is a form of theatre in which the self is 'acted out' in order for it to recognise itself in the acting. There is no 'self' before the riot, only a self 'created' through the act of rioting which is (nowadays) acknowledged by the televisual eye of CCTV. This acted-out self appears to be invulnerable and invincible precisely because it is, at one and the same time, invisible (being part of the anonymous crowd) and yet visible (acting for the television, mobile phone and CCTV cameras). Such action provides the status sought by many. It provides a cognitive model of beingness through owning rather than being through the inward gaze of the mind. The public world of social activity and being seen is everything.

Such actions have little or no consequences, it being a matter not of moral propriety (something understood inwardly) whether one steals or not, but of stupidity if one gets caught (a simple pragmatics of action). Being in the crowd provides the absolution needed as the loss of moral inhibitors begins to have effect. Last, but not least, these actions and this model of the experiencing self happen in a continuous present moment of empowerment ('I am rioting, beating the police and own the street') and of disempowerment ('I am out of work and have no future'). Both these states are experienced simultaneously as the coordinates of the rioting self. The rioters rioted precisely because, for them, there is no internal model of a self that is impelled towards a more positive future, but rather one stuck in the debasement and humiliation of a continuous here and now forever replayed in the generational lives of family and friends.

Thus, we are brought to ask why rioting appeals to some sectors of society and not others. The 'salutogenesis' model of wellbeing focuses on a sense of self-coherence, comprising an idea of comprehensibility (that things happen in an orderly and predictable way), manageability (that you have the skills to cope with life) and that actions are seen as meaningful and have purpose. Rioting or directed violence often provides such a sense of wellbeing in the release of tensions. The government's sense of wellbeing ('the Big Society') derived from these former ideas focuses instead on an idea of contentment ultimately derived from Sophocles and directly opposed to the sense just described, hence the mismatch. The students rioted to restore equilibrium; the summer rioters to permanently disturb it.

What are we now to do in order to stop rioting of this type in England again? The government has set out various policies and suggestions; the mood is one of punishment and retribution, possibly right for now, but of no use at all in the long term. The current heavy sentencing is both a deterrent and a warning by the establishment. For the most part, heavy sentencing is in line with the seriousness of the disturbances: incitement to riot and looting should not expect the same sort of punishment as inciting political protest or mere burglary. Indeed, one of the problems is how to effectively sentence those under age or those who were looting, but for whom only a sentence of aggravated burglary is possible, there being no crime of looting on the statute book.

If we must punish, we must also take responsibility for rehabilitation, but we have no facilities in which to do so. Ordinary prison will only put people in the way of nastier criminal possibilities. We have long given up the harsh regimes of the borstal era, but young offenders need both a sense of discipline as well as a sense of community and responsibility. Jonathan Aitken, talking on *Sky News*, no stranger to prison life himself and now involved with Christian Solidarity Worldwide, put forward the military prison in Colchester as a proven model for the successful engineering of social rehabilitation; a regime of authority and discipline and team building. This is a bitter pill to swallow for those of us who baulk at the boot camp approach.

Such militarised solutions scare liberals, but they may, despite everything, give back a sense of purpose and moral compass to the worst offenders who have been in and out of court all their lives, getting away with petty crime, and these disturbances are (despite the four potential murders, all of which have their specific circumstances) just petty crime on a very large scale. Indeed, pilfering, burglary, mugging and burning cars have been the staple of crime in Tottenham, Hackney and estates across England for over 20 years. In the next few years, if nothing changes, this will again be the pattern, only spilling out of the ghetto at inconvenient intervals.

We do not know if a prison regime would restore the dignity that the offenders have forfeited. We might prefer to see large-scale community work for most, but observing this in practice is disheartening and the results are poor. Could such groups regenerate their neighbourhoods by such work? The answer just might be yes if those who live and offend on these estates are asked what needs to be done to improve their lives and are given back a sense of 'family' and responsibility beyond the confines of the gang.

But are we ready to ask criminals their opinion on anything? To gain a voice that is not simply violent or destructive may indeed restore a sense of self-respect in a community. To get the inarticulate to talk *by their deeds* may be therapeutic and anger releasing – we do not yet know – but they cannot be left the passive recipients of other people's attitudes. To get such people to act in concert (in their peer group if not in their actual gang group) for the good of society instead of the bad may have lasting effects. The point is that we have to work *within the current structures of ghettoised life* before we can move on.

Such a viewpoint offers little consolation to the victims and, without economic and infrastructural support, will soon be valueless unless there is the highly problematic added incentive of visible extra policing and public authority beyond the confines of the community (of whatever kind).

The actual police are distrusted by many communities, but self-policing will exacerbate criminality and give carte blanche to criminal behaviour. The psychological 'no-go' areas have to be expunged, as does the police habit of 'trade-offs' with gangs that have escalated into intra-community violence and teenage knife and gun crime. The secrecy and inwardness of these communities needs to be broken, but the consumer tastes in trainers, electronic goods or mobile phones does not. We are all materialists.

A new type of policing has to be developed. Naturally, there is the straightforward possibility that the testosterone of teenage boys will simply diminish as they age, a point well made by Anthony Burgess in *A Clockwork Orange*, his book recounting the social disintegration of the 1950s. Adolescent rebellion has, of course, happened before.

Do we have the economic, environmental and social resources to curb the trouble from a 'lost' generation who belong to an underclass (sometimes self-defined) that is resentful and alienated but also consumerist and egocentric, sharing many of the traits of the wider society but in distorted form? We can deal with certain issues now, but rehousing the ghetto in decent accommodation, proper welfare support which no longer requires a model of the family to propel it, and a clear indication that a cash culture backed by violence is not preferable to a salary, home and hobbies is going to be hard to sell to a generation whose 'corrupt' attitudes are apparently replicated by the social betters, bankers, politicians, media people and policemen who are, nevertheless, immune from the punishment of the poor.

This latest set of disturbances may be an aberration, but we are likely to see more not less low-scale disturbances as the economic downturn continues and as the authorities increase security towards the Olympics and after, but have fewer resources. Unexpected threats will continue, especially from virtual space (the political arena) and actual space (violence on the street). However, the classes involved will be different. Large-scale unrest comes from smouldering disaffection and an immediate flashpoint which may not be related. The current circumstances show that clearly. The disaffection was not directly related to the death of Mark Duggan. Relative poverty has been shown to be more dangerous than absolute poverty.

The solutions to the twofold threat of political dissent on the streets and actual looting remain related but different. Political dissent in action on the streets or via cyber-attack is much more likely in institutional, infrastructural, banking and business organisations, with organised street attack more likely in clothing, gambling and electronic retail – the poor rebelling by stealing what is easily bought by themselves as well as what they cannot afford; the rich making the revolution by undermining the resources that underpin businesses they consider corrupt, the poor by stealing from those who humiliate them by 'ignoring' their needs and their presence. As such, the real threat is probably from those with a political motivation, not a pecuniary one, but there is the ever-distant promise and ever-looming threat of the alliance of the two:

> And these words shall then become
> Like Oppression's thundered doom
> Ringing through each heart and brain,
> Heard again – again – again –
>
> Rise like Lions after slumber
> In unvanquishable number –
> Shake your chains to earth like dew
> Which in sleep had fallen on you –
> Ye are many – they are few.[39]

APPENDIX 1
1968: THE REVOLUTIONARY MODEL REDEFINED

The revolutionary avant-garde was a product of the nineteenth century, constituted by the politics of socialism and the advancements of technology. It was specifically determined by its struggle with the liberal state and the economics of capital. The struggle between revolutionary avant-gardism and reactionary avant-gardism constitutes the history of the avant-garde in its most dynamic and theoretical form.

The avant-garde was the permanent, marginal base of oppositional culture dedicated to the *struggle* to free the morally self-contained subject into a space of *liberated self-fulfilment*. In so doing it fought against capitalism; the state; militarism; institutionalism; religion; managerialism; racism; imperialism; sexism; autocracy; and totalitarian authority. It was in essence and at every moment international; emancipatory; existential; theoretical; syncretic; technological; utopian; anti-conservative; anti-aesthetical; anti-banal; proletarian (urban and rural); and anti-exploitational. Its heroes were as much Darwin as Freud; Marx as Bakunin; Engels as Thoreau; Max Stirner as Kropotkin; as much the masses as the egotistic self.

The means of the avant-garde enshrined themselves in the proliferation of critique: pamphlets; fly posters; manifestos of every shade and -'ism'; acts of violence; disgraces and outrages; theoretical outbursts and spectacular demonstrations, all in order to embrace rupture and disjunction (especially with history, and art traditions, with consensus, with bourgeois sentiment, with the banal). The aim – to make us see otherwise and through alienating activities abolish alienated subjectivity.

Avant-gardism was dedicated to a future not yet realised – the future of itself *as* realised. But this realisation was the impossible moment of the avant-garde, for avant-gardism was always a potential, not a realization of anything, not an end in itself. It was precisely the premonition, anticipation and inauguration of itself, the declaration of its own beginning prior to its actual beginning. It could be traced only in manifestos and declarations of intent. This was not a failure but exactly as it should have been. Avant-gardism was the process of *defeated becoming*; realised *in history*, it nevertheless opposed the historical only in order the more to determine it. Avant-gardism 'suspend[ed] linear time, and its excess constitute[d] ecstatic time'.[1] Ecstatic time became the time of suspension between the defunct past and an unrealised future. As such, ecstatic time was not merely the present lived forever (as suspension of history and therefore the defeat of avant-garde aspiration) but an abysmal moment in which history was liberated on behalf of the future.

The revolt of the 1960s was the culmination of the nineteenth-century struggle against liberalism, parliamentary democracy and gradualist reform. The year 1968 saw the culmination of the activities of the nineteenth-century avant-garde movement. It marked the end of the transcendent libertarian avant-garde and its socialist double, the end of a dual movement which was politically anarcho-communist and personally individualist and egostistical. The struggle for all forms of political and personal freedom conducted under the banner of these ideals was defeated as much by outside pressures as by internal contradictions: the realisation of the avant-garde was also the abolition of the avant-garde by forces both beyond itself and at *its own hand*.

The future as an ideological project dedicated by the left to enlightened versions of socialism and libertarianism finished in 1968–9 and gave way to frustration – the politics of art gave way to acts of terror and futility. In the ashes of art were born the movements of terrorism: the Simbionese Liberation Army; the Red Army Faction; Weatherman Collective (later the Weather People); the Manson Family; the Molotov Cocktail Party; the Motherfuckers; the Angry Brigade.

For Jean-Francois Lyotard, '1968 was an *abyss* in which the genre of democratic liberal discourse seem[ed] to disappear'. As for ideology, the abyss constitutes an origin from which history was extruded but into which it cannot now return. The abyss is death – a black hole of signification and disruption but also generator of the future from a silent past; a break, rupture, condition of history but not in history. The abyss constitutes a mythic sublime and beatific point of validation for the speaking of history, and it remains in effect a hallucination recognisable in its effects (i.e. historical process and change) but without a proper past to itself or a future. It is the moment of myth. This sublime moment is the empty miraculous – voiding the contents of its own space into a moment *after*, from which and only from which it can be viewed. For Lyotard, it is the unspeakable from which the heterogeneous emerges.

For Jean Baudrillard, 'the grand epoch of subjective irony or radicality ha[d] come to an end' somewhere around 1970. This is the moment of crystallisation, 'the crystal' as Baudrillard called it – 'the pure object' and 'the pure event … no longer with any previous origin or end'. Here is 'something that disappears without a trace, that erases its origins and its end, and that is no longer caught up in linearity'. The *crystal* is the *object* of post-modern hyper-reality and thus the 1960s becomes the infinitely consumed post-modern object – signifying only the *now* of its presence and bringing *no* history with it. An *abysmal* or sublime effect of itself.

The emergence of theory during the 1960s coincided with the end of 'history'. For Baudrillard, theory, unlike history, now became *narrative*: a 'departure' from history per se. It was in this atmosphere that around 1970 both Marxism and Freudianism 'buggered off' in the total 'confusion of things', as he put it. For John Lennon, disillusioned after a long decade, it seemed that all that occurred was that 'everyone dressed up but nothing changed'. It was Michael Foucault who in 1972 noted that the old project of the avant-garde had 'collapsed', generating in its place 'new zones' of activity 'that [perhaps] no longer conformed to the model that Marxist tradition had prescribed. Toward an experience and a technology of desire that were no longer Freudian … the combat shifted and spread into new zones'.

The collapse of the old order of the avant-garde led to a 'new' version of subversive activity, for if reality had itself collapsed into simulacrum, the only subversion was now that of acts of *displacement*. To ask now, in the twenty-first century, whence does the revolution come, who makes history and in what way does *myth* generate the subversive act is to ask questions that seem redundant. And this sense of critical redundancy is itself a legacy of the rejection of the 1960s ethos, a rejection which was ironically generated from within the original milieu. This redundancy is rather the result of a refusal to reopen the case of the 1960s and to reconsider its questions, those questions and attitudes assigned either to a nostalgic but irrecoverable past or to a past seen as anything from slightly embarrassing to disastrous. The point is not to see the 1960s as merely historical enactment but to reassess the potential of the 'project' of the 1960s has for a reconstituted avant-gardism. If the 1960s is an ontological experience, then it is not only the experience of refusal for those of a certain age but it is also part of a historical dynamic whose consequences we still live with now.

The intellectual of the 1960s was embarked on a quest: to find the ideal agent of 'permanent challenge' (Marcuse) whose refusal of the consensual status quo would start the revolution. From the beginning, the quest was frustrated by an inability to identify the insurrectionary class or clearly theorise its role after the initial act of insubordination. Who could act as the ideal social mutineers? If the student body, with its heightened awareness, was to act as the vanguard, a 'detonator' of change (as in France) or the precipitating factor (as in Britain), it was nevertheless true that they were too young and too poor to create lasting change. As transitional workers, students had neither a permanent stake in change nor a traditional or stable economic base. Only the organised working class could offer these, but these traditional agents of change were also agents of stability and conservatism, in cahoots with capital itself. Indeed, the very egos of the traditional working class rattled with internalised capital.

The old avant-garde came from Europe. Hitler and Stalin put an end to that. The fulcrum of 1960s radicalism was the USA. Everything sprang from there and reflected back to there. It was the site and generator of the 1960s experiments and Europe reflected nothing less than the subsequent shock waves which stirred European radicals to action. Such radicals were therefore bound to have a different sense of themselves and radicalism itself soon ceased to have a direct connection to its origins in the struggles of the past. For Abbie Hoffman, the proletariat were essentially irrelevant to the insurrection of the New Left alliance as anti-authoritarianism was individualistic, not class-based. Ridicule not respect was the order of the day – the laughter of carnival its signature. Indeed, Hoffman was happy only to embrace the socialism of the Marx Brothers' variety (including Karl) and during the Paris May Day Riots of 1968, posters proclaimed the Marxism of the Groucho variety!

Habituated to inactivity and reaction, the working class had become respectable, had a stake in society and embraced the bourgeoisie. The temporary alliance of students and workers was little more than an illusion in Europe and non-existent in America. The old white, territorial, *closed* working-class community was to be opposed by the new *post*-proletarian organic communalities based on gender ambiguity, ethnicity and youth. The perforation line split history into pre- and post-World War mentalities. This revolution of *and in* the ordinary person would bring liberation despite Marx, not because of him.

For many intellectuals and radicals, especially those from the margin, Marxism had simply failed to offer a correct analysis of the late twentieth century. It seemed to be unable to account for advanced capitalism, lack of revolutionary activity in advanced capitalist states, the 'absorption' of the working class into the structures of capitalist reaction and the rise of consumerism; it failed to account for co-option, had an outdated idea of the intellectual and a sinister respect for the party machine. Moreover, it had no psychology to match its critique of political economy. In the USA this led the New Left towards the abandonment of *theoretical* positions in an open set of alliances without ideological frameworks or conceptual preconditions.

The 'beyond' of Marxism – its supercession in the contemporaneous – would lead radicals to re-examine new sources of possible rebellion and assertion. For many American intellectuals and radicals, such assertions could be drawn more effectively from American soil than European. American New Leftism was much more likely to be inspired by anarcho-libertarianism or rural communalism than Marxist-Leninism, as indeed it was during the nineteenth century, despite Marxian leanings.

The widespread belief that there is only one revolutionary politics of the left and that that is essentially Marxist-Leninist has obscured the importance of other radical political positions which were repressed in the East yet continued to flourish inside capitalism as both critiques and positive alternatives. The opportunity was thus lost to create a wide spectrum of left-wing beliefs which would include anarchist socialism and anarchist libertarian thought and practice. This narrowing of focus, the domination of Cold War politics and the dominance of party-led oppositional forces, as well as the often violent repression of left-wing alternative movements, policies and actions, has restricted the knowledge of the nature of the left and those debates that might have flourished if its leaders and thinkers were as well known as Marx in academic and political circles.

Historians of the left too easily dismiss the varieties of anarchist politics because they failed to conform to the Marxist-Leninist model, whereas it was precisely this model that failed. Anarchist tendencies, with their spontaneous, amorphous, popular, untheoretical, individualistic, local and self-help approaches and values, are central to ecological, feminist, gender, ethnic and devolutionist debates and are the backbone of charitable organisations working against world hunger, poverty and disease. They are also to be found in animal liberation movements and in 'spontaneous' demonstrations against authority and the state. Anarchism, rather than Marxism, has proved to be more flexible in its practical opposition to capitalism and the state, and, because it retains a strong belief in the individual, it has proved that it can work in the *interstices* of capital as a moral force. Eric Hobsbawn thought it obvious that 'anyone with the slightest knowledge of ideological history could recognise the spirit of Bakunin or even Nechaev in the student radicals of 1968'.[2]

The American New Left was formed around real and pressing issues (civil rights, the Vietnam War, state repression) uniting a broad spectrum of beliefs into a loosely knit but effective mass movement. In contrast, the British New Left was an onlooker to those issues, was narrow in political focus (Marxist) and recruited from a restricted band of enthusiasts. The most successful elements of the British counter-culture were those outside the New Left, through their embracing anarchistic-individualist critiques which were both personal and social. The New Left's cultural critique was therefore far more successful than its political critique, which in a period of high employment, rising wages and a successful Western state was utterly lacking in those domestic targets available in the USA. The British New Left would have remained the British Old Left if these American pressures had not existed.

The troubles which began at the London School of Economics in the autumn of 1966 and which escalated in the spring of 1967 were initiated by a South African student union president and American students and lecturers. The initial cause of the demands for greater student democracy was the appointment of a Rhodesian to the post of Director. Indeed, the major policy adoptions of the National Union of Students in early 1967 were centrally concerned with Vietnam and Rhodesia, not internal British political problems. LSE had a significant level of foreign students, including many from the USA who considered issues in the light of American experience (at Berkeley, etc.) and 'civil rights' – something many British students regarded as totally alien to their experience. The 'Radical Student Alliance' stood for more than its British context and the problems that year at LSE could not really bear the weight of questions of international importance. The specific question of student democracy was a translation into parochial terms of a wider international debate in which the American émigré New Left led the indigenous socialist New Left.[3]

Abbie Hoffman (writing as 'Free') would encapsulate the idea of New Leftism as a 'second American revolution', Bobby Seale would demand 'constitutional rights' under the First Amendment and Tom Hayden would talk of 'the principles embodied in the Declaration of Independence', and all could claim that 'the root concept of the American Revolution remained: "power to the people" – a claim made concrete by its reference to the First Amendment'.

Much of this 'left' non-Marxist radicalism could trace its source back to debates over hipsterism and the extreme nonconformism of the underground in the 1950s. For Norman Mailer the hipster, living on the margin, like the black jazz musician, was a 'philosophical psychopath' whose religious purpose ('one must be religious') was the 'existential' conquest of the borderland. As 'a frontiersman in the Wild West of American Night Life', the hipster fought totalitarianism, conformity and co-option in order to release the sensual transcendent ego.

Whilst the New Left would have scoffed at Ayn Rand's hysterical fear of 'full totalitarian socialism' in the USA, it was quite happy to exercise its own fear of full totalitarian *fascism*. It is not surprising then that many New Left and hippy leaders came closer to Rand's analysis and conclusions than they might have wished to admit. For Rand's 'psycho-epistemological' approach, the only answer to 'Atilla' and 'the witchdoctor' (i.e. totalitarianism) was free market capitalism – a wholesale return to the pioneer-entrepreneurialism of the early republic, hence:

> The professional businessman and the professional intellectual came into existence together, as brothers born of the industrial revolution. Both are the sons of capitalism – and if they perish, they will perish

> together. The tragic irony will be that they will have destroyed each other; and the major share of guilt will belong to the intellectual.
>
> (Ayn Rand, *For the New Intellectual*)

It cannot be overemphasised that the contradictory position of the New Left forced it to embrace both the 'fully integrated' personality of the intellectual in 'the freedom of the market-place of ideas' whilst rejecting the same for actual businessmen or for the market-place of economic goods:

> A society based on and geared to the *conceptual* level of man's consciousness, a society dominated by a philosophy of reason, has no place for the rule of fear and guilt. Reason requires freedom, self-confidence and self-esteem. It requires the right to think and to act on the guidance of one's thinking – the right to live by one's own independent judgement. *Intellectual* freedom cannot exist without *political* freedom; political freedom cannot exist without *economic* freedom; a *free mind and a free market are corollaries.*
>
> The unprecedented social system whose fundamentals were established by the Founding Fathers, the system which set the terms, the example and the pattern for the nineteenth century – spreading to all the countries of the civilised world – was *capitialism.*
>
> To be exact, it was not a full, perfect, totally unregulated *laissez-faire* capitalism.
>
> (Ayn Rand, *ibid.*)

The rejection of laissez-faire capitalism either forced radicals back into a defence of gradualism and reform or turned their intellectual market zeal towards anarcho-communalism and small-scale eco-politics (and the entrepreneurial self-sufficiency that would lead many to become millionaires by the 1980s).

Revolution was, in essence, the realisation of capitalism's once *repressed* potential in its pioneering phase before the intervention of the *state* and the *corporation*. It is no surprise that the 'contradiction' implied by its definition of the market was one that was *not* a contradiction outside Marxist circles. The tradition of refusal in American radical individualism and communalism was a tradition of 'leftism' happily devoid of Marxist-Leninism and closer to Emma Goldman, Alexander Berkman or Rudolf Rocker. Left anarchism always (ironically) found a welcome home in the USA, compatible as it was with much of that country's tradition of seditious free thinking. Theoretical anarcho-communism was the unconscious of left-radical politics in Europe whilst lived out in practice by an American refusenik youth. Utopian socialism and practical communalism found a ready home in the land of Fourierism and agrarian communalism.

For Carl Oglesby, the new way of the left would be 'radical democratic communitarianism', while for Jack Newfield there 'seemed something Emersonian about the SDS', and even Eldridge Cleaver could argue that the role of the Black Panthers was as instigators of a new 'American revolution', whose credo included a return to the centrality of self-determination. For Cleaver, as for American liberal democrats, 'liberty [was] indivisible'.

This was the left without Marx, a tradition that emerged in Europe too in the actual *practice* of insurrection. Indeed, the New Left, in its non-compliance with the 'old' left ideology, found itself unwittingly bypassing Marxist doctrine and rediscovering (albeit most unconsciously) a European tradition of anarchism that had largely arrived in the USA during the earlier half of the nineteenth century and which gathered itself in Chicago and New York amongst Jewish, *mittel*-European and Slav immigrants. It found its most vociferous voices in Emma Goldman and Alexander Berkman.

These Russian exiles, with their *melange* of theoretical influences from Proudhon, Herzen, Kropotkin, Bakunin, Tolstoy and the novelist Chernyshevsky (author of *What is to be Done?*), as well as their debt to Narodnik agitation, became the most famous (and perhaps notorious) anarchist voices of America. They exemplified *oppositional culture*. Nevertheless, this opposition was never fully expressed as a theory of revolution; rather, it was an attempt to produce a life of *virtue* based on political struggle dedicated to the *negation of politics* (i.e. the power of the state). Their blend of communist-anarchism always hovered between community and individual demands, demands that they felt were addressed neither by Marxist-Leninism (despite Goldman's problematic dalliance with the idea of a 'vanguard' party) nor by the extreme individualism of Max Stirner, nor the utopian religiosity of Tolstoy.

For Alexander Berkman, anarchism meant 'Life without compulsion [which] mean[t] liberty; it mean[t] freedom from being forced or coerced, a chance to lead the life that suits you best'. And Emma Goldman could sum up her philosophy by explaining that 'civilisation [was] to be measured by the individual, the unit of all social life;

by his [sic] individuality and the extent to which it [was] free to have its being, to grow and expand unhindered by invasive and coercive authority. [And because] all forms of government rest on violence, and [were] therefore wrong and harmful they [were] always opposed to free individuality'.

From Kropotkin, these revolutionaries took the evolutionary idea of 'mutual aid' rather than survival of the fittest and from a host of historical influences they argued that cooperation amongst humans (the production of mutual-aid communities) always led to virtuous individualism, provided that impediments such as the state were not allowed to take root. For Goldman, the future was a return to an organic past. 'In his [sic] natural condition, man existed without any State or organised government ... Human society then was not a State but an association; a voluntary association for mutual protection and benefit.'

The central importance of the individual ('the centre of gravity in society is the individual') could lead to Max Stirner's form of 'owness', exemplified by individualist-transcendentalists like Ralph Waldo Emerson or David Thoreau, but it could equally lead to Tolstoyan 'unity and love'. In language more suggestive of theosophy than revolution, Berkman and Goldman could exhort followers 'to be like [the] God whom we know only through love and reason ... in order to be rid of suffering, to be tranquil and joyful [and] open ... *the divine life which is in us*'. For Alexander Berkman, this all meant freedom of expression and art, 'freedom from compunction (from whatever quarter), equal rights and liberties, brotherhood [sic] and harmony'.

Both Berkman and Goldman wavered in their original anarchistic beliefs, and Goldman lost faith in the spontaneous action of the proletariat and slowly turned against the unimpressed masses of America, but both retained a fear of, and distaste for, Marxist-Leninism and especially Bolshevism.

The New Left retained Berkman and Goldman's fear of all authority, whether it came from the state or the party, the government, the military or organised religion. New Left radicals also shared a hatred of monopoly capitalism and exploitation and, just like Berkman and Goldman, they supported individualist freedom based on free association. When it came to its ambivalent attitude towards the intellectual 'vanguard', the New Left agitated and demonstrated only in the hope of a spontaneous uprising. For such an uprising, 'politics' as traditionally practised would be abolished, replaced by ethical individualism and virtuous communal responsibility. For Alexander Trocchi, this amounted to an 'invisible insurrection' (Sigma 2), a revolution in the 'broad sense cultural', not a *coup d'état* but a *coup du monde*. Indeed, 'political revolt' was nothing less than an anachronism in the face of 'coming revolution and buddhism' (Gary Snyder) and the 'cosmic buzz' (Dave Stevens).

If the 'ethical revolt' had by the late 1960s become *political*, it retained its appeal to non-political disaffected groups and outraged individuals. Open and 'ecumenical' movements called to those who wished to demand freedom for the self above all else. Distrustful of intellectuals, the American New Left never created a stable and coherent theory of revolutions, nor did it feel the need for one.

Even in Europe the relationship between the left-wing revolutionary and radical subversion and Marxism was far from clear. In 1969 Herbert Marcuse claimed that as capitalism had 'invaded' the mind, the young were now the new psychic proletarian warriors. Yet he could also argue that it would be 'refusal' and 'rebellion [distrustful] of all ideologies, including socialism' which would bring the 'self-determination' that was at the centre of radical struggle (*New Left Revue* 56, July/August 1969). A year previously, *Black Dwarf* (July 1968) saw the students as a 'revolutionary vanguard', even if, as Ernest Mandel demonstrated, the 'university was bourgeois'. If the aim for Danny Cohn-Bendit was the 'overthrow [of the] regime', the means were not clear. Alain Geismer (who had not yet read Marcuse in May 1968) felt that one could not rely on Marxism as it had no theory of advanced capitalism and as such the revolution would be made spontaneously 'as one goes'. For J. Sauvageot, the uprising of 1968 was the direct result of 'the heritage of the [continuous] French Revolutions of the nineteenth century' – Proudhonian rather than Marxian.

The practical and piecemeal nature of the revolution were at one with its *necessary immediacy* and exuberance. Danny Cohn-Bendit proclaimed that 'our movement's strength is precisely that it is based on uncontrollable spontaneity', a variation on Carl Oglesby's formulation of the 'permanent terror of the accidental' and yippy theatrics. It is hardly surprising that student action in Europe rarely met with Communist Party approval or union co operation. The spontaneity of the revolution precluded the traditions of opposition in both party and union which lent themselves to conservative hesitation and bureaucratic proceduralism. The spontaneous insurrection required the urgent re-evaluation of Marxist analysis, a project which occupied Louis Althusser from the early 1960s through to his incarceration in a mental hospital. Quite simply, there was never a structured attempt by any group to seize political power from the government: the revolution was as much 'in your head' (Hoffman) as on the street.

Technology, whilst *essential* to revolution, was also too easily tied to current oppression – an oppressiveness seen not in the oppression of production but rather in the hallucinatory goals of consumer goods. The revolution was not to be anti-consumption, but it was anti-consumerist, attacking the 'obscene' (Marcuse) society of overconsumption of unnecessary goods, of the banal and spectacular (the Situationists). Any political revolt also had to be an aesthetic revolt, a turn against the *banal* and a return to authentic sensual pleasure. The technology of self (drugs) and the technology of communication (media) would all, sooner or later, be used to attack the technology of production.

Technology always remained an intractable and double-edged problem. On the one hand, in the possession of the establishment, it was a tool of repression – as demonstrations at Berkeley proved in 1966 and 1967. On the other hand, certain forms of technology could be utilised on behalf of liberation. For Abbie Hoffman, the 'only pure revolution [was] technological', speeded up by the *release* of innovations (on behalf of leisure) that had been artificially restricted to increase capitalist exploitation (both of class and world). It was technology, after all, that created LSD, itself exploited by the 'Merry Pranksters' and Timothy Leary.

Electronic media, especially television, could be put (unwittingly) to the task of *publicising* the revolution through news and current affairs. 'We are theatre', hippies declared, as both yippies and hippies became media celebrities using Situationist tactics to get their Dada-esque protests into millions of homes. The revolution, in one sense, actually was theatre: Artaud's 'theatre of cruelty' and John Latham's Skoob Towers mixed willy-nilly with love-ins, sit-ins, happenings and be-ins.

Marshall McLuhan believed he saw the significance of the electronic media revolution in such phrases as 'the global village' and 'the medium is the massage [sic]'. In his focus on the non-linear, acoustic and spontaneous, McLuhan believed electronic culture to be a return to the 'global village' now freed from its hierarchy and ignorance into a mixture of Athenian democracy and village-pump politics. In his idealisation of the pre-literate, he actually echoed much debate around 'Cambridge English' and especially the ideal of the lost organic community of F.R. Leavis (who had taught him). The global village was little different from Leavis' Shakespearean community. For the Situationist Guy Debord, McLuhan's ideas were the idealisation of parochialism and ignorance, while for some contemporary commentators, his ideas were subject to blindness to facts, distortion of history and lack of awareness of the role of print culture in its *decisive* influence on electronic culture and its content.

In America, as elsewhere, revolutionary expectations concretised around individual identity. For Tom Hayden and Abbie Hoffman, the gagging of Bobby Seale (and Chicago '69) was nothing less than the persecution of those with 'disrespectful identity' seen by the authorities as 'out of control' (Hayden). The revolutionary war was one fought out in the politics of self; the revolution lived 'in the body' as ontological revolt.

Nowhere was this to be more obvious than in the alliance, or attempted alliances, between radical White positions and Black slum dwellers. The new proletarians were the Black marginal ghetto dwellers – the Third World in the First and at its heart. The fight against capitalism was also to be the fight against imperialism. Such alliances would, it was hoped, bring insurrection out from the heart of capitalism, its invisible heart, that of the disenfranchised who were without a stake in democracy or liberal society. Such protest was, however, to be bought at the expense of the traditional (Marxist) proletariat whose alienation would throw them into the arms of reaction. Third World and ghettoised revolt, revolt from the margins, was the activity of the unassimilated, an absolute refusal of conformism which capitalism *could not absorb* for its own benefit.

For many in the 1960s, there could be no permanent change or any meaningful political realignment without a change in the individual; if you could free subjectivity (ego), it was felt that you freed the community (the political realm). Reformists, civil rights assimilationists and liberal well-wishers would now find that from the margins of the marginal came only terrorism (political insurrection) and Dadaism (aesthetic insurrection). The marginal united all the forces of disruption and in so doing it also gave them an identity and offered them as a target. Despite this, such marginal alliances offered new conditions for the self and gave meaning to 'disrespectful identity' in which the self became the embodiment of an absolute refusal of reformism or compromise.

If the fight against cooperation on behalf of a liberated self had gone on until 1968, by that same year it had also been joined to an active social fight against authoritarianism and the state. By 1969, the refusal of the marginalised had become the chorus of the radicals.

From the neglected margin (Lenin saw the marginal as a mere 'reservoir'), a 'new type of popular culture' (UNEF Manifesto) would emerge determined by its 'non-marketable' nature (David Gilbert). Student 'specialists in provocation' (Hervé Bourges) would successfully create the 'permanent contestation' of power and culture only if a clear alliance was made between disaffected White culture (hippies, SDS, etc.) and ghettoised Black culture (the Panthers). To achieve liberation through 'non-marketable culture' – a product of the disenfranchised and disaffected underclass – Whites would have to dispute class exploitation, Blacks dispute racism and colonialism and women dispute gender identity. To remove exploitation (of classes) and oppression (of races), it would be necessary to abandon reformism, to avoid the 'clichés' of Marxist dogma and literally become *lumpen*: in Eldrige Cleaver's phrase, 'we're all niggers now'.

In finding the concept of ethnicity, radicals also found the missing term in Marxism. For Marx and Engels, the marginal were the reactionary pawns of aristocratic authoritarianism, thuggish dupes and 'social scum ... a bribed tool of reactionary intrigue'. For the New Left, it was precisely from here that the new culture would arise. National liberation movements became the visible corollary of class warfare.

The aim of such intellectual and practical exertion was the creation of free individuals possessing integrated minds in a commonwealth of mutual aid. Opposing the integration of mind, body and community was the integrated *state*. For most intellectuals and artists of the 1960s, the state stood for sheer brutalism, its integration designed to contest, enslave and compartmentalise, spreading propaganda and alienation in order to create *disintegrated* individuals bereft of self-possession and therefore bereft of effective oppositional action (the production of so-called 'weak' citizens). Against this, radicals posed the *integrated personality*: enlightened, empowered and liberated. Such integration could come from an inner quest through drugs and psychedelia or through social struggle on behalf of marginal communities.

Inner struggle tended to be mystic, environmental, communalistic and anarchic, while outer struggle tended to be 'socialist' – anarchist, ethnic and organised (in some loose fashion). The aim was to challenge *state control of consciousness* with self-control of consciousness. If the inner struggle tended also to happen in White 'bourgeois' circles, then the outer quest was directed through the poor and ethnically marginalised. In both cases the struggle was given its impetus by a *necessary paranoia*: a search for deep and hidden wells of meaning unavailable to those for whom liberation was most urgent. Educational methods and literary productions were the main targets for those looking to liberate minds. Thus, campuses were occupied, 'free' universities were created and teach-ins were conducted. From John Calder's *Death of the Word* conferences to John Latham's Skoob project through to John Lennon's frustration at 'endless fucking words', logorrhoea was hunted into silence in order to silence the vehicle of state propaganda. The false word of the state was to be challenged, so radicals thought, by the true 'language' of self – a language of *embodiment* and *action*.

In the 1960s no one was yet willing to accept the idea (itself defeatist and deeply *conservative*) that, as Michel Foucault pointed out, 'there [was] nothing outside the text'. Foucault's declaration, which for a decade or more seemed to liberate language and rob discourse of its 'myth' function, played into the hands of the state and of capitalism. The free play of signifiers was little less than the corollary of exchange; the lack of a signified being the necessary means to avoid ever having the 'buck' stop at your desk!

For most radicals whose optimism hadn't yet turned sour, the attack on the state and its cultural origins (especially the complicity between art and state and corporate patronage) would create a 'personal revolution', a 'new sensibility' and a 'transvaluation of values' (Marcuse) enshrined in 'the liberation of language' (Joseph Ferrandino). Hervé Bourges mused 'if we can avoid revolution we shall not avoid spiritual resurrection'. In the socialisation of production it was hoped would be found the desegregation of art and life – a life now possible as authentic and aesthetically pleasing. The virtuous life would now integrate art and lived experience.

In order to cure the alienation of totality (the monolithic bourgeois totality of capitalist exploitation and banality), it would be necessary to take alienation to its extreme possibility, thereby promoting *shock*. To create shock (the sudden awareness of the possibility of the New), only that art which could dislodge and dislocate would do: Dada happenings; spontaneous Dada theatricals; terroristic and oppositional Dada – anti-cooperative, non-recuperable and evanescent.

This would be samizdat art from the street, the ghetto and the refusenik. In this way, oppositional culture would unite with oppositional politics, itself anarchic and driven by the samizdat manifesto and painted slogan. The result of this symbiosis, this cultural embodiment of the political and the aesthetic (*coup du monde* rather than *coup d'état*), would be a new totality of fluid possibilities and of an art merged into life. The dislocation of aesthetic vision (renewed again and again throughout the twentieth century) was to be the necessary prelude to unity – a unity which transcended precisely because it had been achieved *through* alienation.

The goal of these upheavals and disturbances was the new *self*, both liberated and authentic (capable of *direct* experience of reality). Everywhere one finds a belief in the need to defend or reconstruct a version of *totality* or wholeness and a continuum of mind and body which would finally be free of state control, consumption and capitalism. The new self was to exist in *total self-awareness* and self-fulfilment – a quest many saw in spiritual terms but which was essentially humanistic in its means and its intent. If there was a god, it was the god of the transcendentalists rather than of any organised religion. The first rule of evolution was 'organise your head', if indeed the necessary changes were to be experienced in the revolutionary body. Hoffman's 'I am the Revolution' was indicative of the process of embodiment which was both a prerequisite and a social condition of actual social *reconstruction*.

The political was to start with the individual and end with the individual, changing the status of both as change was brought about. The multiplicity of liberated 'selves' and *self-determined* opportunities was not mere non-focus or crude cultural non-identity, or a concept of hazy identity boundaries (even if it often ended as little else), but an attempt to shift away from the tedium and banality of the conformist I. The I of agency, central to the practical politics of New Leftism, was not to be confused with the subject 'I' or the philosophical (i.e. intellectual) ego. It was the triumph of the 1960s radicals that this alternative 'self' could be imagined and occasionally lived and experienced; it was the tragedy that revolutionary identity could never resolve romantic subjectivity and socialist agency. Too easily the practical (romantic and socialist) concept of transcendence was mistaken for the sublime (romantic and reactionary) in which to go beyond was to step into the vertiginous free fall of the abyss of silence.

To create the necessary psychic changes, the radical gaze turned to its gods: Wilhelm Reich and Carl Jung, Timothy Leary and R.D. Laing. The mind was to be subjected to experimentation as the body became a laboratory for altering consciousness. From Leary and Reich came psychedelia and the orgone. The (aptly named) 'trip' was to be the means of re-seeing the world, of reuniting its parts and of escaping the banal. In its ethnographic dimension it linked the Western intellectual to the shaman and the native, and in its technological dimension it linked the intellectual body to the subversive end of the chemical industry (LSD). From Laing and Jung came anti-psychiatry, psychic symbolism and the experience of psychosis. Madness, schizophrenia and chemical-induced hallucination were to be the weapons (and diagnostic tools) to fight the actual madness and psychosis of regular society – mad without being aware of it. Only through self-induced disorientation and alienation could actual alienation be defeated.

These experimental activities were all attempts to go beyond in order to locate an *authenticity* lost or mislaid. To experience the true self, the actual self would have to be negated and transcended. The true self was holistic, self-determining, free and rational. This enlightened self was to be contrasted to its benighted, socialised predecessor, whilst its holistic self-awareness was to be contrasted with the fragmented, psychologised self of the state's institutions. The body became a theatre in which, and through which, the self experienced its own presence in space and time.

The origins of organic unification – the holistic approach just outlined – which saw a direct relationship between the individual, the social and the creative had its origins in nineteenth-century philosophy and aesthetics, and was strongly associated with revolutionary socialist thought and, more problematically, exemplified by Wagner's theory of the *gesamtkunstwerk*. The desire for unity and communalism enthusiastically embraced the alternative lifestyle of the commune or the harmonious urban 'village'. A wide spectrum of alternative communities sprang up or were redefined. There was Timothy Leary's Castalia Federation; Ginger Island; digger co-ops; ashrams and squats. The British realist drama *Coronation Street* (first shown in December 1960 and later to become a soap opera) seemed to exemplify the nature of an authentic Englishness: self-sufficient, self-healing, self-reliant – a Mancunian corollary of Ronnie and Reggie Kray's cockney East End. The Situationists dreamed of building the 'hacienda' and of dwelling in 'cathedrals', whilst the rain fell at Woodstock and Richard Brautigan's bucolic utopians went trout fishing in America.

In Soviet Russia the avant-garde was defeated when Proletcult was suppressed by the Leninist co-option of Western 'bourgeois' culture on behalf of the Bolshevik vanguard (the party apparatus), as it attempted to suppress Russian Asiatic tendencies during the 1920s. In the West, utopian liberation aesthetics and culture were defeated by the power of liberal democratic co-option and the theoretical swerve away from sociological analysis towards identity politics (and the dissolution of the subject) – all of which accompanied the Cold War phase, 'evil-empire' phase and collapse of Soviet politics and the death of Soviet Marxist-Leninism.

The defeat of the sociological analysis of everyday life (itself a product of nineteenth-century liberationist theories) led to the aesthetic analyses of identity, gender and subjectivity. The brilliance of these analyses masked their incapacity to reinvent a left-liberationist philosophy. The decline of a vision of a socialised history as a unified narrative (against which other unified histories might be tested) was in inverse proportion to the rise of *unified* theory which *acted as narrative*. The coherence of theory replaced the coherence of history (and its explanation) and subversive reading replaced subversion. By the 1980s, it was common to find critical work which had substituted for the politics of the everyday the mere subversion of the aesthetic.

The critique of the nature of everyday lived culture and its representations eventually turned into the critique of representation *as* lived culture: the condition of the simulacrum (which the Situationists feared and execrated) finally came to represent the *only* reality rather than the dominant reality, which remained still open to challenge. Moreover, theory itself, seen in (and only as) its rhetorical dimension, seemed forever trapped in a tautological and continuous undoing, resistant even to itself. The critique of discourse and representational (i.e. linguistic) ideology soon substituted masculinity, imperialism and the spectacle of consumption for Marxist categories of class division. Women, ethnic groups and the popular now acted as the new proletariat on behalf of whom personal identity 'politics' would act in the place of revolutionary socialism.

The central position of language and its capacity to represent the world (the nature of the real) was the first to find itself under radical scrutiny – if the actual state could not be assaulted, then perhaps it could have its orders and self-seeking representations undermined instead. Yet language was precisely *all* that radicalism could use in its representations of actual experience. Without language (and its ability to *speak differently*), opposition was impossible. All statements were now to be taken as *contrary* to themselves, undermining their own validity and therefore useless as analytic tools (hence Jacques Derrida's fascination with the supplementary, silence, lacunae). The subversion of codes turned all concerns over identity into a fight with 'otherness' which was both internalised and psychologised, but it succeeded in making all forms of resistance merely relative, thus confusing the need for priorities, authority and conformity. Such a situation inevitably reinforced 'natural' and political conservatism, mimicking the mores and motives of the market in an often uncanny way.

APPENDIX 2
UNDER THIS SIGN CONQUER: THE VISIBLE REPUBLIC OF LONDON

Until the seventeenth century, the disempowered had no virtually no symbol of their oppression; nothing, that is, to identify them as a coherent body of people with political or social demands. During the Peasants' Revolt of 1381, those that marched in opposition to the status quo left no evidence of marching under any particular banner of freedom. Perhaps some may have marched under a loaf of bread on a pole, symbolising, in a way, the essence of their demands, but although this sign was to be used by later protesters, we have no record of a unifying symbol for the cause of the peasants in the fourteenth century.

It was not until over a century later that German peasants marched under the unifying symbol of the *bundschuh*, a villager's shoe hoisted on a pole which was paraded through villages and taken into battle. The preacher Thomas Müntzer had a rainbow flag, whilst other banners show peasants' tools or tokens of labour. Many years later, the strange peasants' revolt at Dunkirk in Kent, led by the eccentric messianic figure of John Thom known as William Courtney, during 1839 marched to its own Armageddon not under a peasant's banner, but under Thom's personal pennant: a gold lion rampant surrounded by olive branches on a white background with blue borders at the top and bottom. Found on the site where Thom was killed, its meaning has never been explained.

The device of the *bundschuh* did not, however, travel to British shores and the protesting spirit of the poor was left unsymbolised for over 100 years, that is, until the Civil War, when Diggers and Levellers adopted 'commoner's green', the colour of the earth which belongs to all. Green remained the colour of protest for another 100 years. The followers of the Earl of Shaftesbury wore green cockades in the later seventeenth century as symbols of their opposition to Toryism and the crown; green remains a symbol of republican virtues and has been combined with orange to symbolise both Protestant loyalty and its opposite, Irish nationalism. Green was adopted in the twentieth century as the colour of the uniforms of the rather strange scouting club known as Kibbo Kift, with the implication of green renewal and back-to-the-earth politics, and, of course, Lincoln green is the colour most associated with Robin Hood and his proto-socialist methods of appropriation.

The London and Yorkshire gentlemen's associations of the late eighteenth century seem to have sported symbols of their clubs as a sort of freemasonry of opposition to the crown, although the evidence is really only to be found in lampoons and caricatures. Fanciful flags are prominent in illustrations of the time, showing county crests on a white background with founding dates of the association such as that of the County of York or union flags in the top right-hand canton with slogans such as 'England United' painted in and the names of collegiate groups such as London, Newcastle, Bristol and Westminster listed below.

Opposition of any sort needs unifying symbolism and in the eighteenth century this was the cockade worn in a hat: Jacobite cockades were white, government cockades black, Wilkite cockades blue. A blue cockade may have also been associated with the American revolutionists, although their use of general recognition cockades was at first entirely haphazard. The secret sign really became important in the late seventeenth and early eighteenth centuries when Jacobites began using secret iconography as a token of the return of the true monarch. Such signs would include encrypted messages on wine glasses or fans, diamond-shaped rings with reversed inscriptions and anamorphic pictures which look like a smudge until a reflecting cylinder is introduced, transforming the smudge into a portrait of the exiled king.

In the seventeenth and eighteenth centuries a candle visibly displayed in a window would save a house from demolition; a blue ribbon deftly hung upon a rich person's garments saved the wearer from a drubbing from the mob. An eighteenth-century illustration of fighting in front of the Mansion House shows Sir John Hawkins, the Tory friend of Samuel Johnson, in an altercation with rioters holding aloft a double gallows from which are suspended a riding boot and a petticoat.

During the Gordon Riots of 1780, the protesters adopted blue cockades with tags of white paper attached, with slogans such as 'No Popery' embroidered on the tags, rioters forcing these upon recalcitrants when they encountered them in the street as a show of solidarity with their cause. Personal tokens worn either openly or covertly have been a feature of suppressed organisations ever since. Between 1800 and the 1830s, republicans may have worn the common violet of wild heartease as a buttonhole. In Wales its name of 'trilliw' sounds like a transliteration of the French word 'tricolour', the plant itself having two upper petals of purple, lower petals of yellow-white and a green stalk.[1] Purple was also a secret symbol of sympathy with republicanism in its Napoleonic guise. The last true personal tokens of political solidarity are, surprisingly, the various stick pins of the British Union of Fascists during the 1930s, although cheap badges with ban the bomb symbolism or a slogan were also popular in the 1960s.

A contemporary coloured illustration of the demolition of Newgate Gaol in the Gordon Riots shows, perhaps, the first examples of red and black flags in British history, but, equally, the limited colours used on the print may suggest a lucky coincidence by the colourist. Nevertheless, there may be some evidence to suggest that black flags, at least, were flown in the riots as symbols of 'no quarter', shorthand for the revenge of the Protestant mob against a government that had betrayed them to the papists.

Such feelings of betrayal were summed up by the adoption of various American revolutionary flags during the Gordon Riots and after, the politically oppressed of England making cause with their liberated cousins across the Atlantic. The most popular of these flags seems to have been that adopted from the Culpepper Minute Men, a group of volunteers in Virginia whose flag was white with the device of a rattlesnake and the words 'Don't Tread on Me' and 'Liberty or Death' emblazoned underneath; the slogans themselves may have been adopted from Patrick Henry's 'treason' speech of 23 March 1775, which led Virginia into revolution and, as such, the words clearly suggested the idea that 'treason' was actually in this case patriotism.

The slogan went around the world as a watchword of revolution. Irishmen transported after the risings of 1798 and working as convicts in Australia began an insurrection with the cry of 'Now my boys, Liberty or Death'. The massacres that followed their defeat were designed to show rebellious subjects 'what the declared slogan liberty or death really meant'. It was a lesson that was heeded for over 50 years. Such flags and their slogans were revolutionary through and through, and suggested that the contagion of the American disease had truly come to the heart of London. American flags were displayed at rallies for at least the next 30 years and appeared at Spa Fields as late as 1816. In Ireland, American republicanism joined French revolutionary thought to create an Irish fusion. Thus, during the uprising of 1798, there was a catechism for republicans which went as follows:

> Question: 'What have you got in your hand?'
> Answer: 'A green bough.'
> Question: 'Where did it first grow?'
> Answer: 'In America.'
> Question: 'Where did it bud?'
> Answer: 'In France.'
> Question: 'Where are you going to plant it?'
> Answer: 'In the crown of Great Britain.'[2]

American flags and sloganising were important, but other flags of revolution were coming into vogue. Notwithstanding its possible appearance in front of Newgate, the red flag makes its first verifiable historical appearance in British political history during the mutinies at Spithead and the Nore in 1797. The sailors at Spithead had run up red flags as visible signs to other ships of mutinous intent and possible Jacobinism which had seeped over from the French Revolution. The flags at Spithead were ignored by the authorities and the grievances were settled, but the reappearance of red flags and the declaration of a 'floating republic' by Richard Parker, the self-proclaimed leader of the Nore mutiny which followed on the heels of Spithead, suggested to the authorities that red flags had a peculiar and sinister import.

What was the significance of the hoisting of red flags on the main masts of all the ships in revolt? Although often used as a sign of no quarter (black flags were more often used), the use of the flag as a symbol was sufficiently strange to require explanation at Parker's trial. All agreed that the use of a red flag was one of 'defiance' and 'mutiny'. One officer quizzed by his lordships was asked 'have you ever understood what the red flag meant?'. His reply was itself a matter of personal confusion, for he had been told that the sailors 'wished to establish it and fight under it, for the Dutch had stolen it from the English and they [the sailors] wished to restore it ... that was the reply made to me'.[3]

The actual meaning of the red flags may have been simpler in origin, as the fleet was divided into 'red, white and blue' divisions, identifiable by the colour of the stern flag and the position of the ship in the line of battle. Perhaps the sailors with lots of big red flags found them easy to display. Either way, it was to be the symbol of revolution from then on, even if its history was never entirely certain.

Spithead and the Nore followed the red flag being hoisted by Lafayette (hero of the American Revolution) over the Champ de Mars in 1791 or the introduction of the red Phrygian cap in spring 1790. Indeed, the Phrygian cap or its British variant, the 'liberty cap', had been an established symbol of British radicalism since the time of John Wilkes and was then adopted by the American colonists. Phrygian caps of the French type were specifically adopted, however, by the Suffragette movement on their marches during 1911, but were noted 50 years before by Eleanor Marx.[4] The British use of red may therefore go back to the use of red flags as images of defiance (to be used when an enemy has raised the black flag). It was the various French revolutions that explicitly turned a flag of defiance into a flag of revolution.

The first use of a red flag as identifiably associated with working-class protest in Britain was in 1811 or 1812 around Middleton near Oldham, where local protesters marched through villages led by a man who 'waved a sort of red flag'.[5] The next recorded instance of the use of a red flag as a flag of working-class rebellion was not until 1831, when the iron workers of Merthyr Tydfil decided that they had no choice but to fight in order to get redress for their poverty. A bull was slaughtered on Hirwaun Common and its blood used to dye a white cloth, each man being required to pronounce their loyalty holding the bloody material in what was clearly a binding blood oath designed to keep the men together and tie them by fraternal loyalty even in death. The red flag in this instance had the clear symbolism of a medieval guild with all its religious significance – a secret and sacred combinatory union of the oppressed.

The red flag would have remained ambiguous in both meaning and potency without the intervention of the French Revolutions of 1789, 1848 and 1871, after which it stood exclusively for revolutionary left-wing politics, for socialism, communism, anarchism and trade-union syndicalism. The showing of a red flag to disperse demonstrators was first recorded in the Revolution of 1789, the flag being adopted in a show of defiance by the Jacobin Club who wished to honour the Revolution's martyrs. During the Reign of Terror, the flag took on a semi-official meaning, but it was during the 1848 Revolution that it was adopted by socialists as the flag of revolutionary France instead of the tricolour. The government saw the red flag as literally soaked in the blood of the people. Alphonse de Lamartine called it the embodiment of 'blood and terror', but the flag remained the visible symbol of revolution, used again by the communards on the Parisian barricades in 1871. British radical enthusiasm for the French meant that it would become a socialist revolutionary symbol in Britain too, appearing at rallies and marches from the 1880s onwards until finally adopted by the Communist Party of Great Britain in its developed Soviet version in 1923.

The revolutionary song that accompanied the flag was written by Jim Connell in 1889, having been inspired by the revolutionary events of that year:

> One thousand eight-hundred and eighty-nine was the year of the London dock strike. It was the biggest thing of its kind that occurred up to that date and its leaders: H H Champion, Tom Mann, and John Burns aroused the whole of England by the work they did and the victory they won. Not many years previously the Irish Land League aroused the democracy of all countries. I am proud to be able to say that I founded the first branch of the Land League which was established in England. This was the Poplar branch and I remained its secretary until the League was suppressed, and was a member of the Executive during the whole of the time. About the same time the Russian Nihilists, the parents of the Bolsheviks, won the applause of all lovers of liberty and admirers of heroism. Under the rule of the Czar ... the best men and women of Russia were deported to Siberia at the rate of 20,000 a year. Young lady students were taken from their classrooms and sent to work in horrible mines, where their teeth fell out and the hair fell off their heads in a few months. Nobody could fight this hellish rule with more undaunted courage than did the Nihilists, men and women. There happened also, in 1887, the hanging of the Chicago anarchists. Their innocence was afterwards admitted by the Governor of the State of Illinois. The widow of one of them, Mrs Parsons, herself more than half a Red Indian, made a lecturing tour of this country soon afterwards. On one occasion I heard her telling a large audience that when she contemplated the service rendered to humanity she was glad her husband had died as he did. The reader may now understand how I got into the mood which enabled me to write.[6]

Connell actually wrote the first few stanzas in more mundane circumstances: a train ride from Charing Cross to New Cross in south London after attending a meeting of the Social Democratic Foundation. Connell sent the final version to Harry Quelch, who published the lyrics as 'A Christmas Carol' in *Justice* on 21 December 1889. Thereafter the words were sung at political rallies, at the news of the Russian Revolution, on the Clyde during its most militant trade union period, by Labour MPs before the First World War and by miners about to be executed in South Africa.[7] The song was sung in its entirety by Clement Attlee and the government after the 1945 General Election.

The lyrics were originally intended to be sung to an old Irish revolutionary tune, *The White Cockade*, but this was changed when A.S. Headingley put the words to the German hymn *Tannenbaum*, which is also the American tune *Maryland*, thus joining the revolutionary movements across the globe in a tune which was universal. Connell, however, stuck to *The White Cockade*:

> There is only one air that suits *The Red Flag* and that is the one which I hummed as I wrote it. I mean *The White Cockade*. I mean moreover the original version known to everybody in Ireland fifty years ago. Since then some fool has altered it by introducing minor notes until it is now nearly a jig. This later version is the one on sale in music shops today and it does not, of course, suit my words. I suppose this explains why Adolphe Smythe Headingley induced people to sing *The Red Flag* to *Maryland*. *Maryland* acquired that name during the American War of Secession. It is really an old German Roman Catholic hymn. It is church music and was no doubt composed, and is certainly calculated, to remind people of their sins and to frighten them into repentance. I daresay it is very good music for the purpose for which it was composed but that purpose was widely different from mine when I wrote *The Red Flag*. Every time the song is sung to *Maryland* the words are murdered. The very slightest knowledge of elocution will show that the words are robbed of their proper emphasis and true value and meaning when sung to that air. The meaning of the music is different from the meaning of the words. Headingley may as well have set the song to *The Dead March in Saul*.[8]

The first four verses capture the mood of solidarity, internationalism, resistance and martyrdom:

> The people's flag is deepest red,
> It shrouded oft our martyred dead,

And ere their limbs grew stiff and cold,
Their hearts' blood dyed its ev'ry fold.

Then raise the scarlet standard high.
Within its shade we'll live and die,
Though cowards flinch and traitors sneer,
We'll keep the red flag flying here.

Look 'round, the Frenchman loves its blaze,
The sturdy German chants its praise,
In Moscow's vaults its hymns are sung
Chicago swells the surging throng.

Then raise the scarlet standard high.
Within its shade we'll live and die,
Though cowards flinch and traitors sneer,
We'll keep the red flag flying here.

The song was sung regularly until 1999, when New Labour rebranded itself as a centre-left party, but was nevertheless sung at the centenary celebrations in 2006, the red flag itself having been ditched in 1986, when the Labour Party Conference dropped Clause IV of its constitution and adopted the red rose symbol of a European centre-left party.

Clause IV was the central plank of the constituted Labour Party and as such attached it wholeheartedly to the ultimate success of socialism. Drafted by Sidney Webb in November 1917, it was adopted by the Party in 1918. It argued that the Party existed:

> To secure for the workers by hand or by brain the full fruits of their industry and the most equitable distribution thereof that may be possible upon the basis of the common ownership of the means of production, distribution and exchange, and the best obtainable system of popular administration and control of each industry or service.

The clause was last used as a rallying cry in the manifesto of 1983, a strongly worded call for nationalisation and a return to old-fashioned collectivist ideals to be set against Margaret Thatcher's ideal of privatisation. Labour's Gerald Kaufman called it the 'longest suicide note in history', the last charge of nineteenth-century socialist values broken against the equally nineteenth-century ideal of Smilesian self-help. The perceived confusing language of the clause led to its modification after being redrafted by Tony Blair's advisers when he assumed leadership of the party in 1994. The new clause, finally adopted in 1995, read as follows:

> The Labour Party is a democratic socialist party. It believes that by the strength of our common endeavour we achieve more than we achieve alone, so as to create for each of us the means to realise our true potential and for all of us a community in which power, wealth and opportunity are in the hands of the many, not the few, where the rights we enjoy reflect the duties we owe, and where we live together, freely, in a spirit of solidarity, tolerance and respect.

The black flag, on the other hand, has a much less significant history in the British Isles. Originally associated with absolute destruction, it was also a sign of defiance, of pirates and of the negation of the nation state. It also has a shorter history than its red counterpart. Barring its dubious appearance at Newgate in 1780, it is first recorded in Britain at the first Spencerian insurrectionary meeting at Spa Fields where John Castle carried a black flag on 15 November 1816.

The flag takes on its more modern libertarian and socialistic meaning after flying during silk riots in Lyons in 1831 and it also appeared in hunger riots ten years later in France. During the early 1880s, the anarchist paper *Le Drapeau Noir* used it as its name and logo and the Black International may have used it as its symbol when it formed in London in July 1881. The flag certainly flew over the Paris Commune and Louise Michel led rioters in 1883 carrying a black flag.[9] Michel said the standard stood for 'strikes and those who are hungry', whilst after demonstrations and police violence in the Haymarket in Chicago, it seemed to stand for 'the fearful symbol of hunger, misery and death'.[10] Interestingly, the bisected red (socialism) and black (anarchism) flag with its superimposed circled 'A' logo of the modern anarchist movement dates only from the mid- to late 1970s.

By far the most frequent type of flag at demonstrations during the nineteenth century was the one that carried a message on a white or coloured background. These were often banners rather like those carried by the modern trade unions. Perhaps the only survivor from the early nineteenth century is the Skerlmanthorpe 'flag' held at the Tolson Museum in Kirklees in Yorkshire. The flag or banner was intended to be mounted onto two poles and to be carried in front of local political processions.

Made of cotton in secret by villagers (probably women) in Ratcliffe Street, Skelmanthorpe in 1819, the banner is divided into quarters or cantons, each carrying a message. In the left-hand top canton is the slogan 'Skelmanthorp [sic] will not rest Satisfied with the Suffrage being anything but Universal', a demand of working men since the days of the corresponding societies. Next to that, on the right hand at the top, is 'Truth and Justice Pouring Balm into the wounds of the Manchester Sufferers', a reference to the Peterloo Massacre in Manchester in 1819 which occurred in the year of the banner's manufacture. In the bottom-left canton are the words 'May never a cock in England Crow, Nor never a Pipe in Scotland blow, Nor never a Harp in Ireland Play, Till Liberty regains her Sway', a continuous demand of the period for justice and liberty for all, especially with the draconian punishments meted out to Irish rebels and Scottish Jacobins. Finally, at the bottom right, the more remarkable for its importance to the international dimension of artisan's rights, is the picture of a kneeling and chained Black supplicant looking up to the eye of heaven surmounted by the motto 'am I not a man and a Brother [sic]', the image taken and reversed from William Hackwood's or Henry Webber's designs for Josiah Wedgwood's famous anti-slavery medallion of 1787. Remarkably, the banner therefore covers the entire gamut of British radical and artisanal political interests up to the period of Chartism.

First paraded at a meeting at Almondbury Bank in November 1819, it was also at the monster reform rally at Roberttown near Wakefield in 1837 and again at a meeting celebrating the end of the highly unpopular Crimean War in 1856 and the American Civil War in 1865. Frequently hidden and having the religious connotation of an icon for local radicals, concealed in wagons and buried like a sacred relic until needed, it was last paraded at a reform meeting in Huddersfield in 1884, thereafter being effectively forgotten and left lying in a warehouse until it was rediscovered in 1924 and donated to the Tolson Museum.

Such banners and flags were important symbols of unrest and magistrates were keen to seize them wherever possible. Such was the case at the second Spa Fields rally held on 2 December 1816, when Bow Street Runners directed by Sir Nathaniel Conant seized 'flags and banners' in frustration at the mood of the meeting. This concentration on seizing the symbols of insurrection or radical dissent carried on throughout the early nineteenth century, especially at Chartist rallies between the late 1830s and the 1850s, when parade banners carrying slogans were at their height. Such banners, flags and streamers carried the very essence of political unrest and were therefore the embodiment of the radical refusal to kowtow to the status quo. Some, like that at Skelmanthorpe, became sacred in their meaning, to be displayed at times of crisis as a talisman.

The flag that infuriated the authorities the most was the tricolour of revolutionary France, adapted across England, Wales and Ireland as the flag of rebellion, its colours changed to suit local needs. The tricolour *was* revolution, symbolic of everything Jacobinical, and was therefore prime evidence of nefarious intent. Such flags had to be seized at all costs. At the trial of Spencerians, much was made of the flags and banners displayed on the day of the Spa Fields Riot. What indeed was the intent in displaying a 'green, white and red' tricolour other than provocation and incitement, especially when the banners declared 'Justice, Humanity and Truth' or 'Nature, Truth and Justice', as John Stafford, chief clerk at Bow Street, attested when acting as prosecution witness? Stafford's opinion under questioning was that these flags stood for a call to 'insurrection'.

The flag of the 'English' republic was red, white and green in horizontal bars to allow for a slogan or the same colours displayed as in the French flag. It is possible that some variation of these colours were displayed at Peterloo. At the time of Jeremiah Brandreth's revolution in Derbyshire during 1816, Oliver ('Oliver the Spy') had spoken of 'Sir Francis Burdett waiting in the wings to lead the new British Republic with its red, white and green tricolour'. The Chartists adopted the tricolour and its colouring from the late 1830s onwards. Claims that they made horizontal the vertical form of the French flag are unlikely, as the horizontal version existed to allow for slogans, which they certainly employed. The Chartists did, however, sometimes use the French version of the tricolour. James Linton's Chartist journal *The Cause of the People* carried the flag with the wording 'Fraternity – Liberty – Humanity'. As such, the importance of flags and banners was most significant during the Chartist disturbances between 1839 and 1848.

Robert Wedderburn was an unorthodox preacher who certainly used the tricolour for political as well as rebellious effect. The son of a slave and her Scottish owner, Wedderburn wrote *The Horrors of Slavery*, knew Thomas Spence and shared his radical ideas, but followed that radical tradition of dissent that was so important in uniting religious and political radicalism. Although his choice of religious dissent was vaguely conservative, he had been a Methodist and become a Unitarian, his approach to religion marked by an eccentric and fiery political edge. Where the altar would normally have been in a church, there were pictures of Tom Paine, Toussaint L'Ouverture, a skull and crossbones, a red flag and the red, white and green flag of the British Republic. Fiercely passionate about his origins, he wrote to the slaves in Jamaica urging them to rebellion and the setting-up of a republic, by implication arguing for revolution at home.

However, all tricolours owe their origin not to heraldry or conquest but to the rationalist and deist principles of the Enlightenment, where proportion and colour stood for equality of relationship and the symbolic unification of people, nation and principle. The Suffragettes adopted the tricolour to the green, white and violet as standing for 'Give Women Votes', but in their case they used the stripe vertically, as is clearly shown on Pathé newsreels made at the time of large demonstrations in 1911 and 1913, the violet or purple element in their flags being facilitated by the chemical manufacture of 'Perkin's purple'. Suffragettes also used the Phrygian cap and the arrows of prison uniforms as banner decorations and wore miniature badges pinned on bodices. The 'Florence Lockwood banner' from Huddersfield was remodelled after 1907 from 'Votes for Homes' to 'Votes for Women', showing the flexibility, usefulness and longevity of political banners, which could be adopted for a number of causes.

Nevertheless, it was in Ireland that the tricolour was finally adopted. After their failure to instigate the 1848 Rising, the revolutionaries William O'Brien and Thomas Meagher were arrested but released on bail. They fled to Paris in the hope of making an alliance the newly re-established French Republic. Whilst in Paris they met the acting president, Alphonse de Lamartine (who had himself accused the revolutionary French red flag of being soaked in blood and being a betrayal of the tricolour), who presented them with a green, white and orange flag based on the French design. It had originally been designed by Meagher, became the flag of 1916 and eventually the flag of the republic in 1922. The English tricolour and its colours were still being carried as late as George V's silver jubilee in 1935, where two maverick households spoiled the celebrations by flying the red, white and green of the revolution.

The flag has never been fully adopted by revolutionaries in Britain, partly, one suspects, because of its flexibility in terms of what symbolic colours are chosen and what they are meant to suggest, but that is not to say that it has been entirely forgotten. In 2011 the Republican Socialist Party in Southwark, south London proudly displayed a tricolour of red, purple and green. Nevertheless, the internationalist emblems of revolution, the red and black of defiance and the socialist libertarian cause remain the standards of choice. Yet this is not all.

A new image of radicalism has emerged in the twenty-first century. It is the anonymous and stylised Guy Fawkes mask from the 2006 film *V for Vendetta* in which a masked hero, part Phantom of the Opera, part Joker and Mr Punch and part superhero vigilante, sacrifices himself to liberate 'England' from the tyranny of a fascist dictator in the mould of Big Brother from George Orwell's *1984*. The final scene, as Parliament blows up, is mirrored in 1,000 copycat masks as the people watch the fireworks, finally liberated out of their collective anonymity into individual freedom. Fawkes went through a remarkable ideological transformation in the comic strip *V for Vendetta*, which led to the film.

The strip was originally written for a comic called *Warrior* by Alan Moore and illustrated by David Lloyd during the 1980s, a warning against the excesses of Thatcherism and the rise of the right. Here he became not a fanatical Catholic bent on returning England to a repressive papacy, but a freedom-loving anarchist trying to destroy a totalitarian government which believes itself to be the saviour of civilisation. With the release of the film in 2006, the anarchist's mask was adopted as a symbol of revolution by the protest alliance called Anonymous and became the disguise of choice by anarchists on the streets, who by donning the enigmatic features of the mask see themselves as fighting for freedom, liberty, community and peaceful existence. A symbol of everyman, 'freedom fighters' and the 'revolutionary spirit', 100,000 copies of the mask are sold every year worldwide.

APPENDIX 3
A LITTLE RIOTOUS CHRONOLOGY

AD 60 or 61: Boudicca and the Iceni tribe attack the newly built London. The Roman historian Tacitus records 30,000 dead in the massacre. The skulls of three victims recovered from the Walbrook stream (near present-day Walbrook in the City of London) are preserved in the Museum of London. For many years historians believed Boudicca's last battle was on the site of King's Cross Station. 'Boadicea's' statue with her chariot has guarded Westminster Bridge since 1902.

1196: William Fitz Osbert or William with the Long Beard preaches against fraudulent banking practices. He is soon executed.

1381: the Peasants' Revolt is led by Wat Tyler. The rebels are welcomed into London and burn down John of Gaunt's palace at the Savoy and seize the Tower, but when Tyler meets Richard II at Smithfield, he is betrayed and killed as he seeks sanctuary in the church of St Bartholomew the Great. Smithfield was a place of execution; William Wallace was executed there. A memorial records the event.

1554 : Sir Thomas Wyatt leads the men of Kent to depose Mary I, but is stopped in Southwark when the gates of old London Bridge are barred and the guns of the Tower are trained on Borough. The rebels cross at Westminster and fight a bloodless battle at Charing Cross. Wyatt gives himself up in hope of a pardon but is beheaded. Southwark Cathedral and the Clink prison, which was burned down in the Gordon Riots, are nearby.

1668: the Bawdy House Riots occur in which protests against the maladministration of the royal household (and the rents from brothels) turn to radical republicanism. Such rioting was accompanied by bonfires, bell ringing and 'Pope'-burning rituals amongst journeymen and apprentices. The seventeenth century seethed with republican sentiment, and riots and revolution after the Civil War were endemic across Britain.

1780: Lord George Gordon leads the Protestant League in the Gordon Riots in a week's orgy of destruction. Catholics are especially targeted. Much of London is set ablaze and hundreds die as a result of the violence. The uprising is finally quelled by soldiers in Threadneedle Street when the rioters threaten to storm the Bank of England. Gordon is eventually jailed and converts to Judaism. Recent protests against the bankers saw the death of Ian Tomlinson by the Royal Exchange very near the Bank.

1816: the banner of reform is raised in Spa Fields near Exmouth Market, Clerkenwell. The mass demonstrations end with a march on the Tower of London. The years following this are those of increasing disturbance and government repression. Spa Fields is still there, although blocks of flats take up much of the space. Clerkenwell was a centre of radical dissent and the site of a number of notorious prisons. The Marx Memorial Library is still located on Clerkenwell Green.

1820: those leaders of the Spa Fields riot who were not imprisoned form a gang under Arthur Thistlewood and meet in a stable in Cato Street near the Edgware Road to plot the kidnap and killing of the Prime Minister and his cabinet. The stables are stormed by soldiers and Bow Street Runners, and the gang is captured. A blue plaque marks the building. Very near is Paddington Green Police Station, where modern terrorists are often interrogated.

1848: the Chartists, demanding parliamentary reform, meet on Kennington Common, then a waste ground. Over 40,000 people meet to hear speeches and march on Parliament. A photographer captures the very first picture of a political rally. Soon afterwards, the Common is turned into a park to make the area 'respectable'.

1887: a rally by socialists, including the poet William Morris, meet to protest against the imprisonment of an Irish 'home ruler' in the new open space of Trafalgar Square. The police and two cavalry squadrons defend Nelson's Column. The protest is put down with great force by police and soldiers, resulting in many injuries and three deaths. The day becomes known as 'Bloody Sunday'. A police observation post may still be found in the corner of Trafalgar Square.

1910: a gang of Latvian Bolsheviks and anarchists bungle a raid on a jewellery shop in Houndsditch, resulting in the death of three policemen. The subsequent police investigation ends in the 'Siege of Sidney Street' off Commercial Road in January 1911. The incident becomes as legendary as the Jack the Ripper murders. There is a memorial in Cutler Street behind where the jewellers stood; the flats at the corner of Sidney Street are named after the terrorists!

1936: trade unionists, communists and Jewish leaders organise the biggest rally to date in order to stop the British Union of Fascists under Oswald Mosley marching through the East End. An estimated crowd of between 75,000 and 100,000 people march under the banner 'They Shall Not Pass' and battle police at Gardener's Corner near Aldgate Station. The fascists take another route but are thwarted in their aims. The nearby Altab Ali Park is named after another victim of fascism killed in the 1970s.

1958: the first post-War race riot in London begins in Notting Hill and ends after a week's intermittent violence. The rise of post-War fascist parties comes to a head in the 1970s and results in mass demonstrations by anti-fascist groups. In 1974 Kevin Gateley is trampled by police horses in Red Lion Square and in 1979 Blair Peach is killed in Southall whilst attending an anti-fascist rally.

1968: the anti-Vietnam movement has two rallies and attempts to storm the American Embassy in Grosvenor Square. Protesters hope to capture the embassy and raise the North Vietnam flag or gain a 'martyr' trying. This is the first real media riot.

1981: disturbances take place across Britain after police harassment in Brixton.

1985: the Broadwater Farm riots following a police 'killing' leads to extreme levels of violence, including the death of PC Keith Blakelock, the first policeman to be killed in a riot since 1830.

1992: a huge bomb planted by the Provisional IRA demolishes the Baltic Exchange building at Mary Axe, a nearby medieval church and damages many other buildings. Three people are killed. A year later, another bomb rocks Bishopsgate and the police throw up the 'Ring of Steel', a set of barriers across main roads, the first wall around London since medieval times. The stain-glass windows from the Baltic Exchange are now in the National Maritime Museum in Greenwich.

2000: the modern anarchist movement makes its first May Day appearance on the street with the 'Guerrilla Gardening' occupation and 'remodelling' of Parliament Square.

2005: a bomb destroys a bus in Russell Square after other bombs have destroyed Underground trains. In all, 56 people are killed, including the four bombers. The inquest into the attacks opened in 2010 and is ongoing. There are memorials in Russell Square and Hyde Park and a tree dedicated to a student victim outside Birkbeck Library in Malet Street.

2010: student protests against tuition fees occur. Students manage to attack Conservative Campaign Headquarters and attack the car carrying the Prince of Wales. This marks the beginning of a new wave of militant action.

2011: the summer riots across England following the death of Mark Duggan affect large parts of London, including Tottenham, Hackney, Walthamstow, Ilford, East Ham, Dalston, Brixton, Woolwich, Peckham and Ealing. Outlying areas such as Croydon, Romford and Woodford were also affected.

NOTES

1 2000: PREFACE TO DISORDER IN THE TWENTY-FIRST CENTURY

1 V.I. Lenin, 'Theses on the Question of the Immediate Conclusion of a Separatist and Annexationist Peace', in *The Revolutionary Phase* (Moscow: Progress Publishers, [7 January 1918] 1972), 7.

2 'Adapting to Protest – Nurturing the British Model of Policing', www.statewatch.org/news/2009/nov/uk-hmic-adapting-to-protest.pdf (date accessed 19 March 2012), 51.

3 The apparent abandonment of many poorer areas in the UK has led to the rise of self-help vigilante groups such as the EDL. These groups effectively 'police' and 'protect' their areas once normal police practices have been abandoned. Such areas are essentially 'lawless' or, more properly, outside the law. Professor Hamid Ghodse, the head of the United Nations International Narcotics Control Board, accused the UK of moving towards, or actually already having, 'no-go' drugs areas, an accusation quickly refuted by a number of senior police constables and Members of Parliament. See *I*, 29 February 2012.

4 *Intelligence and Security Committee Report 2007–8* (London: Stationery Office, 2008), 17–18.

5 *The Paper*, Edition Minus 1, February 2011 (Hato Press and Centre for Ethics and Politics, Queen Mary College, University of London), 8.

6 Escalate collective manifesto, University of London, www.escalatecollective.net (date accessed 19 March 2012), 3.

7 *Ibid.*, 5.

8 *Daily Mail*, 12 November 2010.

9 *Evening Standard*, 17 January 2011.

10 *Metro*, 29 March 2011.

11 *The Paper*, February 2011, 8.

12 www.pirateparty.org.uk and various other PP websites.

13 Escalate collective manifesto, 5.

14 *Ibid.*, 5.

15 *The Paper*, February 2011, 5.

16 Escalate collective manifesto, 5.

17 *Ibid.*, 4.

2 2010: OCCUPY EVERYTHING

1 The trial of Gary Dobson and David Norris for Lawrence's murder began at the Old Bailey on 14 November 2011, following a re-examination of the evidence. They were both convicted, but have now filed appeals. Despite the convictions, Black Britons are wary of the judicial system, being far more likely to be its victims. A poll carried out by *The Voice* (5–11 January 2012) directly after the sentencing found that 83 per cent of Black people thought that nothing had improved since the death of Stephen Lawrence and only 17 per cent thought that race relations had improved, and this despite the recommendations of the Macpherson Inquiry of 1999. Nevertheless, on 5 April 2012, the Deputy Commissioner, Craig Mackey, had to issue a statement regarding alleged racist incidents in the Metropolitan Police Service and referrals to the IPCC:

> The Commissioner made it clear after the first alleged incident came to light last weekend that we take the issue of racism extremely seriously. I want to reiterate – there is no room for racism in the Met ...
>
> The Met has around 50,000 staff, including 32,000 officers, who were deployed to over 1.3 million incidents last year on behalf of Londoners. The vast majority act with the professionalism and high standards we expect. The Met does not tolerate racism.
>
> Breakdown of cases with a racist element that have been referred to the IPCC:
>
> 1 Allegation that a PC racially abused a prisoner on 11 August 2011 in Newham (the officer has been suspended), and that two PCs assaulted the prisoner on 11 August in Newham (the officers are not suspended or restricted in relation to this matter but one of the officers is restricted on an unrelated matter).
> 2 Allegation that a PC assaulted a prisoner on 11 August 2011 in Newham; the officer has been placed on restricted duty (this is the officer involved in above incident).
> 3 Allegation that a A/PS & two PCs working on Newham borough used racist language between Jan and March 2012 (all three officers are suspended).
> 4 Allegation that a PC working in Central Communication Command mishandled calls (racial element) in 2010 (the officer is on restricted duties). This is a re-referral as this matter had previously been referred to the IPCC and we had been advised local investigation.
> 5 Allegation that a PC and a member of police staff in Islington used racist language, reported on 26 March 2012 (both the PC and the member of police staff are suspended).

6 Officer was convicted at court on 23 March 2012 of racially aggravated public order offences that were investigated by British Transport Police. This is a mandatory referral to the IPCC (the officer is suspended).
7 Allegation of bullying in Wandsworth borough by a number of police officers and staff against PCSOs over an 18-month period (two officers are presently suspended). This is a re-referral as this matter had previously been referred to the IPCC and we had been advised local investigation.
8 Allegation from a member of the public of a racist assault involving five officers from the Territorial Support Group against several juveniles in Hyde Park in 2011 (all 5 officers remain on full duties at this time). This is a re-referral as this matter had previously been referred to the IPCC and we had been advised local investigation.
9 Allegation from a member of the public that he was racially abused by an unidentified police officer whilst in Camden borough on 6 January 2012. This is a re-referral as this matter had previously been referred to the IPCC and we had been advised local investigation.
10 Allegation that a PC working on Westminster borough used racist language between May 2010 and August 2011 (the officer is presently on restricted duties).
11 Allegation against a TSG officer using racist language towards a member of the public and officer(s) assaulting a member of the public. The allegations relate to the arrest of a 26-year-old man on suspicion of an immigration offence in Leytonstone High Road at approx. 23:30hrs on 24 September 2011.

Surprisingly, therefore, after so much effort to erase institutional racism from policing especially, a gay black policeman, Kevin Maxwell, allegedly suffered a mental breakdown after prolonged harassment from colleagues between 2009 and 2010. He satisfied Judge Byrne at his employment tribunal that there had been a violation of '[his] dignity' and that he was forced to work in 'an intimidating, hostile, degrading, humiliating or offensive atmosphere'. More worryingly, Maxwell was employed at Heathrow as a counter-terrorism officer working within Counter Terrorism Command Special Branch. Scotland Yard ordered an internal investigation. See the *Evening Standard*, 21 February 2012.

2 *The Paper*, Edition Minus 1, February 2011 (Hato Press and Centre for Ethics and Politics, Queen Mary College, University of London), 9.

3 *Ibid.*, 6.

4 *Ibid.*, 12. The article was first published in the Australian student paper *Rabelais*, where it was the subject of an unsuccessful prosecution.

In January 2012, the celebrity chef Anthony Worrall Thompson was arrested for shoplifting at a supermarket. Instead of the punishments handed out in the normal course of events, he was treated as a celebrity; in other words, his actions were seen as an aberration brought on by anxiety, stress and loss of self-determination resulting in the need for a self-asserting but illegal act in order to restore balance. See *The Sun* (9 January 2012) for a humorous treatment of this case.

5 *Ibid.*, 12.

6 Broadhurst now directs the 2012 Olympics Gold Command.

7 *Evening Standard*, 25 November 2010.

8 *Metro*, 5 January 2011.

9 A *Strong Britain in an Age of Uncertainty: The National Security Strategy*, Cm 7953 (London: HMSO, 2010), 3–4.

10 *Evening Standard*, 24 November 2010.

11 *Evening Standard*, 25 November 2010.

12 *Metro*, 5 January 2011.

13 *Evening Standard*, 30 November 2011.

14 Yvette Cooper, House of Commons Parliamentary Debates (*Hansard*), 11 August 2011, col. 1145.

15 *Evening Standard*, 15 September 2011.

16 Her Majesty's Inspectorate of Constabulary, *The Rules of Engagement: A Review of the August 2011 Riots*, www.hmic.gov.uk/media/a-review-of-the-august-2011-disorders-20111220.pdf (date accessed 21 March 2012), 79. Of the ten key principles governing the use of force, the following six points are most pertinent. They comprise a 'distillation' of the law only, but are applicable in all circumstances whether or not it is one of public disturbance:

1. When force is used, it shall be exercised with restraint. It shall be the minimum honestly and reasonably judged to be necessary to attain the lawful objective.
2. Lethal or potentially lethal force should only be used when absolutely necessary in self-defence, or in the defence of others against the threat of death or serious injury.
3. Any decision relating to the use of force which may affect children, or other vulnerable persons, must take into account the implications of such status.
4. Police officers should plan and control operations to minimise, to the greatest extent possible, recourse to lethal force, and to provide for the adoption of a consistent approach to the use of force by all officers. Such planning and control will include the provision to officers of a sufficient range of non-lethal equipment and the availability of adequate medical expertise to respond to harm caused by the use of force.

5. Individual officers are accountable and responsible for any use of force, and must be able to justify their actions in law.
6. In order to promote accountability and best practice, all decisions relating to the use of force, and all instances of the use of force, should be reported and recorded either contemporaneously, or as soon as reasonably practicable.

17 *Evening Standard*, 8 November 2011.
18 *Ibid*. However, not all was sweetness and light. As time progressed, the St Paul's staff and clergy began to complain of abuse, over-loud music, graffiti and falling congregations because of the camp: *Evening Standard*, 31 January 2012.
19 'Occupy the City', anonymous leaflet.
20 During January 2012, a poll for Bloomberg showed that a large proportion of financiers and bankers felt that banks had lost their 'moral compass' and 70 per cent predicted rioting because of economic instability. Fifty per cent saw inequality as the greatest problem, as well as a lack of investment in youth. At least 60 per cent agreed, partly at least, that bankers were driven by 'greed': *Metro*, 26 January 2012.
21 The early Tudor historian Robert Fabyan recorded in Henry Craik (ed.), *English Prose*, vol. I, *Fourteenth to Sixteenth Century* (Oxford University Press, 1916), 136.
22 *Evening Standard*, 25 February 2011.
23 *Rolling Stone*, 5 April 2010.

3 2010 TO 2012: THE CONSTANT THREAT AND THE DISTANT FEAR

1 *The Independent*, 30 December 2011.
2 *Securing Britain in an Age of Uncertainty: The Strategic Defence and Security Review*, Cmd 7948 (London: HMSO, 2010), 15.
3 *Morning Star*, 23 November 2010.
4 *Evening Standard*, 12 September 2011.
5 See *A Strong Britain in an Age of Uncertainty: The National Security Strategy*, Cm 7953 (London: HMSO, 2010).
6 *Ibid.*, 14.
7 The Prime Minister's annual review of 2010, *Strategic Defence and Security Review* (7 December 2011), cols. 31–32WS. Report in deposited papers, http://www.parliament.uk/deposits/depositedpapers/2011/DEP2011-1996.pdf (date accessed 21 March 2012).
8 *The Independent*, 18 April 2012; *Evening Standard*, 11 April 2012.
9 *The Times*, 9 November 2010.

10 www.studentrights.org.uk (date accessed 21 March 2012). See also the cautionary argument of Baroness Deech (*The Times Higher Education* magazine, 22 March 2012). The Muslim student community is often the subject of the liberal establishment's patronising attitude. As such, Malcolm Gillies, Vice Chancellor of London Metropolitan University, proposed banning alcohol because it might offend some Muslim students who saw its sale as 'immoral'. The suggestion was rigorously opposed by other Muslims at the University: *Evening Standard*, 19 April 2012.

11 *Evening Standard*, 8 December 2011.

12 *Securing Britain in an Age of Uncertainty: The Strategic Defence and Security Review*, 26.

13 *Ibid.*, 49.

14 *A Strong Britain in an Age of Uncertainty: The National Security Strategy*, 17,

15 *Securing Britain in an Age of Uncertainty: The Strategic Defence and Security Review*, 49.

16 *Ibid.*

17 John Tomlinson, *Left, Right: The March of Political Extremism in Britain* (London: John Calder, 1981), 13.

18 *The Paper*, Edition Minus 1, February 2011 (Hato Press and Centre for Ethics and Politics, Queen Mary College, University of London), 4.

19 *Ibid.*, 10.

20 The European Court of Human Rights ruled in March 2012 that kettling at the 2001 May Day 'Monopoly' demonstrations was lawful. The case had been brought by a group of people merely caught up in the cordon and a person who took part in the demonstration, all of whom claimed that they had been unlawfully 'deprived of their liberty' under Article 5 of the European Convention on Human Rights. The ruling suggests that 'containment' for reasons of 'security' may on occasion have precedence over the liberty of the person.

21 Liberty, 'Liberty's Report on Legal Observing at the TUC March for the Alternative', March 2011, www.liberty-human-rights.org.uk/materials/libertys-report-on-legal-observing-at-the-tuc-march-for-the-alternative.pdf (date accessed 21 March 2012), 14. See also the police response to the report: http://content.met.police.uk/News/MPS-response-to-Liberty-report/1260268848994/1257246745756 (date accessed 21 March 2012).

22 In debate with the author, Bishopsgate Institute, London, 7 July 2011.

23 *Evening Standard*, 8 April 2011.

24 *The Times Higher Education* magazine, 2 May 2011.

25 *The Guardian*, 20 July 2011.

26 *Evening Standard*, 31 October 2011.

27 *Daily Telegraph*, 31 December 2011.

28 *Daily Telegraph*, 12 January 2011.

29 *Metro*, 14 April 2009; *Evening Standard*, 11 January 2011.

30 *Channel 4 News*, 29 November 2011.
31 *Evening Standard*, 20 October 2011.
32 *Evening Standard*, 3 November 2011.
33 See Tomlinson, *Left, Right*. The original division of parties and ideologies in England dates to the seventeenth century. The Earl of Shaftesbury's followers and those opposed to the Duke of York were accused of being like Scottish thieves or 'Whigs' and they in turn called the king's party Irish wreckers or *Toraidhe*, contracted in English to 'Tories'. The terms 'left' and 'right' date to the French Revolution.
34 Assange later vociferously denied the accusation, which apparently arose from a conversation with the editor of *Private Eye*. The editor did not apparently keep written notes of the conversation.
35 http://en.wikipedia.org/wiki/Redmond-Bate_v_Director_of_Public_Prosecutions (date accessed 21 March 2012).
36 *New Statesman*, 1 March 2011; *Evening Standard*, 5 September 2011.
37 As explained by Tim Godwin, Deputy Commissioner of the Metropolitan Police, at New York University's tenth anniversary conference to commemorate 9/11, held on 3 October 2011 at the Senate House, University of London.
38 *Evening Standard*, 29 March 2012.
39 *Evening Standard*, 15 December 2011.

4 2010: THE CRISIS AND THE STUDENT RIOTS

1 Garrett Epps, 'Huey Newton Speaks at Boston College, Presents Theory of "Intercommunalism"', *Harvard Crimson*, 19 November 1970.
2 Paul Mason, *The Guardian*, 3 January 2012.
3 *The Paper*, Edition Minus 1, February 2011 (Hato Press and Centre for Ethics and Politics, Queen Mary College, University of London), 4. As student numbers fell and as the fears over student fees increased, Ed Lester, who was head of the Student Loans Company, was offered a pay deal without tax deductions because he was employed through a private personal service company, allowing him to save on taxes and expenses.
4 David Cameron, speech to the Conservative Party Conference, Birmingham, 6 October 2010. See www.conservatives.com/News/Speeches/2010/10/David_Cameron_Together_in_the_National_Interest.aspx (date accessed 23 March 2012).
5 David Cameron quoted in *The Guardian*. See www.guardian.co.uk/politics/2010/oct/06/david-cameron-speech-tory-conference (date accessed 23 March 2012).
6 Dan Hancox (ed.), *Fight Back! A Reader on the Winter of Protest* (London: OpenDemocracyviaOurKingdom, 2011), 24.
7 *Evening Standard*, 10 November 2010.
8 *The Guardian*, 11 November 2010.

9 *Evening Standard*, 11 November 2011.
10 *Ibid.*
11 *Ibid.*
12 http://blogs.news.sky.com/frontlineblog/Post:25a1d1f5-a371-4130-abab-bbeb70b3cb98 (date accessed 23 March 2012).
13 http://www.guardian.co.uk/uk/2010/dec/03/police-minister-students-protests (date accessed 23 March 2012).
14 *The Guardian*, 26 November 2010.
15 *Daily Mail*, 10 December 2010.
16 *Sunday Times*, 12 December 2010.
17 *Ibid.*
18 *Evening Standard*, 29 November 2010.
19 *Evening Standard*, 25 November 2010.
20 *Evening Standard*, 7 November 2010.
21 *Educational News*, October/November 1889. For the full story of school protest, see Clive Bloom, 'Schoolchildren on Strike', *BBC History Magazine*, 12(9) (September 2011).
22 *Metro*, 26 November 2010.
23 Personal communication with the author, 2 April 2012.
24 *Evening Standard*, 14 March 2011. The IPCC passed a file of evidence to the CPS in February 2012, following an investigation into allegations that three Metropolitan Police Service (MPS) officers conspired to wrongly arrest a 20-year-old male and that one of those officers also assaulted the male during student demonstrations in London on 9 December 2010. The IPCC undertook an independent investigation following a referral from the MPS Directorate of Professional Standards on 16 February 2011. As part of their inquiries, IPCC investigators interviewed the three police constables, two from the London Borough of Bexley and one from Lewisham, under caution. It is now a matter for the CPS to determine whether or not criminal charges will follow (IPCC reply to author request, 5 March 2012).
25 *Evening Standard*, 14 December 2010.
26 *The Times*, 13 December 2010.
27 *Evening Standard*, 14 December 2010.
28 *Mail Online*, 21 December 2011.
29 *Evening Standard*, 24 February 2011.
30 *Evening Standard*, 22 March 2011.
31 *Sunday Telegraph*, 27 March 2011.
32 Conversation between the author and a protester whose name is withheld.
33 *Sky Online*, 26 March 2011.
34 *Metro*, 28 March 2011.
35 *Daily Mail*, 27 March 2011; see also debate with the author at the Bishopsgate Institute on 7 July 2011.

36 *Evening Standard*, 28 March 2011.
37 *The Paper*, April 2011, 10.
38 *Metro*, 30 November 2010. On a similar theme, Len McCluskey, Secretary General of the public sector workers' union Unite, suggested the use of 'civil diobedience' by the low paid during the Olympics: *The Guardian*, 28 February 2012.

5 2011: THE SUMMER RIOTS – A COLD WIND IN AUGUST

1 See the full Independent Police Complaints Commission correspondence and reports on the death of Mark Duggan at: www.ipcc.gov.uk/search/Results.aspx?k=mark%20duggan (date accessed 27 March 2012).
2 *Evening Standard*, 8 August 2011.
3 *Morning Star*, 13–14 August 2011.
4 *Evening Standard*, 8 September 2011.
5 For the sequence of events, I have followed Her Majesty's Inspectorate of Constabulary's report, *The Rules of Engagement: A Review of the August 2011 Disorders*, Appendix D, 112–24, available at: www.hmic.gov.uk/publication/rules-engagement-review-august (date accessed 27 March 2012).
6 *Daily Mail*, 8 August 2011.
7 *Evening Standard*, 8 August 2011.
8 It is possible that the Metropolitan Police will purchase more specialised armoured vehicles to cope with any further trouble. Although they already possess 13 armoured trucks (called 'Jankels') which were deployed during the riots, they would like to explore the possibility of buying more armoured vehicles. Officers discussed the option at the International Armoured Vehicle exhibition at Farnborough on 21 February 2012. See *Evening Standard*, 22 February 2012.
9 *Daily Mirror*, 8 August 2011.
10 *Evening Standard*, 9 August 2011.
11 *The Times*, 9 August 2011.
12 *Daily Telegraph*, 10 August 2011.
13 *Metro*, 22 August 2011.
14 *The Sun*, 10 August 2011.
15 *Daily Express*, 10 August 2011.
16 *Weekly Gleaner*, 11–17 August 2011. *The Voice* carried stories and articles relating to the breakdown of community trust within ethnic areas (11–17 August 2011).
17 *Daily Express*, 10 August 2011.
18 *Evening Standard*, 20 October 2011.

19 *Jewish News*, 11 August 2011.
20 A number of arrests followed both the initial attack and the fake 'good Samaritan' help which followed, but which was actually when the student was mugged. Beau Isagba, who broke the student's jaw and stole his bicycle in the initial attack, was convicted on 16 February 2012. The thieves who mugged Rossli, Reece Donovan from Romford and John Kafunda of Ilford, were found guilty of robbery and violent disorder on 2 March 2012 and both were sentenced to long prison terms on 14 March 2012. Another violent offender, Karl Smith, was sentenced to five years' imprisonment on 14 February 2012 for threatening diners at a McDonald's in Brixton with an axe before helping others to loot the restaurant. The longest sentence was reserved for Andrew Burls, who was jailed for eight years after being convicted of burglary and arson in Peckham. He was arrested because his bandana failed to disguise the fact that he is cross-eyed. Gordon Thompson, who allegedly set fire to the House of Reeves furniture store in Croydon, appeared at the Old Bailey charged with 'arson with intent to endanger life' and 'arson being reckless as to whether life was endangered'. Thompson was sentenced to 11 and a half years on 11 April 2012, the longest term so far of any rioter.
21 *Daily Express*, 13 August 2011.
22 *Evening Standard*, 18 November 2011.
23 House of Commons Official Report, Vol. 531, No. 92 (11 August 2011), col. 1202.
24 *Ibid.*, cols. 1051 and 1078.
25 *Ibid.*, col. 1052. The general public were more inclined, despite the evidence of their own eyes, to support the police version of events, as a poll in *The Guardian* indicated (13 August 2011). In the wake of increasing hostility, Cameron quickly modified his language to that of lavish praise of the police.
26 *Ibid.*, col. 1052.
27 *Daily Telegraph*, 11 August 2011.
28 House of Commons Official Report, Vol. 531, No. 92 (11 August 2011), col. 1054.
29 *Ibid.*, col. 1053.
30 *Ibid.*, col. 1055.
31 *Ibid.*, col. 1051.
32 *Ibid.*, col. 1071.
33 *Ibid.*, col. 1057.
34 *Ibid.*, col. 1060.
35 *Ibid.*
36 *Ibid.*, col. 1083.
37 *Ibid.*, col. 1105.
38 House of Lords Official Report, Vol. 729, No. 188 (11 August 2011), col. 1510.

39 *Ibid.*, col. 1511.
40 *Ibid.*, col. 1516.
41 *The Independent*, 12 August 2011.
42 *The Sun*, 10 and 11 August 2011.
43 *Metro*, 22 September 2011.
44 *Evening Standard*, 14 December 2011.
45 *Evening Standard*, 15 August 2011.
46 *The Times*, 13 August 2011.
47 *Ibid.*
48 *Daily Telegraph*, 16 August 2011; *Daily Mail*, 20 August 2011.
49 Hysteria was not confined to the papers. Sky presenter Colin Brazier posted a blog on the news desk's website in which he stated that the most troubled 120,000 families for whom the government has set aside £450 million should be deported to the Sandwich Islands as a cost-saving exercise: *Evening Standard*, 23 January 2012.
50 *Daily Telegraph*, 12 August 2011.
51 *Daily Mail*, 20 August 2011.
52 *Financial Times*, 9 August 2011.
53 Metropolitan Police Service, *Strategic Review of MPS Response to Disorder: Early Learning and Initial Findings*, http://content.met.police.uk/cs/Satellite?blobcol=urldata&blobheadername1=Content-Type&blobheadername2=Content-Disposition&blobheadervalue1=application%2Fpdf&blobheadervalue2=inline%3B+filename%3D%22367%2F144%2FCO553-11Initial_Findings.pdf%22&blobkey=id&blobtable=MungoBlobs&blobwhere=1283531305435&ssbinary=true (date accessed 27 March 2012). See also Metropolitan Police Service, *Operation Kirkin: Strategic Review, Interim Report*, http://content.met.police.uk/cs/Satellite?blobcol=urldata&blobheadername1=Content-Type&blobheadername2=Content-Disposition&blobheadervalue1=application/pdf&blobheadervalue2=inline;+filename%3D%221006/646/CO553-11InterimreportKirkin.pdf%22&blobkey=id&blobtable=MungoBlobs&blobwhere=1283535860204&ssbinary=true (date accessed 27 March 2012).
54 *Ibid.*
55 *Ibid.*
56 *Evening Standard*, 7 October 2011.
57 Metropolitan Police Service. *Strategic Review of MPS Response to Disorder: Early Learning and Initial Findings.*
58 *Evening Standard*, 7 September 2011.
59 *Daily Telegraph*, 5 August 2011.
60 *Evening Standard*, 20 October and 14 December 2011.
61 *BBC News at Six*, 30 December 2011.
62 *Newsnight*, 12 August 2011.
63 *Evening Standard*, 16 November 2011.
64 *Evening Standard*, 5 October 2011.

6 1668, 1780 AND 1981: CONTEXTS AND EXPLANATIONS

1 Metropolitan Police Service, *Strategic Review of MPS Response to Disorder: Early Learning and Initial Findings*, http://content.met.police.uk/cs/Satellite?blobcol=urldata&blobheadername1=Content-Type&blobheadername2=Content-Disposition&blobheadervalue1=application%2Fpdf&blobheadervalue2=inline%3B+filename%3D%22367%2F144%2FCO553-11Initial_Findings.pdf%22&blobkey=id&blobtable=MungoBlobs&blobwhere=1283531305435&ssbinary=true (date accessed 27 March 2012).
2 *Evening Standard*, 16 March 2012.
3 *Evening Standard*, 22 March 2012.
4 *New Statesman*, 15 August 2011.
5 Darra Singh, Simon Marcus, Heather Rabbatts and Maeve Sherlock (eds), 'After the Riots. The Final Report of the Riots Communities and Victims Panel', 28 March 2012, http://riotspanel.independent.gov.uk/wp-content/uploads/2012/03/Riots-Panel-Executive-Summary-and-Recommendations.pdf (date accessed 2 April 2012), p. 1.
6 *Ibid.*, p. 1.
7 *Ibid.*, pp. 1–2.
8 *Ibid.*, pp. 4 and 5.
9 *Ibid.*, p. 2.
10 www.ask.co.uk/how/how_many_lottery_tickets_are_sold_each_week (date accessed 2 April 2012).
11 'After the Riots', p. 3, emphasis in original.
12 *The Guardian*, 30 March 2012.
13 *Ibid.*
14 *Evening Standard*, 2 February 2012.
15 *Evening Standard*, 26 January 2012.
16 *The Guardian*/LSE, 'Reading the Riots', www.guardian.co.uk/uk/interactive/2011/dec/14/reading-the-riots-investigating-england-s-summer-of-disorder-full-report and Guardian (date accessed 2 April 2012).
17 *Irish Times*, 13 August 2011.
18 *New Statesman*, 15 August 2011.
19 *The Spectator*, 13 August 2011.
20 Howard Tumber, *Television and the Riots* (London: British Film Institute, 1982), 15. For the reaction of the Black community to the verdict on Stephen Lawrence's killers and, therefore by implication, the August riots, see the poll conducted by *The Voice* in which 83 per cent of those polled said that things had *not* improved since the murder (5–11 January 2012).
21 *Ibid.*, 13.

22 *Ibid.*, 14.
23. The idea returned after the riots when the Employment Minister, Christopher Grayling, called for employers to employ a 'hoodie' to beat the unemployment of young people which had reached its highest level since 1992: *Evening Standard*, 18 April 2012.
24 *Irish Times*, 13 August 2011.
25 Tim Harris, *London Crowds in the Reign of Charles II* (Cambridge University Press, 1987), 83.
26 John Paul de Castro, *The Gordon Riots* (Oxford University Press, 1926), 33–4. The violent orchestrated war against 'papists' that marked the sixteenth and seventeenth centuries had boiled over and then subsided by the late eighteenth century. By then the very idea of persecuting Catholics was considered anathema and something from a barbarous age. Believing such hatred to be a dead letter, Parliament proposed a Catholic Relief Bill in May 1778, which aimed to free Catholic Scots Highlanders from the old draconian Oath of Allegiance brought in during William III's day and to allow their recruitment into the army. It was a cynical move. The annulment of the 1699 Act would effectively allow for the creation of extra regiments to be sent to fight the growing strength of the rebellion in America.
27 *Ibid.*, 41.
28 *Ibid.*, 62.
29 *Ibid.*, 72.
30 *Ibid.*, 77.
31 *Ibid.*, 89–90.
32 *Ibid.*, 90–1.
33 *Ibid.*, 131–2.
34 *Ibid.*, 136.
35 *Ibid.*, 162–3.
36 Christopher Hibbert, *King Mob: The London Riots of 1780* (New York: Dorset Press, 1958), 103.
37 *Ibid.*, 103.
38 Paul Edwards and Polly Rewt (eds), *Letters of Ignatiez Sanchez* (Edinburgh University Press, 1994), 15.
39 Percy Bysshe Shelley, *The Mask of Anarchy* (1819).

APPENDIX 1
1968: THE REVOLUTIONARY MODEL REDEFINED

1 Paul Hegarty, unpublished research paper (1999).
2 Eric Hobsbawn, *Age of Extremes: The Short Twentieth Century, 1914–1991* (London: Abacus, 1995), 52.

3 See Harry Kidd, *The Trouble at LSE, 1966–1967* (Oxford University Press, 1969).

APPENDIX 2
UNDER THIS SIGN CONQUER: THE VISIBLE REPUBLIC OF LONDON

1 Information on revolutionary flags courtesy of David Lawrence, although the interpretations are my own. Lawrence has also unearthed information regarding a Chartist flag of 1838, which had a sunburst pattern and was carried at Newport in 1839 and later adopted by W.J. Linton, but without the sunburst in 1851 as the flag of the English Republic.
2 This information is taken from Clive Bloom, *Restless Revolutionaries: A History of Britain's Fight for a Republic* (Stroud: The History Press, 2010), 75.
3 *Ibid.*, 85.
4 Yvonne Kapp, *Eleanor Marx*, vol. 1 (London: Virago, 1972), 90, 206.
5 Bloom, *Restless Revolutionaries*, 125.
6 Andrew Boyd, *Jim Connell, Author of the Red Flag* (London: Socialist History Society, 2001), 7–8.
7 *Ibid.*, 9.
8 *Ibid.*, 11.
9 Louise Michel, *Red Virgin: Memoirs of Louise Michel* (University of Alabama Press, 1981), 168.
10 Paul Avrich, *Haymarket Tragedy* (Princeton University Press, 1984), 145.

INDEX